ENGLISH LITERATURE
IN
THE TWENTIETH CENTURY

ENGLISH LITERATURE

IN

THE TWENTIETH CENTURY

By

JOHN WILLIAM CUNLIFFE

Essay Index Reprint Series

 BOOKS FOR LIBRARIES PRESS

FREEPORT, NEW YORK

First Published 1933
Reprinted 1967

INTERNATIONAL STANDARD BOOK NUMBER:
0-8369-0355-2

CONTENTS

ENGLISH LITERATURE
IN
THE TWENTIETH CENTURY

CHAPTER I

INTRODUCTORY

THE death of Queen Victoria in the first year of the twentieth century marks with a convenient definiteness the beginning of a new age. In international politics England's position of "splendid isolation" was abandoned in favor of an *entente cordiale* with France, which the new sovereign, Edward VII, had a considerable share in arranging. Great Britain had emerged from the Boer War victorious, but with diminished prestige; the German Emperor's congratulatory cablegram to President Kruger had aroused British animosity, and the British Government's counter stroke of sending the White Squadron out into the North Sea had excited German fears. Germany set about the increase of her own fleet to a strength that caused further irritation of British susceptibilities, and Europe seemed to be divided into two armed camps. All that the diplomatists could do was to defer the outbreak of the inevitable conflict to 1914.

The Great War suspended every peaceful human activity, and reduced the arts, including literature, almost to silence. Indeed the period for all Europe might be divided into pre-war and post-war, for the whole world is still suffering from the results of the disaster. The delicately balanced economic and financial relations by which the world's business was carried on were upset and have not yet recovered their equilibrium.

In the conduct of domestic policy a change was brought about in 1906 by the defeat of the Conservative Government which had conducted the Boer War, and the return of the Liberals to power, 376 strong, with 54 Labour members at their back, in place of two Labour members when the century began. Sir Henry Campbell-Bannerman, the new Premier, had declared before the General Election, that twelve millions of the population of Great Britain were in the grip of perpetual poverty and on the verge of hunger. In an attempt to mitigate, if not to remedy, this state of things, the Liberals passed a number of measures of a Socialistic character—Workmen's Compensation Act (1906), Small Holdings Act (1907), Old Age Pensions (1908), National Insurance Act (1911), Minimum Wage Act (1912). Expenditure, chiefly for social services, rose from 149 million pounds to 209 millions before the War, and has increased enormously since. Lloyd George, who had sponsored the National Insurance Act, speaking at Glasgow on Scottish Land Reform not long before the outbreak of the Great War, said: "You have hundreds of thousands of men working unceasingly for wages that barely bring them enough bread to keep themselves and their families above privation. Generation after generation they see their children wither before their eyes for lack of air, light, and space, which is denied them by men who have square miles of it for their own use. Take our cities, the great cities of a great Empire. Right in the heart of them everywhere you have ugly quagmires of human misery, seething, rotting, at last fermenting. We pass them by every day on our way to our comfortable homes. We forget that divine justice never passed by a great wrong. You can hear, carried by the breezes from the north, the south, the east, and the west, ominous rumbling. The chariots of retribution are drawing nigh.

How long will all these injustices last for myriads of men, women, ar:d children created in the image of God—how long? I believe it is coming to an end."

The War transformed Lloyd George from "the orator of the new social order" into "the organizer of victory," and when peace came, his power crumbled along with that of every other statesman who had endeavoured to patch up the miseries of a disordered world by the Treaty of Versailles (1919). His Coalition Government gave place to a Conservative administration, which was speedily defeated at the General Election of 1923. The Labour Government, which succeeded, stayed in for less than a year, and the difficulties either party—Conservative or Labour—experienced in attempting to govern the country, without a sufficient majority in the House of Commons, culminated in 1931 in the appointment of a second Coalition Government, headed by a Labour Premier, Mr. Ramsay Macdonald, but depending for its existence upon Conservative support. The financial and economic problems of peace proved even more incapable of solution than the problems of war. The European Governments found themselves alike unable to pay the debts they had incurred to the United States and the debts they had incurred to each other, including the reparations to which the Germans had unwillingly submitted as the price of peace. The result was a world-wide dislocation of financial and commercial relations which involved every nation except Russia in acute distress through the universal fall in prices, destruction of values, and consequent unemployment. In England the expenditure on unemployment relief, begun as insurance and extended by grants from the Government under the unhappy name of "the dole," proved a greater burden than the nation could carry, and brought about an enforced depreciation of the currency.

The maintenance of the gold standard, effected at great sacrifices too soon after the end of the War, had to be abandoned by the Coalition Government which was formed to preserve it.

It is evident that the state of political and social unrest in England which preceded and followed the War was unfavourable to the production of imaginative literature, and the effect of these unfavourable conditions was enhanced by a decay of religious faith. Sidney Low and Lloyd C. Sanders, summing up the achievements of the Victorian era at the beginning of the twentieth century, record the impression: "To some pessimists the orthodoxy of economics, the orthodoxy of science, and the orthodoxy of faith seemed alike 'bankrupt.'" Even so acute a thinker and so detached an observer as Professor Henry Sidgwick, writing at the end of the nineteenth century and looking back over the victory for liberalism he had helped to win, said: "Well, the years pass, the struggle with what Carlyle used to call 'Hebrew old clothes' is over, Freedom is won, and what does Freedom bring us to? It brings us face to face with atheistic science: the faith in God and Immortality, which we had been struggling to clear from superstition, suddenly seems to be *in the air*." This attitude, though characteristic of the twentieth century intellectuals, was not confined to them. Writing of England after the War, Charles E. G. Masterman says: "Shortly after the War, a report was issued, signed by members of all the religious bodies, of the experience of chaplains in dealing with the ordinary adult male soldier during the War. The report, if pessimistic, had at least the merits of candour. The general testimony was that, with occasional distinguished exception, this great mass of British male young adult life was facing death and being killed without any of the conviction of a spiritual

existence, a dominating Providence, or a future life, which
have been entertained unchallenged for nearly two thousand years. It was not the War which had made this
change. England, according to these testimonies, was no
longer Christian, and had become pagan; and the great
majority of the male population of England had completely ceased to believe in the faith of their forefathers."

This statement of the spiritual condition of English
youth in 1914–18 may seem to some exaggerated. But
similar testimony is given by leading representatives of
English orthodoxy. To E. F. Benson, son of the Victorian Archbishop, writing in 1932, it appeared too mild
a phrase to say that "a wave of irreligion" swept over the
young generation in the years 1914 to 1918. "For some
years already a growing indifference to religious matters
had been sweeping over them: it might be called a wave,
or it might be called a tide. . . . Already, before the
War, the national indifference to matters of religion had
been on the increase, and the Church had been losing
hold, and these four years had vastly accelerated the
process. Some, those chiefly who had seen service, rejected it with scorn and bitterness, but apart from them,
the attitude of the mass of the nation was to turn from it
as from some topic that lacked interest and reality. There
was no slogan or crusade against it; it was merely a bundle
of discarded and obsolete pieties, rubbish that lay littered
in the house of life, and had perhaps better be cleared
away, lest the microbes that bred in those medieval rags
should again infect the spirit of man with fevers of childish superstition. The house must be cleaned and set in
order, made habitable for a race that now looked on the
world with a more enlightened eye." "All around," said
the Bishop of Birmingham in his charge to the clergy at
his episcopal visitation of 1932, "they saw decay of faith.

Of the great institutional systems, Anglican, Free Church, Roman Catholic, Unitarian, not one escaped. Ingenious advertisement, confident assertion, violent misrepresentation, conservative tenacity, earnest social enthusiasm—all failed to avert loss, both of adherents and of prestige. Profound doubts had developed, not merely as to particular details of Christian dogma, but as to the most fundamental of Christian beliefs—the existence of God. A widespread feeling existed that Christianity was antagonistic to that free and splendid progress, the glory of the thought and life of the present era, a feeling that in the churches intellectual incompetence was associated with spiritual insincerity." The fact of paramount importance in the spiritual life of England, he asserted, was the "loss of religious certainty."

This sense of spiritual uncertainty was also of paramount importance from a literary point of view. There was no longer a common body of religious belief to which writers of imaginative literature could appeal in confidence that they would find a general response in the hearts and minds of their readers. When Hamlet says "there's a special providence in the fall of a sparrow," and

> There's a divinity that shapes our ends,
> Roughhew them how we will,

Shakespeare knew that this expression of faith in divine Providence would find an echo in the hearts of all. So, too, Wordsworth, two centuries later could set forth his assured belief

> That the procession of our fate, howe'er
> Sad or disturbed, is ordered by a Being
> Of infinite benevolence and power;
> Whose everlasting purposes embrace
> All accidents, converting them to good.

Midway in the nineteenth century ('In Memoriam,' 1850), Tennyson could only

> stretch faint hands of faith, and grope,
> And gather dust and chaff, and call
> To what I feel is Lord of all,
> And faintly trust the larger hope.

By the end of the nineteenth century even this "faint trust" in a beneficent Providence had largely disappeared from the minds of thinking men, and there was no longer any general expectation of a future life in which the woes of suffering humanity would be relieved, and its wrongs redressed.

From a merely literary point of view the lack of Christian faith might have been less serious if some other form of belief had commanded general acceptance. But, as was ironically remarked by the Bishop of Southwark, "Our ethical teachers—the novelists—are agreed only on the absurdity of the Christian faith. They completely disagree, however, upon what should replace it." If the mechanistic determinism which had been the favourite philosophy of evolutionary science in the nineteenth century had continued to gain ground in the twentieth century, the poets and novelists might have accommodated their minds to it; but it went almost completely out of fashion. The dogmatic faith in science as the guide of life, characteristic of so much of nineteenth century thinking, faded away under the light of twentieth century research, especially in astronomy and physics. Two Oxford professors, Sir James Jeans and Sir Arthur Eddington, are the leading exponents of the new science which, according to the distinguished Cambridge mathematician, Bertrand Russell, is "undermining the whole structure of applied reason and presenting us with a world of unreal and fantastic dreams in place of the Newtonian solidity." "Science now presents nothing but the most disorderly, random, and preposterous universe of events, connected by little except a structure composed of human concepts." Sir James Jeans, at the conclusion of 'Eos, or the Wider Aspects of Cosmogony" (1929), writes that the picture the scientist sees may be merely a creation of his own mind, in which nothing really exists except the mind itself; "the universe which we study with such care may be a dream, and we brain-cells in the mind of the dreamer." Professor John Scott Haldane, another Oxford scientist, while avowing himself a free-thinker because he cannot accept the creed of any existing church, sees no hope in science as a revelation of the significance of human life. "Science by itself cannot guide us, since from its very nature it does not deal with the values which are supreme. Science is not enough. Reason in its highest form as religion, and real religion extending into every part of our lives is what the world has most need of, and particularly just now, with old theological beliefs, which to a large extent embodied religion, disintegrating in every direction along with old scientific beliefs as well as old political beliefs."

Even in the power of applied science to better man's condition, the engineers themselves are losing faith. Sir Alfred Ewing, the veteran of English engineering, in his address as President of the British Association for the Advancement of Science in 1932, said: "More and more does mechanical production take the place of human effort, not only in manufactures, but in all our tasks, even the primitive task of tilling the ground. So man finds this, that while he is enriched with a multitude of possessions and possibilities beyond his dreams, he is in great measure deprived of one inestimable blessing, the necessity of toil.

We invent the machinery of mass-production, and for the sake of cheapening the unit we develop output on a gigantic scale. Almost automatically the machine delivers a stream of articles in the creation of which the workman has had little part. He has lost the joy of craftsmanship, the old satisfaction in something accomplished through the conscientious exercise of care and skill. In many cases unemployment is thrust upon him, an unemployment that is more saddening than any drudgery." Other observers of English society have come to the same conclusion. Professor G. M. Trevelyan, in his 'British History in the Nineteenth Century' writes that "the life of the poorest agricultural labourer in 1760 was, though narrow, ignorant, and rough, nearer to beauty and poetry than it has since become in a world driven by machines and vulgarized by hustle and advertisement." A recent article in the 'Manchester Guardian' asserts as an "undoubted fact that for large numbers of people, not only in England but all over the world, life becomes daily more intolerable. It is no use arguing, as many people will, that the poorest out-of-work man in England today has within his reach pleasures and comforts unknown to the workingman, and indeed to the bulk of the middle class, when George III came to the throne. That may be true, but it is quite irrelevant. A man's discontent is due not to what he has or lacks but to what he sees others enjoying while he goes without."

Along with the general discontent and the decay of religious beliefs went the weakening of the standards of morality to which those beliefs gave the supports of an authoritative sanction and an impelling motive. In 'A Corner of England' (1932), an intensive study of a London slum by John Martin, the author states that the slum-dwellers have ceased to recognize the sanction of the rights of property. "A man loses little and may easily gain in local prestige if he is thought to be a burglar or a motor bandit." And outside of the slums, among self-respecting and respectable working people throughout the length and breadth of England, there has been a noteworthy falling away from ancient standards.

Hopes of heaven or fears of hell no longer appeal to men as sufficient reasons for a life of self-restraint and virtuous industry. Englishmen continue, indeed, to work hard—though perhaps not so hard as before—from motives of self-interest, from social ambition, from habit, or from a desire for public approbation; but they no longer have the consciousness that possessed their forefathers that in so doing they were fulfilling the will of God. Even before the turn of the century there was a notable increase in the desire for pleasure, and in the twentieth century the "earnestness" of the Victorians passed into a byword with the younger generation. The theatre came into favour again, not merely with one class, but with all classes, and the cinema, first as a "movie" and then as a "talkie," became universally popular as a form of entertainment. The devotion to sports, which in former times had been regarded as an aristocratic privilege, came to be accepted as a legitimate interest even for the poorest. The proportion of sporting news in the papers increased to an enormous extent, and so serious an organ of opinion as the London 'Times' could announce "Tennis Finals" as the main item of interest it was able to provide, even for the most intelligent section of the British public; the cheaper papers came to rely very largely on sporting and betting news to keep up their circulation. Amid all the disasters and distresses that followed the Great War, there were millions of people every week attending football matches or listening to accounts of them over the radio or scanning the odds of the racing reports in the evening papers.

This is not to say that the English people in the twentieth century are a degenerate race as compared with their forefathers in the nineteenth, or any preceding century. The English rank and file during the War, and during the privation and anxiety that followed the War, showed the same tenacity and patient endurance as was characteristic of their ancestors. But they were different. They were—if not more intelligent—better educated; they were more sober and cleaner in their habits; they had a higher standard of comfort; they were less brutal and less cruel. If, as has been suggested above, they were less religious and less industrious, they were more humane and more conscious of their solidarity with their fellows. It is noteworthy than when the system of National Insurance against unemployment broke down after the War, and had to be supplemented by the "dole," the administration of the funds was keenly criticized, but there was no concerted effort to abolish the national grant of relief to the men and women out of work. Nor was there any marked jealousy of the large number of women who came into occupations hitherto closed to them, although they must have, to a considerable extent, displaced men. The populace, under the trying conditions of war and peace, continued to display the good-humoured tolerance and quiet courage which had brought the nation through so many crises in the past.

The times were certainly such as to try men's souls. Even before the end of the nineteenth century England's exports in the staple industries of textiles, iron, and steel, in which she had so long led the world, were beginning to fall off, if not in actual amount, at any rate in comparison with the achievements of her competitors. The War, by dislocating trade relations and upsetting financial arrangements for the interchange of commodities, dealt to British commerce a blow from which recovery seemed impossible. Widespread distress led to fewer marriages and a lower birth rate, though the check on the increase of population was in part offset by the lower death rate and the consequent extension of the average length of life. According to Sir George Newman, the Chief Medical Officer of the Ministry of Health, the expectation of life, which in 1841 was 40 years for a boy and 42 for a girl, and in 1871 was 41 and 44 years respectively, in 1931 had reached the astonishing figures of 56 for a boy and 60 for a girl. In spite of the depressing conditions of trade, England was a healthier, a stronger, and, one is inclined to believe, a happier population in the twentieth century than in any previous period of her history. Writing in 1931 of the nineteenth century Socialists, William Morris and Walter Crane, as dreamers "of a better-dressed and more beautiful proletariat, their labour interchanged with pageantry, and with dancing and singing to pipe and tabor," Sir William Rothenstein remarks: "Well, there is something to be said on behalf of this dream. If we haven't as yet adopted pastoral dress, I have seen, during the last 40 years, ragged, barefooted boys and sluttish, untidy girls vanish from the London pavements; and with dirt and rags, drunkenness, too, disappeared."

Thus, though spiritual conditions seemed unpropitious to genius, the material conditions were by no means unfavourable to literary production. The extension of elementary education to the whole population, achieved before the end of the nineteenth century, was followed in the twentieth by the bringing of secondary education within the reach of the masses and by the provision of scholarships which opened the way for the poorest to the universities. There was no excuse for any "mute inglorious Milton" to perish unknown for lack of literary opportunity, and on the other hand, the reading public was so immensely enlarged as to increase the demand for literature and the profits of authorship to a degree undreamt of in previous centuries. The establishment of international copyright in the last decade of the nineteenth century added the American to the English market, and, especially in the novel and in the drama, gave the English author an opportunity such as had never before existed in the history of the world. The greatly improved facilities for international communication brought the ideas and methods of foreign authors speedily to the attention of the British public and British craftsmen, and writers in twentieth century England were no longer hampered by the national prejudices and Puritanical restrictions which had beset the frank description of and comment on life in novels and plays almost to the end of the Victorian era. The twentieth century novelist or playwright had all the liberty that he deserved or desired, and took full advantage of it. Henry James, as early as 1914, commended the younger English novelists of his time for their courage in hugging the shore of the real in matters of sex instead of flying to the open sea of sentiment at the least sign of difficulty. The popularity of psychoanalysis led to further frankness in this regard, and the twentieth century dramatist or novelist not only recovered the chartered liberty of eighteenth century literature but went beyond it.

Meanwhile, the bashful maiden whose blushes Mrs. Grundy wished to spare, had done something for her own emancipation with the aid of the bicycle, the tennis racket, the hockey stick, and the golf club. The greater opportunities offered by the War for women of all classes resulted not merely in the grant of the parliamentary suffrage, but in a greater feeling of independence. This was emphasized by the adoption of more sensible styles of dress, first for games and then for everyday wear. Fashions of hairdressing also became simpler, and the young women of the twentieth century were obviously taller, stronger, and more self-reliant than their predecessors in any age known to history. The opportunities for secondary and college education which were organized for women in the last thirty years of the nineteenth century were still further developed in the twentieth, and the professions of law and medicine, which had been wholly or partially closed to them, were thrown open. Changes in legislation or in the interpretation of the law gave married women a greater degree of personal liberty in addition to the control of their own property, and placed them on the same level as men in the divorce court. All these outward evidences of liberty and equality were accompanied by an inner conviction in the minds of women which gave them a greater sense, not only of personal freedom, but of personal responsibility.

Literature (and still more, journalism) had a great deal to do with bringing about these changes and with conveying the knowledge of them to the unenlightened. Books, especially those which had a wide sale, dealt more and more with current issues; the novel and the play were made use of for all kinds of propaganda; and the circulation of serious discussions of political and economic questions, through cheap printing and free libraries, increased to an enormous extent. By the side of a great mass of printed matter of merely ephemeral interest, there were more books than ever dealing with serious questions in a serious way. Never before did problems of politics, economics, and sociology gain such widespread attention.

At the time of writing the immediate future of Great Britain in commerce and industry seems far from encouraging. But if we take a longer view, comparing the condition of the English working-class before the financial crisis of 1931 with what it had been a generation earlier, we find a record of improvement. 'The New Survey of London Life and Labour' made in 1929–30, gives the results of a careful investigation which affords a sound basis for comparison with the inquiry into the condition of the London poor conducted by Charles Booth forty years earlier. Booth at that time defined "the poor" as "those who have a sufficient regular though bare income, such as eighteen shillings to twenty-one shillings per week, for a moderate family"—roughly about five dollars a week in U. S. currency at that date. The more recent investigators, after a study of price changes for the primary necessaries of life according to the standard of living in East London, drew the poverty line at thirty-eight to forty shillings a week—rather under ten dollars. On this basis they calculated that distress in the most poverty-stricken metropolitan districts has decreased; in Poplar the percentage of the population living in extreme poverty sank from 36.5 to 24.1; in Bethnal Green, from 44.6 to 17.8; in Shoreditch, from 40 to 18; in Bermondsey, from 42.2 to 17.5; in Shepney, from 35.7 to 15.5. It is, of course, regrettable that in the richest city in the world—with the possible exception of New York—there should be sections in which about one-fifth of the families should be living on incomes below the line of a bare subsistence. In the London area there are still between twenty and twenty-five thousand "homeless poor," by occupation hawkers, casual labourers, pedlars, newsvendors, sandwichmen, street musicians, costermongers, and unskilled workmen, living in common lodging-houses, casual wards, or free shelters;

they "include a large element of the vagrant, criminal, mentally deficient, and physically abnormal." In Shoreditch one-fifth of the working-class population are living three or more to a room, so that the housing question is still a problem. Of the street traders who to the foreign visitors offer one of the most picturesque features of the English metropolis, many are in extreme poverty; the lowest class is that of the sandwichmen; of these there are some 750, who rarely earn more than a pound a week, equivalent to a little under five ·dollars before England went off the gold standard and to still less since.

The problem is part of the continued urbanization of England—a movement which began more than a century earlier and has apparently not yet reached its apex. In the nineteenth century the process of transformation of rural areas into towns went on most rapidly in the manufacturing districts of the Midlands and the North of England; in the twentieth century it is most marked in the neighbourhood of London—not so much in the central portion referred to in the last paragraph, known as the administrative county, as in the "Outer Ring" of Greater London, the area covered by the City of London and Metropolitan Police districts, occupying roughly a circle of 15 miles radius with Charing Cross as a centre. At the census of 1931 the population within the Greater London area amounted to 8,203,942 persons—one-fifth of the total population of England and Wales. The increase in Greater London during the ten-year period 1921–31 was 723,741—equivalent to adding to the metropolitan area the population of one of the great northern cities, such as Manchester or Liverpool. This increase took place entirely in the "Outer Ring." The central administrative county, which increased during the nineteenth century from less than a million to nearly five millions, has fallen off in population continuously during the twentieth century; the "home counties" of Middlesex, Surrey, Hertfordshire, and Essex are those which show the most striking increases. The administrative county of Middlesex, which lies entirely within the Outer Ring, has increased its population in ten years by over 30 per cent; the town of Hendon alone has increased by over 100 per cent. The extra-metropolitan population of the ancient county in 1801 was 71,411; it is now 1,638,728 persons, and of these the urban districts account for over a million and a half. An area once entirely rural has become almost entirely urban. The census returns for Surrey, Hertfordshire, and Essex tell substantially the same story. The size of the family has decreased, and one-half of the total families are now composed of only two or three persons; large families (eight or more persons) now account for only 3 or 4 per cent of the total. Everywhere the female sex predominates. In Surrey females outnumber males in every constituency, the excess averaging 17.1 per cent for the population and 22.8 per cent for the electorate. The twenty constituencies of Essex report in all except two cases more women electors than men.

This massing of the population around London has been accompanied—and in part caused—by an increasing "socialization," effected partly by the central government, partly by the local municipality with the aid or consent of the central government. A very large number of these dwellers in the outskirts work in London and live in houses provided by the London County Council; they get primary and secondary education in municipal schools, read in municipal libraries, amuse themselves in municipal museums, picture galleries, cinemas, parks, recreation grounds, and public baths. The State controls radio, telegraphs and telephones; it supplies medical and dental attendance; it fixes hours of labour, conditions of employment, and sometimes wages; it provides pensions for old age, and payments for sickness, accident, or unemployment. During the last half-century the expenditure by municipalities on social services has increased sevenfold, and the amounts paid by the central government up to 1931 brought the country to the verge of bankruptcy. The Labour Government paid for the financial débâcle by resignation, disorganization, and subsequent defeat at the polls, but the development of the social services was by no means entirely their doing. Conservative, Liberal and Coalition governments had all had a share in increasing expenditure for social purposes, and the end is not yet. As long ago as 1890, Sir William Harcourt, a leading Liberal politician, said "We are all Socialists now," and if the remark was, at the time, half ironical, it has become the simple truth by the passage of years. The Coalition Government was enabled, under the stress of the financial crisis of 1931, to put a brake on the national expenditure, but with the return of more normal times, the process of socialization will be resumed. It is a way on which, under democratic government, there is no turning back.

These changes, involving the disappearance of the aristocracy and the county families from the English countryside and the displacement of the centre of electoral power from the middle class to the working proletariat, are in themselves significant as affecting both the producers of literature and the people for whom it is produced; but their main effect is probably the creation of an impression of uncertainty and instability. England, in the nineteenth century apparently the most solid and secure of modern democracies, is now obviously in a state of transition, and no one knows what is going to happen next—in politics, in finance, in commerce, in religion, in art, in literature. In these conditions of constant and often sudden change, the intellectual life—and the literary production which depends upon it—become peculiarly difficult. Professor John Dewey put this very clearly in his recent book 'Individualism Old and New': "In static societies—those which the industrial revolution has doomed—acquiescence had a meaning, and so had the projection of fixed ideals. Things were so relatively settled that there was something to acquiesce in, and goals and ideals could be imagined that were as fixed in their way as existing conditions in theirs. The medieval legal system could define 'just' prices and wages, for the definition was a formulation of what was customary in the local community; it operated merely to prevent exorbitant deviations. It could prescribe a system of definite duties for all relations, for there was a hierarchical order, and occasions for the exercise of duty fell within an established and hence known order. Communities were local; they did not merge, overlap, and interact in all kinds of subtle and hidden ways. A common church was the guardian and administrator of spiritual and ideal truth, and its theoretical authority had direct channels for making itself felt in the practical details of life. Spiritual realities might have their locus in the next world, but this after-world was intimately tied into all the affairs of this world by an institution existing here and now. Today there are no patterns sufficiently enduring to provide anything stable in which to acquiesce, and there is no material out of which to frame final and all-inclusive ends. There is, on the other hand, such constant change that acquiescence is but a series of interrupted spasms, and the outcome is mere drifting. In such a situation, fixed and comprehensive goals are but irrelevant dreams, while acquiescence is not a policy but its abnegation."

In such a period we may expect to find very wide divergence of opinion and the advocacy of measures which must seem to many people extravagant. The more daring, radical thinkers have something to suggest which may be worth consideration or may be utterly impracticable, but is at any rate more likely to be of interest than a mere plea for the maintenance of things as they are. The air is full of the consciousness of new conditions, such as the world has never faced before, and there is a general expectation of impending change, both in national and international affairs. In the conduct of its domestic policy and in its contributions for the solution of international problems, Great Britain has endeavoured to combine enterprise with moderation, and the English literature of the period, although much of it is transitional and journalistic, has features which are both of immediate and of permanent interest.

CHAPTER II

VICTORIAN SURVIVORS

EVEN in a period of turbulent change, more is continued than is uprooted, or life would be impossible. The main characteristic of early twentieth century literature was perhaps a revolt from Victorianism, but for some years at any rate the surviving Victorians still occupied the centre of the stage. George Meredith on his seventieth birthday, just before the close of the nineteenth century, was acclaimed as the foremost man of letters of the English-speaking world, and the acclamation was renewed on his eightieth birthday, the year before his death in 1909. In the interim he had published a long philosophical poem 'A Reading of Earth' (1901) and a volume of shorter poems, but it cannot be said that these or his posthumous works, 'Celt and Saxon' and 'The Sentimentalists,' added to his reputation, which rested on what he had achieved, in prose and in verse, during the nineteenth century.

Samuel Butler (1835–1902) and George Gissing (1857–1903) belong clearly to the nineteenth century; what Gissing published after 1900 was his least characteristic work, and although Butler's 'Way of all Flesh' (1903) had a great influence on twentieth century literature and twentieth century thought, it was written before 1884 and falls chronologically within the Victorian period.

THOMAS HARDY (1840–1928)

It was different with Thomas Hardy, whose novels and poems divide themselves, with reasonable compactness, between the nineteenth century and the twentieth. The novels were all published in the n'neteenth century, though they held their own with the reading public and in the critical opinion of the twentieth century better than Meredith's. Hardy's first volume of poems appeared in 1898, though its contents were written mainly in 1865–70; but his reputation as a poet was made in the twentieth century. The publication of successive volumes of poems up to the year of his death, and his imposing funeral in Westminster Abbey, with leading representatives of the academic, political, and literary world as pall-bearers, impressed the popular imagination. His shy avoidance, especially in the last years of his long life, not only of publicity but of ordinary social intercourse, made him an appealing and romantic figure; and his dark, fatalistic philosophy fell in with the temper of the time more readily than Meredith's transcendental optimism. His great poetic drama, 'The Dynasts,' was published in three parts in the years 1904, 1906, and 1908, and was rightly regarded as a very remarkable achievement for a man who was over sixty when it was begun and nearly seventy when it was finished. It is a huge spectacle in nineteen acts and one hundred and thirty scenes, intended for "mental performance alone" (though part of it has been successfully staged). The list of characters for each of the three parts covers two or three pages, beginning with "certain impersonated abstractions, or Intelligences, called Spirits" and ending with Wessex peasants enlisted as soldiers against Napoleon and still lowlier camp

followers. The "forescene in the Overworld" represents
the Immanent Will as working "with an absent heed,"

> like a knitter drowsed,
> Whose fingers play in skilled unmindfulness.

The Will winds up Napoleon and other "flesh-hinged
manikins" "to click-clack off Its preadjusted laws," but
all are merely puppets, pulled by invisible strings. Then
follows in ever-changing procession a panorama of the
successive events of the epoch and the actors in it, great
and small; we see Nelson on the deck of his ship, Pitt
taking counsel with George III, Napoleon in every con-
ceivable relation, the English House of Commons in debate, the common soldiers of both sides on the battle-
fields, on the march, and in their cups. It is a combination
of the method of Shakespeare's historical plays, with
that of Goethe's 'Faust,' but with less humour than is
afforded by either, and the Wessex scenes hardly give
sufficient relief for the intolerable length of the parliamentary speeches and diplomatic discussions. The philosophy is that of the Wessex novels and of the poems,
though in the closing lines the Chorus of the Pities
breathes a hope that the Immanent Will, "That neither
good nor evil knows" may "wake and understand." If
"God's Education" is to come about at all, Hardy sets
forth in a poem published contemporaneously with 'The
Dynasts,' it must be brought about by men. "Theirs is
the teaching mind." God is without pity, as he is without
aim or purpose.

> "My labours—logicless—
> You may explain; not I:
> Sense-sealed I have wrought, without a guess
> That I evolved a Consciousness
> To ask for reasons why.

> "Strange that ephemeral creatures who
> By my own ordering are,
> Should see the shortness of my view,
> Use ethic tests I never knew,
> Or made provision for!"

In a preface written in 1901 Hardy suggests that many of his poems are merely dramatic or impersonative, thought this may not be explicitly stated. Even when they may be rightly regarded as the expression of his individual opinion, they comprise "a series of feelings and fancies written down in widely different moods and circumstances." Similarly, in the "apology" prefixed to the poems of 1922, he protests against the acceptance as his "view" of "a series of fugitive impressions which I have never tried to coördinate." He protested too against the description of this view as "pessimism" and defined his intention as "the exploration of reality, and its frank recognition stage by stage along the survey, with an eye to the best consummation possible: briefly, evolutionary meliorism." He would hold fast to the conviction that pain to all upon earth, "tongued or dumb, shall be kept down to a minimum by loving-kindness, operating through scientific knowledge and actuated by the modicum of free-will conjecturally possessed by organic life when the mighty necessitating forces—unconscious or other—that have 'the balancing of the clouds,' happen to be in equilibrium, which may or may not be often."

Hardy's admission of this small avenue of escape from evolutionary determinism is worth noting; but it is not surprising that certain tendencies of thought, recurring in his novels and poems, have been interpreted as arising from a general attitude towards life. His tone in the later poems is rather one of gentle resignation than of fierce indignation, but his main themes are still the ironies and illusions of life, the inconstancy of man and woman, the disappointment and frustration of human hopes and desires. That his persistent choice of these themes and his occasional comment on them should be described as pessimistic need not be regarded as a reproach. His attitude towards human suffering is intensely sympathetic, and very far from cynical; his keen sensibility is matched with kindness. His imaginative power and artistic skill met with increasing recognition in his later years, and his position as the last great survivor of the Victorian age was one of unique honour and almost universal appreciation. As he sank to rest, he recalled the fame of the great gentlemen of the past who "burnt brightlier towards their setting-day," and wrote his own modest 'Epitaph':

> I never cared for Life: Life cared for me,
> And hence I owed it some fidelity.
> It now says, "Cease; at length thou hast learnt to grind
> Sufficient toll for an unwilling mind,
> And I dismiss thee—not without regard
> That thou didst ask no ill-advised reward,
> Nor sought in me much more than thou couldst find."

RUDYARD KIPLING (1865–   )

While Meredith and Hardy were undoubtedly the great names in imaginative literature at the beginning of the century, the writer whom everybody was reading and discussing was Rudyard Kipling. The son of a British official at Bombay, he had been educated in England and had returned to India as a youth of eighteen to work on the 'Civil and Military Gazette' at Lahore, where his father was Principal of the School of Art. Coming by way of the United States to England in 1889–90, he had brought with him as his main literary baggage 'Plain Tales from the Hills' and six other volumes (already in print) of short stories of Anglo-Indian life. He had written more short stories in London, two longer stories, 'The Light that Failed' and 'The Naulahka' (the latter in collaboration with Wolcott Balestier, whose sister he married), two 'Jungle Books,' two books of verse ('Barrack Room Ballads' and 'The Seven Seas') and a school novel—'Stalky & Co.'—all before he was thirty-five years old. It was an astonishingly brilliant performance, and it is no wonder that the reading public was carried away by it. Both prose and verse had a new movement, a powerful rush, a glow of life—or was it only a mechanical glitter? Some of the grey heads wagged their beards and said it could not last —the young man had no staying power—he could not write a full-length novel. To disprove the accusation, Kipling in the first year of the century produced 'Kim,' which silenced the critics for a while, though soon some of them were saying that the new novel was simply a collection of short stories about the same people.

On returning to England after the Boer War, Kipling settled down at Rottingdean in Sussex and lived in contact with the quieter scenery of Southern England and the gentler sides of English life. As against his abounding vitality, his extraordinary power of invention, his skill in narration and description, the hostile critics had laid stress on the defects of these qualities in his earlier work —a love of striking, even brutal contrasts, the worship of mere force, a lack of sympathy for civilizations outside the English pale, and inability to render the finer sides of life within it. In spite of the apparent range and variety of his characters, the gentler and more intellectual men

and women who represent the human race in its highest
development were always inadequately realized and often
grotesquely caricatured. His psychology was never subtle,
and he succeeded best with primitive peoples, children,
and the coarser specimens of civilized humanity. Even
with the military and official classes whom he knew best,
altogether apart from the cheap cynicism which marred his
earliest work, there was a hard and artificial smartness in
their way of talking and a narrowness in their view of life
which does them less than justice. His common soldiers
had an exaggerated brutality which was unnecessary to
set off their real qualities of hardihood and faithfulness.
His colours were too glaring; his psychology was superficial; his characters did not develop. These were objections naturally evoked by his overwhelming popularity,
and they could not be denied.

But 'Just So Stories' (1902) breathed a homelier and
quieter charm, which was continued, with some loss of
freshness, in 'Puck of Pook's Hill' (1906) and 'Rewards
and Fairies' (1910). By the latter date, however, Kipling's creative vitality seemed to be exhausted—not a surprising result of the extraordinary productiveness of his
youth. Or it may be that by this time the public were
familiar with his style and his matter, and were no longer
attracted by the charm of novelty. It is certain that his
popularity began to fall off, and amid the new interests of
the Great War and the troubles that followed it, he sank
into comparative obscurity. The militant imperialism for
which he stood went out of fashion, except in remote official circles. It was no use exhorting America or indeed
Great Britain, to "take up the white man's burden." The
white man was too much concerned with burdens of his
own to wish to take on any additional burdens for the
relief of his dark-skinned brethren. And the dark-skinned

brethren showed no desire to be relieved—except of the
white man's presence and his government, his manufactures, and his whole civilization.

J. M. BARRIE (1860–   )

Another Victorian Romantic who found himself not altogether at home in the twentieth century was Sir J. M.
Barrie, who wrote all his novels and made his early successes on the stage in the nineteenth century. Born in a
Scottish manufacturing town and educated at the University of Edinbu·gh, Barrie made his way through provincial journalism in the English Midlands to writing for
metropolitan newspapers and reviews. In his address as
Rector of the University of St. Andrews in 1922, Barrie
recalled these days of his early twenties: "The greatest
glory that has ever come to me was to be swallowed up in
London, not knowing a soul, with no means of subsistence,
and the fun of working till the stars went out. To have
known anyone would have spoilt it. I didn't even quite know
the language. I rang for my boots and they thought I said
a glass of water, so I drank the water and worked on.
There was no food in the cupboard so I didn't need to
waste time in eating. The pangs and agonies when no
proof came. How courteously tolerant was I of the post-
man without a proof for us; how McConnachie on the
other hand wanted to punch his head. The magic days
when our article appeared in an evening paper. The
promptitude with which I counted the lines to see how
much we should get for it. Then McConnachie's superb
air of dropping it into the gutter. Oh, to be a free lance
of journalism again—the darling jade!" "McConnachie,"

it should be explained—and it cannot be explained better than in Barrie's own words—"is the name I give to the unruly half of myself—the writing half. We are complement and supplement. I am the half that is dour and practical and canny, he is the fanciful half; my desire is to be the family solicitor, standing firm on my hearthrug among the harsh realities of the office furniture, while he prefers to fly around on one wing."

All through his career Barrie was faced with the problem of reconciling two very different phases of his own personality—the dour, practical, canny Scot who wanted to keep hold of the harsh realities of life and the romantic writer who was inclined to see things through a haze of sentiment. His Victorian public insisted on romance, and he gave it to them in good measure, pressed down and running over, in such novels as 'The Little Minister,' in which a Scottish clergyman is irregularly married to a highborn lady who wanders about "Thrums" (Barrie's native town of Kirriemuir), disguised as a gipsy. The public was delighted, and would no doubt have honoured further demands upon its credulity, but the dour, practical, canny Scot in Barrie apparently became weary of McConnachie's extravagances, and in 'Sentimental Tommy' and its sequel 'Tommy and Grizell' a vein of cynicism mingled with the sentimental romance; Barrie disappointed his old public without gaining a new one, and he turned his attention away from fiction to devote himself to drama, in which he had for some years been experimenting with varied success. Perhaps the most likely work of his first period to endure is the biographic sketch of his mother, 'Margaret Ogilvy.' Even in this, a scrupulous critic might discern an occasional inclination to extract exaggerated humour or pathos out of some familiar detail of domestic life, but in connection with the leading figure, who is realized with unfailing delicacy and charm, any tendency to sentimentality is held in check by the unmistakable sincerity of feeling which inspires the whole. Barrie owed a great debt to his mother, and the difficult task of expressing his consciousness of it is discharged with a tact, sensibility, and refinement which are beyond praise.

His first ventures upon the stage were not happy. In 1891 he produced a romantic drama of the eighteenth century 'Richard Savage' (in collaboration with H. B. Marriot-Watson), an Ibsen burlesque, and a dramatized version of 'Vanity Fair'—all failures. He first made a hit in 1892 with a farce, 'Walker, London,' which sets forth the innocent amatory adventures of a London barber, alone on his honeymoon because there was not money enough for two, and entangled in the superior society of a houseboat on the Thames in the assumed character of an African explorer. It achieved with eminent success its purpose of providing a part in which a popular actor of that day (J. L. Toole) could display his powers.

After an intermediate failure with the libretto of a comic opera (in which he collaborated with Conan Doyle), Barrie scored great popular successes with 'The Professor's Love Story' and his dramatization of his own novel 'The Little Minister,' which were acclaimed on both sides of the Atlantic in spite of (and sometimes perhaps because of) their excessive sentiment and extravagant romance. In 'The Wedding Guest' (1900) Barrie tried, not altogether successfully, to deal with a serious problem seriously, and he returned to the farcical in 'Little Mary,' to the fanciful in 'Quality Street'—the latter a sympathetic reproduction of the sentimental atmosphere of the early nineteenth century; it was highly praised by the critics and stood the test of revival twenty years later. But it

was not until 'The Admirable Crichton' was put on the
stage later in the same year (1902) that Barrie succeeded
in that blend of the ironic with the romantic which is
peculiarly his own. The romance is chiefly in the setting;
irony and satire run all through the treatment of the characters and the plot. The critics treated the play seriously
—perhaps too seriously—and on its revival in 1918 there
were loud outcries against Barrie's attempt to take the
edge off his own satire. A. B. Walkley's protest in the
'Times' deserves quotation: "[Barrie] ought to have been
too conscientious an artist to 'touch up' his old work. He
ought to have left the original ending alone, not merely
because it was the original—though that is reason good
enough—but because it was the right, congruous, appropriate ending. The wheel had come full circle. It was a
case of 'As you were.' The butler of the first act, after being
a superman, had, in the fourth, become the butler again,
and nothing but the butler. He left you with the announcement of his intention of settling down with Tweeny
in a little 'pub' in the Harrow Road. This struck the perfect note, the final word of irony. You didn't need to be
reminded of the superman. You could do that for yourself. But now the author insists upon superfluously re-
minding you. The Harrow Road 'pub' has been dropped
out. Crichton glares at his old island subjects, and they
cower with reminiscence. He glares at the formidable
Lady Brocklehurst, and she, even she, quails. Lady Mary
reminds him of the past, and even a *redintegratio amoris*
is hinted at. In short, the author 'hedges'—'hedges'
against his own old irony, that perfect thing. This *is* a
butler, he seems to say, but remember, Oh, please remember, he *was* a superman. As though we should forget it!
And Crichton is even made to be wise after the event. He
foresees the late war, and predicts that if England should

ever hear the roll of the drums, then all the Bill Crichtons will get their chance. With more about England, &c., Crichton, our imperturbable *homme fort*, turned mouthing, sentimental 'patriot'! Good heavens!"

In the printed versions of the play (1915 and 1918) there is no mention of "the 'pub' in the Harrow Road" and there is no patriotic outburst at the end. "Poor Tweeny" in both versions is deprived (by a stage direction) of any expectation of joining Crichton in married bliss as a London landlady, and Crichton's ultimate fate is left in doubt. In the earlier printed version he is allowed to snub Lady Mary just before the final curtain; in the later one, he remains the imperturbable butler to the end, and simply assures her that he has not lost his courage. The patriotic prophecies of the 1918 revival were doubtless a mistake, accounted for by war excitement, and the author has done well to omit them in the permanent copy. As the text stands, it is still true that "beneath the fun and friendliness of this delightful comedy we get a glimpse of a very queer, very unhappy conception of the world and of human nature."

The 'Times' review, from which the above sentence is quoted, finds again in 'What Every Woman Knows' "a clear cruelty, a strong hint of sneering." "We are shut up in a cage of makeshift, of a clear-sighted, tolerant despair. . . . We can find no faith—not even faith in womanhood, for all Maggie's ability—in 'What Every Woman Knows.'" If this is true—and there may well be some truth in it—it is curious that no hint of it reached the thousands of people in England and America who enjoyed the humour and sentiment of this delightful comedy. No doubt there is more under the surface than the ordinary spectator sees or the ordinary reader discerns, but one doubts whether it is so "bitter, cruel, despairing" as the 'Times' reviewer thinks. As in 'The Admirable Crichton,' the characters and situations are alike impossible, and we get as far off the track by attempting to press their significance to a logical issue as the ordinary theatre-goer does by accepting them for the sake of the humour and pathos and homely wisdom the words and acts convey. The opening situation in 'What Every Woman Knows'—the Scottish railway porter who commits burglary for the acquisition of knowledge—is an admirable example of Barrie's art; both on the stage and in the printed version—half dialogue, half narrative with the characteristic comments of the author—it is a delight, not because of its probability—no one would be bold enough to claim for it that virtue—but by reason of a whimsical relation to fact which is the peculiar charm of Barrie at his best.

When the relation to fact becomes too tenuous, as in 'The Legend of Leonora,' the common sense of the public revolts, though it has shown itself perfectly willing and able to follow Barrie's lead into flights of pure fancy such as 'Peter Pan' and 'A Kiss for Cinderella.' 'Dear Brutus' and 'Mary Rose' occupy again the more difficult intermediate ground between fact and fancy where Barrie's playful tenderness is cunningly combined with a view of life which is stern without being harsh.

One finds the same range and variety in the one-act plays. 'The Will' and 'The Twelve-Pound Look' carry satire almost to the point of cynicism; 'The Old Lady Shows her Medals' touches the deepest springs of human emotion with a hand unfailing in tact and delicacy.

Perhaps there is no author of our own time about whom it is harder to forecast the verdict of posterity. Contemporary differences of opinion about Barrie are a sufficient warning against dogmatism. There are still those who accuse him of a belated Victorian sentimentality; there are others who carry their worship to the other side of idolatry. Professor William Lyon Phelps, of Yale University, suggests that the most intelligent attitude to take towards his work is "unconditional surrender," and goes on to say: "J. M. Barrie is the foremost English-writing dramatist of our time, and his plays, taken together, make the most important contributions to the English drama since Sheridan. He unites the chief qualities of his contemporaries, and yet the last word to describe his work would be the word eclectic. For he is the most original of them all. He has the intellectual grasp of Galsworthy, the moral earnestness of Jones, the ironical mirth of Synge, the unearthly fantasy of Dunsany, the consistent logic of Ervine, the wit of Shaw, the technical excellence of Pinero. In addition to these qualities, he has a combination of charm and tenderness possessed by no other man." ('North American Review,' December, 1920.)

Such praise is at once too general and too extravagant to be helpful; and it is not enough to refer doubters to "the published plays" at large. It is likely that future critics will make careful distinctions between Barrie at his best and Barrie in his off moments. Considered as a whole, his work is curiously uneven, and even in the plays in which his whimsical genius carries us away, especially during stage-presentation, the reader who has not adopted the attitude of "unconditional surrender" will find weaknesses which may not be so readily pardoned by a generation less under the sway of Barrie's popular reputation and personal charm. It hardly seems possible that the plays will follow the novels into comparative neglect. The form he has adopted for their publication—half drama, half novel—is peculiarly suited to his genius, and will probably secure their preservation, even if many of them fail to hold the stage. Barrie's own generation certainly owes him a great debt for numberless hours of unexpected delight. His magic touch has ennobled and endeared the common things of life, and his fancifulness has rarely been completely divorced from common sense. Recent critics have gone too far in ascribing to his plays a cynical interpretation which is probably very far from his intention, but they could not bear that so delicate and true an artist should be classed among the sentimentalists. It is in the combination of tenderness and humour with keen satire that he has made a unique contribution to British drama.

BIBLIOGRAPHY

George Meredith

PROSE WORKS

1856 'The Shaving of Shagpat.'
1857 'Farina.'
1859 'The Ordeal of Richard Feverel.'
1861 'Evan Harrington' ('Once a Week,' 1860).
1864 'Emilia in England' (later called 'Sandra Belloni').
1865 'Rhoda Fleming.'
1867 'Vittoria' ('Fortnightly Review,' 1866).
1871 'The Adventures of Harry Richmond' ('Cornhill,'
      1870–1).
1876 'Beauchamp's Career' ('Fortnightly Review,' 1874–5).
1879 'Essay on Comedy' ('New Quarterly Mag.,' 1877).
1879 'The Egoist.'
1881 'The Tragic Comedians' ('Fortnightly,' 1880–1).
1885 'Diana of the Crossways' ('Fortnightly,' 1884).
1891 'One of Our Conquerors' ('Fortnightly,' 'N. Y. Sun,'
      'Australasian,' 1890).
1894 'Lord Ormont and his Aminta.'
1895 'The Amazing Marriage' ('Scribner,' 1895).
1910 'Celt and Saxon' ('Fortnightly,' 1910).
1910 'The Sentimentalists' (unfinished comedy, 'Scribner,'
      Aug.).

POEMS

1851 'Poems' (First Version of 'Love in the Valley').
1862 'Modern Love.'
1883 'Poems and Lyrics of the Joy of Earth.'
1887 'Ballads and Poems of Tragic Life.'
1888 'A Reading of Earth.'
1892 'Poems' ('The Empty Purse and Others').

1892 'Modern Love, The Sage Enamoured.'
1892 'Jump-to-Glory Jane.'
1898 'Odes in Contribution to the Song of French History.'
1901 'A Reading of Life.'
1909 'Last Poems.'
1910 'Poems Written in Early Youth.'

COLLECTED EDITIONS

1885–7   First collected edition of the novels.
1889–95   New edition.
1896–8   Limited edition (32 vols.—3 of poems).
1897   Selected Poems.
1897–9   Library edition (17 vols.—2 of poems).
1901–5   Pocket edition (18 vols.—2 of poems).
1910–11   Memorial edition (27 vols.).
1912–20   'Standard' edition (17 vols.).
1922   Mickelham edition (17 vols.).

BIOGRAPHY AND CRITICISM

Hannah Lynch, 'George Meredith; a Study,' 1891.
Walter Jerrold, 'George Meredith, An Essay towards Appreciation' (English Writers of To-day Series), 1902.
G. M. Trevelyan, 'The Poetry and Philosophy of George Meredith,' 1906.
M. Sturge Henderson, 'George Meredith: Novelist, Poet, Reformer,' 1907.
    (Chapters XIV to XVII on 'Meredith's Poetry' by Basil de Selincourt.)
J. A. Hammerton, 'George Meredith in Anecdote and Criticism,' 1909.
Ernst Dick, 'George Meredith, Drei Versuche.' Berlin, 1910.
Constantin Photiades, 'George Meredith, sa Vie, son Imagination, son Art, sa Doctrine.' Paris, 1910, Translation by Arthur Price, 1913.
'The Letters of George Meredith,' 1912.
J. H. E. Crees, 'George Meredith. A Study of his Works and Personality,' Oxford, 1918.
S. M. Ellis, 'George Meredith. His Life and Friends in Relation to his Work,' 1919, 1920.

Alice Mary, Lady Butcher, 'Memories of George Meredith,' 1919.

René Galland, 'George Meredith, les Cinquant Premières Années,' 1923.

William Chislett, Jr., 'George Meredith,' 1925.

J. B. Priestley, 'George Meredith' (English Men of Letters), 1926.

M. Gretton, 'Writings and Life of George Meredith,' 1926.

Robert Esmond Sencourt, 'The Life of George Meredith,' 1929.

R. Peel, 'Creed of a Victorian Pagan,' 1931.

There are full bibliographies by John Lane in 'George Meredith: some Characteristics' (Richard Le Gallienne), 1890 (Fifth edition, revised, 1900), and by A. J. K. Esdaile in 'The Literary Year-Book for 1907.'

SAMUEL BUTLER

1862	'Dialogue on the Origin of Species.'
1863	'Darwin among the Machines.'
	'A First Year in Canterbury Settlement.'
1865	'The Evidence for the Resurrection' ('The Fair Haven,' 1873).
1872	'Erewhon.'
1877	'Life and Habit.'
1878	'A Psalm of Montreal' ('Spectator').
1880	'Unconscious Memory.'
1887	'Luck or Cunning as the Main Means of Organic Modification?'
1897	'The Authoress of the Odyssey.'
1901	'Erewhon Revisited.'
1903	'The Way of All Flesh' (wr. 1872–84).
1906	'Essays.'
1912	'Note-Books.'
1913	'The Humour of Homer and Other Essays with Biographical Note.'

BIOGRAPHY AND CRITICISM

C. E. M. Joad, 'Samuel Butler,' 1925.

M. Garnett, 'Samuel Butler and his Family Relations,' 1926.

B. Farrington, 'Samuel Butler and the Odyssey,' 1929.

Clara G. Stillman, 'Samuel Butler: A Mid-Victorian Modern,' 1932.

In addition to the biographical note by Henry Festing Jones mentioned above, there are two volumes of an authoritative biography, 'Samuel Butler' (1919), by the same author and critical books on Butler by Gilbert Cannan (1915), and John F. Harris (1916).

GEORGE GISSING

1880	'Workers in the Dawn.'
1884	'The Unclassed.'
1886	'Isabel Clarendon.'
	'Demos.'
1887	'Thyrza.'
1888	'A Life's Morning.'
1889	'The Nether World.'
1890	'The Emancipated.'
1891	'New Grub Street.'
1892	'Born in Exile.'
	'Denzil Quarrier.'
1893	'The Odd Women.'
1894	'In the Year of Jubilee.'
1895	'Eve's Ransom.'
1897	'The Whirlpool.'
1898	'Charles Dickens: A Critical Study.'
1899	'The Crown of Life.'
1901	'By the Ionian Sea. Notes of a Ramble in Southern Italy.'
	'Our Friend the Charlatan.'
1903	'The Private Papers of Henry Ryecroft.'
1904	'Veranilda.'
1905	'Will Warburton.'
1906	'The House of Cobwebs and other Stories.'

BIOGRAPHICAL AND CRITICAL

Frank Swinnerton, 'George Gissing, A Critical Study,' 1912.
Morley Roberts, 'The Private Life of Henry Maitland,' 1912.
Edward Clodd, 'Memories,' 1916.
Introductions by Frederic Harrison to 'Veranilda,' 1904, and by Thomas Seccombe to 'The House of Cobwebs,' 1906.

May Yates, 'George Gissing, An Appreciation' (Publications
of the University of Manchester, England), 1922.

H. Miles, 'George Gissing,' 1929.

Algernon and Ellen Gissing, 'The Letters of George Gissing to
Members of his Family,' 1931.

Articles by A. S. Wilkins in the 'Owens College Union Magazine,' January, 1904; by H. G. Wells in the 'Monthly Review,'
August, 1904; and by Austin Harrison in the 'Nineteenth
Century,' September, 1906. Selections, autobiographical and
imaginative, from his works, with biographical and critical
notes by his son, and an introduction by Virginia Woolf, 1929.

THOMAS HARDY

NOVELS

1871   'Desperate Remedies.'
1872   'Under the Greenwood Tree.'
1873   'A Pair of Blue Eyes.'
1874   'Far from the Madding Crowd' ('Cornhill Magazine').
1876   'The Hand of Ethelberta.'
1878   'The Return of the Native.'
1880   'The Trumpet Major.'
1881   'A Laodicean.'
1882   'Two on a Tower.'
1886   'The Mayor of Casterbridge.'
1887   'The Woodlanders.'
1891   'Tess of the D'Urbervilles.'
1895   'Jude the Obscure.'
1897   'The Well Beloved.'

SHORT STORIES

1888   'Wessex Tales.'
1891   'A Group of Noble Dames.'
1894   'Life's Little Ironies.'
1913   'A Changed Man, The Waiting Supper and Other Tales.'

POEMS

1898   'Wessex Poems' (wr. 1865–70).
1901   'Poems of the Past and Present.'

1904 'The Dynasts,' Pt. 1.
1906 'The Dynasts,' Pt. 2.
1908 'The Dynasts,' Pt. 3.'
1910 'Time's Laughing Stocks.'
1916 'Satires of Circumstance.'
1917 'Moments of Vision and Miscellaneous Verses.'
1922 'Late Lyrics and Earlier.'
1923 'The Queen of Cornwall.'
1928 'Winter Words.'
1929 'Human Shows, Far Phantasies, Songs and Trifles.'

BOOKS ABOUT HARDY

Lionel Johnson, 'The Art of Thomas Hardy,' 1895. (New editions 1923, 1928.)

F. A. Hedgcock, 'Thomas Hardy, Penseur et Artiste,' 1911.

Lascelles Abercrombie, 'Thomas Hardy' (Contemporary Writers Series), 1912.

H. C. Duffin, 'Thomas Hardy: A Study of the Wessex Novels' (Publications of the University of Manchester, England), 1916.

Samuel C. Chew, 'Thomas Hardy, Poet and Novelist' (Bryn Mawr Notes and Monographs), 1921.

Joseph Warren Beach, 'The Technique of Thomas Hardy,' 1922.

Ernest Brennecke, Jr., 'Thomas Hardy's Universe: a Study of a Poet's Mind,' 1924.

Ernest Brennecke, Jr., 'Life of Thomas Hardy,' 1925

Patrick Braybrooke, 'Thomas Hardy and his Philosophy,' 1927.

J. G. Sime, 'Thomas Hardy of the Wessex Novels,' 1928.

Samuel C. Chew, 'Thomas Hardy, Poet and Novelist,' 1928.

Florence Emily Hardy, 'The Early Life of Thomas Hardy (1840–1891),' 1928.

Henry Major Tomlinson, 'Thomas Hardy,' 1929.

Florence Emily Hardy, 'The Later Years of Thomas Hardy (1892–1928),' 1930.

Ruth A. Firor, 'Folkways in Thomas Hardy,' 1930.

E. C. Hickson, 'Versification of Thomas Hardy,' 1931.

Arthur S. McDowall, 'Thomas Hardy, A Critical Study,' 1931.

Bibliography (1865–1915) by A. P. Webb.

BOOKS ABOUT THE HARDY COUNTRY

Wilkinson Sherren, 'The Wessex of Romance,' 1903.
Charles George Harper, 'The Hardy Country,' 1904.
Clive Holland, 'Wessex,' 1906.
Bertram Windle, 'The Wessex of Thomas Hardy,' 1906.
C. G. Harper, 'Wessex,' 1911.
S. H. Heath, 'The Heart of Wessex,' 1911.
Herman Lea, 'Thomas Hardy's Wessex,' 1913.
R. Thurston Hopkins, 'Thomas Hardy's Dorset,' 1922.
Donald Maxwell, 'The Landscape of Thomas Hardy,' 1928.
A useful little 'Handbook of the Wessex Country of Thomas
  Hardy's Novels and Tales' is published by Kegan Paul
  (London).

RUDYARD KIPLING

1886 'Departmental Ditties' (Lahore). (London, 1897.)
1888 'Plain Tales from the Hills' (Calcutta). (London,
        1890.)
      'Soldiers Three.' 'The Story of the Gadsbys.' 'In Black
        and White' (Calcutta). (Three volumes in one, Lon-
        don, 1895.)
      'Under the Deodars.' 'The Phantom Rickshaw.' 'Wee
        Willie Winkie' (Calcutta). (Three volumes in one,
        London, 1895.)
1890 (U. S.) 'The Light That Failed' (London, 1891).
1891 'The City of Dreadful Night.'
      'Life's Handicap.'
1891–2 'The Naulahka' (with Wolcott Balestier).
1892 'Barrack Room Ballads.'
1893 'Many Inventions.'
1894 'The Jungle Book.'
1895 'The Second Jungle Book.'
1896 'The Seven Seas.'
1897 'Captains Courageous.'
1898 'The Day's Work.'
      'A Fleet in Being.'
1899 'Stalky & Co.'
1901 'Kim.'
1902 'Just So Stories.'

1903   'The Five Nations.'
1904   'Traffics and Discoveries.'
1906   'Puck of Pook's Hill.'
1909   'Actions and Reactions.'
1910   'Rewards and Fairies.'
1911   'A School History of England' (with C. R. L. Fletcher).
1916   'Sea Warfare.'
1917   'A Diversity of Creatures.'
1919   'The Years Between.' 'Verse 1885–1918.'
1923   'The Irish Guards in the Great War.'
1923   'Independence.' (Rectorial address at St. Andrews
          University, October, 1923.)
1923   'Land and Sea Tales for Boys and Girls.'
1926   'Debits and Credits.'
1931   'Selected Poems.'
1932   'Limits and Renewals.'
1932   'His Apologies.'

BIOGRAPHICAL AND CRITICAL

There are many books about Kipling,—a 'Primer,' a 'Guide Book,' and a 'Dictionary'; critical and biographical studies by G. F. Monkhouse (1899), Will M. Clemens (1899), Richard Le Gallienne (1900), Cecil Charles (1911), Cyril Falls (1915), John Palmer (1915), Patrick Braybrooke (1926), and R. Thurston Hopkins (1914, 1916, 1921, 1929 and 1930); Bibliography by E. W. Martindell (1922); Bibliography by F. V. Livingston (1927).

J. M. BARRIE

NOVELS AND SKETCHES

1887   'Better Dead.'
1888   'Auld Licht Idylls.'
1889   'A Window in Thrums.'
1891   'The Little Minister.'
1896   'Margaret Ogilvy.'
          'Sentimental Tommy.'
1900   'Tommy and Grizell.'

PLAYS (*Dates of Production*)

1891	'Ibsen's Ghost.'
1892	'Walker, London.'
1894	'The Professor's Love Story.'
1897	'The Little Minister.'
1900	'The Wedding Guest.'
1902	'Quality Street.'
	'The Admirable Crichton.'
1903	'Little Mary.'
1904	'Peter Pan.'
1905	'Alice Sit-by-the-Fire.'
	'Pantaloon.'
1908	'What Every Woman Knows.'
1910	'The Twelve-Pound Look.'
1912	'Rosalind.'
1913	'The Will.'
	'Half an Hour.'
1914	'The Legend of Leonora.'
	'Der Tag.'
1915	'The New Word.'
1916	'A Kiss for Cinderella.'
	'A Slice of Life.'
1917	'The Old Lady Shows her Medals.'
	'Dear Brutus.'
1918	'A Well-remembered Voice.'
1920	'Mary Rose.'
1922	'Shall we Join the Ladies?'

BIOGRAPHICAL AND CRITICAL

J. A. Hammerton, 'J. M. Barrie and his Books,' 1900, 1902.
H. M. Walbrook, 'J. M. Barrie and the Theatre,' 1922.
Patrick Braybrooke, 'J. M. Barrie: a Study in Fairies and Mortals,' 1924.
Thomas Moult, 'Barrie,' 1928.
F. J. H. Darton, 'J. M. Barrie,' 1929.
J. A. Hammerton, 'Barrie; the Story of a Genius,' 1929.
J. Kennedy, 'Thrums and the Barrie Country,' 1930.
B. D. Cutter, 'Sir James M. Barrie,' 1931.

CHAPTER III

GEORGE BERNARD SHAW (1856–   )

THE most important literary event of the twentieth century was the revival of English comedy under the leadership of Bernard Shaw. The British drama in the nineteenth century had sunk to a depth of decay now hard to realize. In the theatre of the second half of the century, George Henry Lewes testifies, the public looked only for sentimental claptrap, jingles, dances, costumes, bare necks, and grimaces. Matthew Arnold, writing in 1879, said: "In England we have no drama at all. Our vast society is not homogeneous enough, not sufficiently united, even any large portion of it, in a common view of life, a common ideal capable of serving as basis for a modern English Drama." William Archer, who about this time was labouring for the regeneration of the theatre by translating Ibsen and contributing intelligent dramatic criticism to the London press, when he reflected on these endeavours forty years later, confessed that he was "puzzled to conceive how anyone with the smallest pretension to intelligence could in those years seriously occupy himself with the English theatre." Another famous London dramatic critic, A. B. Walkley, stigmatized the theatre of the early Victorian period as without ideas, so ephemeral, so paltry and jejune, that it was impossible to think of it without a yawn. "One shrinks from dwelling on this tedious theme." Even in 1904, when the revival of English comedy was well under way, Walkley, though encouraged, was still far from cheerful about the prospect: "There is a small minority of the playgoing public which shows symptoms of discontent. Its artistic conscience, if not deeply stirred, is, at any rate gently pricked. It signs manifestoes, writes to the newspapers, and in other futile ways gives vent to its suspicions that something ought to be done. But what precisely ought to be done nobody knows. Meanwhile the theatres, music-halls in everything but name and an atmosphere of tobacco-smoke, have it all their own way. The vast majority of the public takes its theatrical amusement, as it takes its newspaper information, in snippets. It is a public without patience, without the capacity for sustained attention, and, like Lady Teazle when she married Sir Peter, it has no taste. To speak of the drama as an art to such a public as this is to talk a language which it does not understand, and has no inclination to learn."

Shaw shared with Barrie—and had much the larger share—in the task of rescuing the drama from the slough into which it had fallen. He had to conduct a prolonged campaign until he was nearly fifty before he established himself as the leading personage in European drama, for the circumstances of his birth, education, and early struggle for literary success and influence were far from propitious. He was born in Dublin of English Protestant middle-class stock. "I am a typical Irishman," he says: "my family come from Yorkshire. My father was an ineffective, unsuccessful man, in theory a vehement teetotaler, but in practice often a furtive drinker." His mother, much more gifted and independent-minded, left Dublin to establish herself as a teacher of singing in London—a fact of cardinal importance in Bernard Shaw's future career. The religious atmosphere of his childhood

—though sometimes enlivened by a heretical uncle—was narrow and dreary, but at the age of ten he gave up going to church, and his first appearance in print was a letter to the newspapers protesting against the methods and doctrines of the popular religious revivalists, Moody and Sankey, who visited Dublin in 1875. His school days were, according to his own verdict, "the most completely wasted and mischievous part of my life. I instinctively saved my brains from destruction by resolute idleness, which, moreover, made school meaningless and tedious to me." But he "picked up at home, quite unconsciously, a knowledge of that extraordinary literature of modern music, from Bach to Wagner, which has saved me from being to the smallest disadvantage in competition with men who only know the grammar and mispronunciation of the Greek and Latin poets and philosophers. For the rest, my parents went their own way and let me go mine. Thus the habit of freedom, which most Englishmen and Englishwomen of my class never acquire and never let their children acquire, came to me naturally."

At fifteen he entered the office of a Dublin land-agent, and stayed there five years; he proved a competent clerk, in spite of his heretical opinions and his devotion to music and art, but it is not surprising that life at a Dublin desk was distasteful to him, and in 1876 he followed his mother to London. He worked for a while with the Edison Telephone Company, but subsisted mainly on his mother's bounty, his earnings during the first nine years by his pen amounting to only six pounds, of which five were paid for writing the advertisement of a patent medicine. These were the years of his novels, of which the first was, "with merciless fitness," entitled 'Immaturity.' The manuscript remained unpublished for half a century, partially devoured by mice, and even they were "unable to finish it." The other four found their way into print in obscure Socialist reviews, and have since been more than once republished, both in England and America, but beyond showing a turn for heresy and paradox, they are of slight literary significance, and their author has always refused to take them seriously. He says: "I recall these five remote products of my nonage as five heavy brown-paper parcels, which were always coming back to me from some publisher, and raising the very serious financial question of the sixpence to be paid to Messrs. Carter, Paterson & Company, the carriers, for passing them on to the next publisher."

Shaw was really engaged in acquiring the education for which he had found no opportunity in Dublin—haunting the National Gallery and the British Museum, hearing good music, joining revolutionary societies and meeting radical thinkers, reading Karl Marx and Henry George, speaking at street corners and in Hyde Park in support of Socialism, vegetarianism, and teetotalism, and so clarifying his opinions by learning how to express them. He gave up novel-writing for reasons he must be allowed to explain himself, for, as he says, "the best authority on Shaw is Shaw": "I had no taste for what is called 'popular art,' no respect for popular morality, no belief in popular religion, no admiration for popular heroics. As an Irishman, I could pretend to patriotism neither for the country I had abandoned nor the country that had ruined it. As a humane person I detested violence and slaughter, whether in war, sport, or the butcher's yard. I was a Socialist, detesting our anarchical scramble for money, and believing in equality as the only possible permanent basis of social organization, discipline, subordination, good manners, and selection of fit persons for high functions. Fashionable life, open on indulgent terms to unencumbered 'brilliant' persons, I could not endure."

Shaw's next venture was into journalism, for which he was admirably qualified by talent and education and in which he scored a brilliant success, first as reviewer for the 'Pall Mall Gazette' (1885–89) and art critic for the London 'World' (1885–88), next as musical critic for the 'Star' (1888–90), then in the same capacity for the 'World' (1890–94), and finally as dramatic critic for the 'Saturday Review' (1895–98). A selection of his dramatic notices, under the title 'Dramatic Opinions and Essays' was published in New York with an admirable preface by James Huneker, himself a very competent critic, and still enjoys a wide circulation on both sides of the Atlantic. It would be difficult to find in any language —and impossible in English—a set of criticisms which contain so much of permanent value. It was a time of crisis in the history of the London stage, which was beginning to emerge from the swaddling bands of sentimentalism and conventionality. A reviving breath came from the Continent in the dramas of Ibsen, and Shaw did his utmost to open the mind of the public to the new inspiration. Pinero and Henry Arthur Jones were writing plays of compromise which attempted to adapt new ideas to the popular palate, and Shaw encouraged or chided them as he found them true or false to the new ideals. The idolatry of Shakespeare, inherited from the critics of the Romantic movement, was an obstacle to progress, and Shaw did his best to destroy it, though he acknowledges that 'Othello,' 'Lear,' and 'Macbeth' are masterpieces, and that Shakespeare is "unsurpassed as poet, story-teller, character draughtsman, humorist, and rhetorician." Rightly considered, and due allowance being made for Shaw's love for the position of devil's advocate, there is little in his criticisms a modern Shakespeare scholar would object to; but at the time they aroused attention by their apparent extravagance—just what the author was aiming at—and ultimately they contributed powerfully to a juster appreciation of Shakespeare's real genius. Nothing is gained by attributing, even to masterpieces, virtues they do not really possess, and much of the Shakespeare worship current at the time had no solid foundation.

Shaw was justly proud of his achievements as a journalist, "convinced that nothing that is not journalism will live long as literature, or be of any use while it does live," but he has nothing but contempt for the journalists who profess that "it is their duty to 'reflect' what they believe to be the ignorance and prejudice of their readers, instead of leading and enlightening them to the best of their ability." When Max Nordau gained a passing popularity by a superficial essay on the degeneracy of modern art, Shaw took a holy delight in reversing his usual rôle and exposing the fallacies of Nordau's devil's advocacy—an easy task for Shaw, with his more thorough acquaintance with modern music, art, and literature and his greater command of invective. This paper, originally published in 1895 as a contribution to an American review, was reprinted in 1908 with a preface and some revisions, and is one of Shaw's most characteristic productions. It is amusing to find him asserting the necessity and usefulness of conventions and warning the "emancipated" young enthusiast who flings duty and religion, convention and parental authority to the winds that she will find herself plunged into duties, responsibilities and sacrifices from which she may be glad to retreat "into the comparatively loose life of an ordinary respectable woman of fashion." We have characteristic outbreaks by the way on the one hand against "the popular conception of God as an omniscient, omnipotent, and frightfully jealous and vindictive old gentleman sitting on a throne above the clouds," and on the other against the "crop of cheap syllogisms excogitated by a handful of raw Rationalists in their sects of 'Freethinkers,' and 'Secularists' and 'Positivists' and 'Don't Knowists' (Agnostics)." An incidental defence of special pleading throws light on Shaw's habitual method—"the way to get at the merits of a case is not to listen to the fool who imagines himself impartial, but to get it argued with reckless bias for and against." This explains much that readers find disconcerting in Shaw as mere extravagance and perversity. But more significant still is a sober and yet eloquent passage in which he sets forth his ideas as to the aim of art: "The claim of art to our respect must stand or fall with the validity of its pretension to cultivate and refine our senses and faculties until seeing, hearing, feeling, smelling, and tasting become highly conscious and critical acts with us, protesting vehemently against ugliness, noise, discordant speech, frowsy clothing, and re-breathed air, and taking keen interest and pleasure in beauty, in music, and in nature, besides making us insist, as necessary for comfort and decency, on clean, wholesome, handsome fabrics to wear, and utensils of fine material and elegant workmanship to handle. Further, art should refine our sense of character and conduct, of justice and sympathy, greatly heightening our self-knowledge, self-control, precision of action, and considerateness, and making us intolerant of baseness, cruelty, injustice, and intellectual superficiality or vulgarity. The worthy artist or craftsman is he who serves the physical and moral senses by feeding them with pictures, musical compositions, pleasant houses and gardens, good clothes and fine implements, poems, fictions,

essays, and dramas which call the heightened senses and
ennobled faculties into pleasurable activity. The great
artist is he who goes a step beyond the demand, and, by
supplying works of a higher beauty and a higher interest
than have yet been perceived, succeeds, after a brief
struggle with its strangeness, in adding this fresh extension
of sense to the heritage of the race."

Associated with Shaw's journalistic activity are two
books, 'The Quintessence of Ibsen' (1891) and 'The
Perfect Wagnerite' (1898). The first interprets Ibsen
from the point of view of Shaw's anti-idealism, and contains many entertaining flashes of light on and about the
struggle then proceeding to secure a foothold for the Ibsen
plays on the English stage; but it is Shaw's philosophy
rather than Ibsen's that is set forth, and the essay is far
from being a sufficient or safe guide to the ideas and
purposes of the Scandinavian poet. In the second volume
the Nibelung cycle is interpreted from the point of view
of Wagner's revolutionary opinions. But Shaw, in spite
of his versatility and keen intelligence, is no more successful than a mere professor in applying an allegorical
key to a work of art. At the time, however, the book no
doubt contributed to a better understanding of Wagner's
genius.

While Shaw was earning his livelihood as a journalist
and doing good service by winning attention for work of
real merit, as well as by exposing old shams and new
bores,—a task for which he had prepared himself by years
of study,—his real intellectual interest (first aroused by
Henry George's 'Progress and Poverty') lay in the social
questions which later became the predominant factor in
his work. He allied himself in 1884 with the more moderate organization of Socialist agitators known as the
Fabian Society and wrote in the last two decades of the

nineteenth century and the early years of the twentieth
a number of Socialistic papers which were published as
Fabian tracts or essays. Within the society, after a brief
period of extravagance, Shaw attached himself to the
more conservative wing, assisting Sidney Webb to resist
the unsuccessful campaign of H. G. Wells in favour of
a more vigorous policy. Meanwhile Shaw had enlarged
his acquaintance with practical problems of administration by six years' service on the St. Pancras Vestry and
Borough Council, the main literary outcome being one
of his most solidly reasoned Socialistic pamphlets, 'The
Common Sense of Municipal Trading' (1904). About this
time his interest in Socialism was waning under the competition of a new enthusiasm for eugenics, but this belongs
to the later period of his success as a dramatist and will
be most conveniently discussed in that connection. In
1911 he declared himself still theoretically in favour of
a "system of society where all the income of the country
is to be divided up in exactly equal proportions," and in
1928 he elaborated and modified this position in 'The Intelligent Woman's Guide to Socialism and Capitalism.'

Of the Shaw of the earlier period Sir William Rothenstein wrote in 'Men and Memories' (1931): "Shaw was a
wild man in public, violent, aggressive, and paradoxical;
in private he was the instinctive gentleman, ever on the
side of the oppressed and unpopular, tender-hearted and
generous, though he had little enough in those days to
be generous with. . . . He held his head high and kept
his temper and poured out his wit. Every gallant cause
has had his support. . . . No step was lighter, eye
fresher, nor tongue freer nor cleaner than Shaw's. No
decadence in him; he was a figure apart—brilliant, genial,
wholesome, a great wit, a gallant foe and a staunch friend,
a Swift without bitterness, sharer and castigator of the

follies of mankind, whose cap, though of Jaeger, was worn as gaily as motley."

As early as 1885, William Archer, who secured for Shaw his first footing in journalism, had attempted to collaborate with him in a play. Its subject was to be the power of money in modern social and industrial organization—the theme of the 'Rheingold,' as afterwards developed by Shaw in 'The Perfect Wagnerite'—and its manner was to be that of the well-made play, a French comedy, '*La Ceinture Dorée*,' being actually chosen for a suggestion of the plot. Archer made the scenario, and Shaw wrote the dialogue for the first act. At this point the two collaborators found themselves hopelessly at variance, but Shaw insisted on finishing the second act and reading it to Archer, who promptly went to sleep. This silent criticism discouraged Shaw more than his collaborator's comments, and he put the manuscript aside. In 1891 there came, in the wake of the new theatre movement abroad and the controversy about the production of the Ibsen plays on the English stage, the foundation of the Independent Theatre in London by J. T. Grein. The opportunity was there, but where were the new English plays? None were to be found, and Shaw bethought himself of his rejected manuscript. He added a third act, gave it the mock-scriptural title of 'Widowers' Houses,' and it was produced at the Royalty Theatre in 1892. "It made a sensation out of all proportion to its merits and even its demerits; and I at once became infamous as a dramatist." The Socialists applauded on principle; the public hooted; the critics followed suit; and the play had only two performances. Shaw himself accurately describes it as "a grotesquely realistic exposure of slum landlordism, municipal jobbery, and the pecuniary and matrimonial ties between it and the pleasant people of 'independent' incomes who imagine that such sordid matters do not touch their own lives." The characters are grotesquely impossible, the plot is conventional romance reversed so as to show all manner of ugliness, the dialogue is adorned with "silly pleasantries" (the author's own phrase). Shaw admits that in these "farcical trivialities" he had not taken the theatre seriously, and he determined to try again. He now felt quite sure of himself as a writer for the stage.

Ibsenism, at this time become a craze, was misunderstood both by its reactionary opponents and its "emancipated" devotees, and Shaw undertook in his next play to show both sides their misconceptions. 'The Philanderer,' of which the central scenes pass in a supposed Ibsen club in London, exhibits in its characters various degrees of infatuated hero-worship and blind condemnation, the heroine, Grace Tranfield, representing the intelligent appreciation of Ibsen's ideas as interpreted by Shaw himself. The play also serves to illustrate the fundamental difference in method between Shaw and the great Scandinavian whom he has been accused of copying. Ibsen is primarily the poet-dramatist, whose aim is "to depict human beings, human emotions, and human destinies, upon a groundwork of certain of the social conditions and principles of the present day." Shaw is first of all a propagandist, who uses the stage as a pulpit to set forth his opinions. In 'The Philanderer,' in addition to the exposition of popular misconceptions about Ibsen, Shaw indulges his prejudices against vivisection and the medical profession. The dialogue shows a considerable advance on 'Widowers' Houses,' but the characters, though more subtly conceived, are still mechanical. Grein declined to produce it on the excuse that it was beyond the capacity of his company, and it remained unacted until its real significance was almost unintelligible to either a New York or a London audience, the Ibsen craze having passed.

Shaw had too much determination and intellectual vigour to be discouraged. He returned to his earlier model in 'Mrs. Warren's Profession,' which purports to deal with the question of prostitution, but really discusses much wider questions of social and commercial organization. Mrs. Warren, in her account of herself first as a poor working girl and then as a successful manager of a white slave syndicate, sets forth the apologue of modern industrialism, as Shaw viewed it. The other characters are much less powerfully realized, and the rifle episode introduces an unnecessary element of melodrama; the doubtful paternity of Mrs. Warren's daughter also introduces unnecessary elements of "unpleasantness," but as a piece of dramatic construction and character drawing the play is by far the best thing Shaw had yet done. The British censor, however, interfered and prohibited its performance; there was a solitary production in London by the Stage Society in 1902, but the censor's ban was not withdrawn for thirty years; when it was put on the public stage, first in Birmingham and then in London in 1925, it received a warm welcome from both the public and the critics, who did not find it at all shocking.

In spite of the failure of 'Mrs. Warren's Profession' to reach the stage in 1894, the year was a fortunate one for Shaw. He was able to give up musical criticism on the 'World' for the more congenial and better-paid task of dramatic critic on the 'Saturday Review.' His first attempt at a "pleasant" play, 'Arms and the Man,' was put on at the Avenue Theatre, London, and ran from April 21 to July 7, at a loss of about five thousand pounds, which was paid by Miss Horniman, the "lady bountiful" of the new drama in London, Manchester, and Dublin; her father, a successful tea merchant, had left her a fortune, part of which she devoted to the encouragement of dramatic originality. 'Arms and the Man' travesties only conventional romanticism and militarism, and as the scene was laid in Bulgaria, about which the British public knew little and cared less, critics and audiences alike were willing to be amused. Its success had the important result of encouraging the leading American actor of the time, Richard Mansfield, who saw it during the London run, to put it on at the Herald Square Theatre, New York, the following September. Mansfield made a hit in the part of Bluntschli and liked the play; he asked Shaw to write another for him. Shaw was at this time trying to persuade Ellen Terry, who was sharing the triumphs of Sir Henry Irving at the London Lyceum Theatre, to induce Irving to put on a play by him, and he wrote for her 'The Man of Destiny,' which was submitted to Irving for his consideration. Shaw was also engaged in falling in love with Charlotte Frances Payne-Townshend, a "charming Irish millionairess with green eyes," who had become an ardent Socialist and a devoted admirer of Shaw, and married him at the West Strand Registry Office on June 1, 1898. Meanwhile Shaw succeeded in finishing 'The Devil's Disciple,' a comedy of the American Revolutionary War, for Mansfield, who produced it at Albany on October 1 and at the Fifth Avenue Theatre, New York City, on October 6, 1897. It had a good run (64 performances), and Shaw was able to write to Ellen Terry that he had received two thousand five hundred pounds in royalties up to April, 1898, with the prospect of receiving as much again. This unaccustomed wealth relieved Shaw of the necessity of further journalistic drudgery, and in the spring of 1899 he gave his position of dramatic critic on the 'Saturday Review' over to Max Beerbohm.

He felt himself, perhaps somewhat prematurely, not merely "a man of wealth and consideration," but "an established playwright." Irving persisted in neglecting to produce 'The Man of Destiny,' which was also refused by Mansfield; 'Candida,' a comedy dealing with Christian Socialism, with an excellent study of Ellen Terry in the part of the heroine, was rehearsed and abandoned by Mansfield; it also failed of production in London, and made no particular impression on a provincial tour on which it was produced by the Independent Theatre Company in 1897–8. Cyril Maude, then manager of the Haymarket Theatre, made a kindly inquiry about it, but Shaw, with characteristic independence, answered that it would not suit the Haymarket, but that he would write one that would. This was 'You Never Can Tell,' which was actually put into rehearsal with Allan Aynesworth in the principal part, but turned out to be, on account of the novelty of its tone and treatment, a piece of pure bewilderment to the actors. Shaw was absolutely uncompromising on all suggestions of changing the play or cutting down the dialogue, and it was withdrawn before it was produced. John Harrison, who was then stage-manager of the Haymarket, recounted the circumstances long after in a letter to the 'New York Times': "The members of the company had not the faintest idea of what they were talking about, and I suppose Shaw was either too lazy or too pained to tell them, and the climax came when Allan Aynesworth and Winifred Emery said to Shaw, 'Why don't you cut these parts?' 'Right!' replied Shaw. 'A rehearsal for cuts at 11 o'clock tomorrow.' The next morning Allan Aynesworth walked on to the stage with the largest blue pencil I have ever seen. God knows where he had got it, but it was about eighteen inches long and about three in circumference. With a beatific smile on his face, he strolled down to Shaw and, handing him his part, said, 'You said you could cut my part, Mr. Shaw; here is a pencil.' Shaw took the part, glanced at the pencil, and without batting an eye took the pencil with a 'Thanks, very much, I've left mine at home,' and deliberately made a downward stroke on every page of the part. There were snickers and muttered conversation all round. Rehearsal was dismissed. Harrison, Maude, and Shaw retired to the office. One hour after Cyril Maude said to me with great glee: 'We're not going to produce the play; ain't that a bit of luck!' Just about three weeks after that I met Ailsa Craig (daughter of Ellen Terry) on the street. She said: 'Hello; your management has turned down the best play written for years!' "

Maude's judgment in rejecting 'You Never Can Tell' was at fault, for it has since proved one of Shaw's most popular productions, both in England and America, combining a delightfully comic waiter and a grotesque barrister (his son), impossible twins, and a dental chair as a novelty in stage device with a modicum of philosophy about the relations of parents and children. But as the frontal attack on the London stage had apparently failed, Shaw tried the flank by publishing his one success, 'Arms and the Man,' and his half dozen failures under the title of 'Plays Pleasant and Unpleasant,' with elaborate stage directions and still more elaborate prefaces, intended for the edification of readers and as "first aid to critics." The success of this venture established the modern practice of publishing plays and gave Shaw access to the English-reading public all over the world—especially in the United States. He repeated the experiment, adding three prefaces this time, in 'Three Plays for Puritans' (1901) —'The Devil's Disciple,' 'Cæsar and Cleopatra,' and 'Captain Brassbound's Conversion.'

'Cæsar and Cleopatra' in the twentieth century was one of Shaw's most successful plays as acted by Sir Johnston Forbes-Robertson's company on both sides of the Atlantic, and in 1925 it was chosen by the New York Theatre Guild to open its new theatre; but in the nineteenth century it could not get itself performed. Mansfield declined it in 1899, and in the same year Forbes-Robertson pondered over it but gave it up for the time being on the ground that the expenses of production involved too heavy a risk. So Shaw finished the century with one English success, 'Arms and the Man,' and one American success, 'The Devil's Disciple,' to his credit. At the beginning of the twentieth century he was still "decisively ostracized" from the London regular theatres.

A voluntary organization for the production of plays which could not get a hearing in the commercial theatre, the London Stage Society, came to Shaw's rescue; they had no regular theatre, paid the author no royalties, and often paid the actors little or nothing; there were no paid admissions, the audience being limited to subscribers or those to whom the subscribers gave tickets. They began in 1899 with a single performance of 'You Never Can Tell'; they gave the first London production of 'Candida' in July, and of 'Captain Brassbound's Conversion' in December, 1900; they produced 'The Man of Destiny,' with Granville-Barker in the title part, in 1901; in January, 1902, greatly daring, they put on the stage 'Mrs. Warren's Profession.' It was still under the censor's ban, but the Stage Society's performances were technically private, and therefore not subject to interference by the authorities.

Then, with startling suddenness, success came to Shaw in full tide. 'Candida,' as published in 'Plays Pleasant and Unpleasant' was acted by amateurs in Chicago and Philadelphia, and attracted the attention of Arnold Daly, who produced it at a "trial matinée" at the Princess Theatre, New York, on December 8, 1903. It was warmly welcomed by the public and the critics, and after running for a hundred and fifty performances went on tour to Boston and elsewhere. In 1904–5 two companies under Arnold Daly's direction carried 'Candida' all over the United States. At first Daly presented 'The Man of Destiny' along with 'Candida,' but as he found this too great a strain for one evening, Shaw wrote for him a "comediettina" ('How he Lied to her Husband'), which, in conjunction with 'The Man of Destiny,' opened Daly's New York season in September, 1904, to be succeeded by 'You Never Can Tell' early in 1905. Daly's 1905–6 repertoire included 'John Bull's Other Island,' 'Mrs. Warren's Profession,' and 'Arms and the Man'; but the great event of this season was 'Man and Superman,' produced with Robert Loraine as John Tanner and the third act omitted. After running throughout the season at New York, with crowded houses, it was taken on tour to the principal cities of the United States.

The success of 'Candida' in New York emboldened Granville-Barker, who had been the moving spirit in the Stage Society productions of Shaw plays in London, to make a renewed effort at commercial production of modern drama at the Royal Court Theatre in conjunction with an experienced professional manager, J. E. Vedrenne. They began in April, 1904, with half a dozen experimental matinées of 'Candida.' The result was, as Shaw put it, "very satisfactory: heaps of press notices, all compliments for the company, and a modest profit for Barker and the theatre, besides some thirty pounds or so fees for the author." The Court Theatre became fashionable, was visited by royalty, and acquired unquestionable prestige: 'Man and Superman,' which had been written in 1901 and published in 1903, was produced by the Stage Society in May, 1905, and immediately taken over to the Court Theatre, which gave also 'John Bull's Other Island,' 'Candida,' and 'You Never Can Tell,' for three weeks each, with remarkable success. By this time Shaw had become the main reliance of the Court management, which began the season of 1905–6 with revivals of 'John Bull's Other Island' and 'Man and Superman.' 'Major Barbara,' the Salvation Army play specially written by Shaw for the Court Theatre, had a successful six-weeks' run, and the season was wound up with 'Captain Brassbound's Conversion,' with Ellen Terry, for whom the play was originally written, in the principal part. In three seasons, beginning in 1904, the Court Theatre gave over 700 performances of Shaw plays; the evening bills were drawn almost exclusively from the Shaw repertory and settled, at any rate for the next ten or twelve years, the issue of his exceptional popularity. He became not merely an "established playwright," but the leading dramatist of the modern stage.

The recognition of Shaw's supremacy in America and England was contemporaneous with his recognition on the European Continent. Through the good offices of William Archer, in 1902 an Austrian playwright made German translations of 'Candida,' 'The Devil's Disciple,' and 'Arms and the Man,' and these were successfully produced at Vienna, Dresden, and Berlin in 1903; other productions quickly followed, and in 1905 Shaw was hailed as "king of the German stage." Then came translations into Swedish, Danish, Magyar, Polish, Russian, and Dutch, establishing Shaw's position beyond question as an international playwright.

'Man and Superman' had been published in 1903 with 'Epistle dedicatory, the Revolutionist's Handbook, and Maxims for Revolutionists.' With the third act ('Don Juan in Hell') omitted, it was the success of the season 1905–6 both in England and the United States. The telling situation in the first act, though against all theatrical tradition (in that the secret of Violet's marriage is held back from the audience) and contrary to popular morality, delighted the public, and the suggestion that woman is the pursuer rather than the pursued had enough truth in it to win favour. Shaw's more serious purpose was to set forth his new doctrine of the Life Force, which impels Ann to seek in John Tanner a father for the Superman. "For art's sake" alone, he tells us in the 'Epistle dedicatory' he "would not face the toil of writing a single sentence." By comparing the Epistle with 'The Revolutionist's Handbook' we learn that what Shaw wished to convey was that education, progress, democracy, socialism are all illusions, and that "the only fundamental and possible socialism is the socialization of the selective breeding of Man: in other terms, of human evolution." The "method" is apparently to be "a joint stock human stud farm" under a State Department of Evolution. It is safe to say that very few of the thousands who enjoyed the play in England and the United States saw anything of this in the submission of John Tanner and Ann Whitefield to "the Life Force" when they "renounce happiness, renounce freedom, renounce tranquillity, above all, renounce the romantic possibilities of an unknown future, for the cares of a household and a family." They said to Shaw, as Ann said to Tanner, "Go on talking," and the final stage direction, "universal laughter," included the audience as well as the actors.

After a political dissertation on the Irish question, 'John Bull's Other Island,'—much more favourably regarded in London than in Dublin, for which it was written,— Shaw returned to sociology in 'Major Barbara.' The introduction of the Salvation Army is merely incidental, and Shaw apparently chose the manufacture of munitions as Undershaft's business because it was the modern industry he disliked most; but behind Undershaft stands the Life Force, regarded no longer as an impulse to propagation but as the Will of God—"a will of which I am a part." The real burden of the play (and of the preface) is, however, the doctrine of the evil of poverty, taken over (with due acknowledgement) from Samuel Butler. In the preface we read: "Now what does this Let Him Be Poor mean? It means let him be weak. Let him be ignorant. Let him become a nucleus of disease. Let him be a standing exhibition and example of ugliness and dirt. Let him have rickety children. Let him be cheap and let him drag his fellows down to his price by selling himself to do their work. Let his habitations turn our cities into poisonous congeries of slums. Let his daughters infect our young men with the diseases of the streets and his sons revenge him by turning the nation's manhood into scrofula, cowardice, cruelty, hypocrisy, political imbecility, and all the other fruits of oppression and malnutrition."

So in the play Undershaft enumerates the seven deadly sins as "food, clothing, firing, rent, taxes, respectability, and children," and describes poverty as "the worst of crimes": "All the other crimes are virtues beside it: all the other dishonours are chivalry itself by comparison. Poverty blights whole cities; spreads horrible pestilences;

strikes dead the very souls of all who come within sight, sound or smell of it. What you call crime is nothing: a murder here and a theft there, a blow now and a curse then: what do they matter? They are only the accidents and the illnesses of life: there are not fifty genuine professional criminals in London. But there are millions of poor people, abject people, dirty people, ill fed, ill clothed people. They poison us morally and physically: they kill the happiness of society: they force us to do away with our liberties and to organize unnatural cruelties for fear they should rise against us and drag us down into their abyss. Only fools fear crime: we all fear poverty."

The public found Shaw's doctrines as expounded by Undershaft much less interesting that 'The Revolutionist's Handbook,' and the Salvation Army lass who was the granddaughter of an earl was no more convincing than the Greek professor who turned from beating the big drum to running a huge concern for the manufacture of munitions. There was a further falling-off in 'The Doctor's Dilemma,' which repeats on a large scale and in a preface of nearly a hundred pages the misrepresentation of the medical profession Shaw had already been guilty of in the earlier sketch of Dr. Paramore ('The Philanderer'). The professional dilemma is non-existent, there being no question as to the conduct of a doctor who kills a patient because he wants to marry the patient's wife; but the problem really posed is "how much selfishness we ought to stand from a gifted person for the sake of his gifts." In the preface to 'The Sanity of Art,' written about this time, Shaw says that he does not believe in allowing license to genius, but in the play the unscrupulous artist makes out a very good case for himself, and dies in "indescribable peace" protesting his faith "in Michael Angelo, Velasquez, and Rembrandt; in the might of design, the mystery of colour, the redemption of all things by Beauty everlasting, and the message of art that has made these hands blessed."

'The Doctor's Dilemma' was acted as soon as it was written, and so were the two plays that followed it. Shaw was in a position to say what he liked, for revolutionary opinion was growing, and many people who enjoyed his fun regarded his paradoxes merely as part of the performance. In 'Getting Married' he not only said what he liked, but said it how he liked. There is no plot —merely the setting of a continuous conversation on marriage, fortified by the customary preface, in which polygyny, polyandry, promiscuity, and every other sexual arrangement are discussed, and the following are offered as practical proposals:

"Make divorce as easy, as cheap, and as private as marriage.

"Grant divorce at the request of either party, whether the other consents or not; and admit no other ground than the request, which should be made without stating any reasons.

"Place the work of a wife and mother on the same footing as other work: that is, on the footing of labour worthy of its hire; and provide for unemployment in it exactly as for unemployment in shipbuilding or any other recognized bread-winning trade."

The play presents the inequalities and subterfuges of the existing marriage system in a sufficiently extravagant fashion, and is remarkable for a passage in which Mrs. George Collins is inspired to picture the raptures of passion with an ardour Shaw succeeded in conveying only in this instance—and that in retrospect.

In 'The Shewing-up of Blanco Posnet' Shaw returned

to melodrama, this time in a Wild Western setting, with the Life Force figuring under the name of God. This the Censor objected to and prohibited the performance of the play; but as the Lord Chamberlain's writ did not run in Dublin, it passed successfully into the repertory of the Irish National Theatre, and was produced by the Irish Players on their American tour without a shadow of offence. Shaw took occasion to make hay of the British censorship, which was then being investigated by a parliamentary committee, in a characteristic preface.

The Censor also fell foul of Shaw's next play, 'Press Cuttings,' which ridiculed the suffragette agitation, then at its height, and represented Premier Balsquith as chaining himself to the scraper at General Mitchener's door. As the Censor had objected to the "sermon in crude Melodrama" because it discussed religion, a forbidden subject for the English theatre, he interposed in this instance another long-standing tradition which prohibited the introduction of contemporary personages on the stage. Shaw protested that he had no intention of caricaturing Mr. Asquith and Lord Kitchener and changed the names to Johnson and Bones; the play is an amusing skit on contemporary political difficulties, but has no philosophic or dramatic significance.

The same might be said of 'Misalliance,' except that it gave the opportunity for a preface on 'Parents and Children' (Samuel Butler again) of more than ordinary length, and of 'The Dark Lady of the Sonnets,' a Shakespearian extravaganza, both of which failed to please; but with 'Fanny's First Play' Shaw scored the most remarkable success of his career up to that time (1911). It had a record run in London, and in the United States ran for an even longer period. Shaw availed himself of the Elizabethan device of "the play within the play" for a setting in which he made fun of the London critics, A. B. Walkley, Gilbert Cannan, and A. E. Vaughan; and the expedient of attributing the play proper to an aspiring amateur enabled him to combine the extravagant heresies he had already inflicted on the public with a conventional plot. The son of a respectable tradesman is sentenced to fourteen days' imprisonment with the option of a fine for assaulting the police, on the same day that the daughter of another respectable tradesman, to whom he is engaged, receives a similar penalty for the same offence, independently committed by her on her way home from a religious meeting. In the end the boy marries "Darling Dora," a "daughter of joy," and the girl a disguised footman who is the brother of a Duke. In the two-page preface, which was all he deemed the play worth, Shaw described it as a mere "pot-boiler," and so it was, in the sense that it contained no propaganda that Shaw had not made before; but the public liked the familiar heresies about family life all the better in a setting obviously absurd, and accepted them as a not unwelcome part of a capital evening's entertainment.

By this time Shaw seemed to have communicated to the public, indirectly and directly, all that he really had to say. He had realized the need for saying it entertainingly, and in some cases the sugar-coating of the pill had been so substantial as to overmaster completely the bitter instruction it was intended to convey, but this was remedied by the prefaces, if people could be induced to read them. There was no subject, however, on which his versatile intellect could not reflect gleams of wit and wisdom, and the temptation of the open stage, to be used as a pulpit to his heart's desire, was too great to be resisted. 'Over-ruled,' which was first entitled 'Trespassers will be Prosecuted,' is a continuation of the interminable conversation of 'Getting Married,' and 'Great Catherine' introduces a Victorian Englishman to the Russian court of the eighteenth century, but both these are mere sketches. The substantial additions to Shaw's dramatic achievement up to the outbreak of the War were 'Androcles and the Lion' and 'Pygmalion,' which had their original production in Germany, 1912–13. Both were put on London and New York stages, and met with enthusiastic approval. 'Pygmalion,' as staged in the spring of 1914 at His Majesty's Theatre by Sir Herbert Beerbohm Tree with Mrs. Patrick Campbell in the part of the flower girl, was an even greater commercial success than 'Fanny's First Play.'

'Androcles and the Lion' presents the Shavian view of primitive Christianity, with some glances at religion in general in the finely conceived character of Lavinia, but its real attraction consists in the dramatization of the nursery tale which 'Sandford and Merton' had made familiar to Shaw's own generation. The Lion (really the principal rôle) and Androcles, both admirably acted, were irresistibly funny, and a comic Emperor with comic subjects (including the Christian martyrs) contributed to the enjoyment of those who did not mind the profanation of subjects traditionally sacred.

'Pygmalion,' "a romance in five acts," presents the conversion of a London flower girl into a possible duchess by three months' training in phonetics. Her trial appearance in a London drawing room provides some excellent fooling, but the real delight of the play is the character of her father, the dustman Doolittle, spokesman of the undeserving poor until a legacy from a misguided American philanthropist lands him in an unhappy respectability. The suggestion of the idle dustman may have come from a recollection of Shaw's boyhood—a cynical tramp who was asked by Shaw's uncle why he did not work and "frankly replied that he was too lazy"; but the conception is worked out with inimitable humour. Oddly enough, this burlesque character is more humanized than that of the boorish professor of phonetics, a caricature of a well-known Oxford don, but so indistinctly realized that Shaw had to add not merely a preface about him, but a supplementary note of sixteen pages to explain the outcome of the educational experiment which forms the centre of the play.

During the War Bernard Shaw's reputation was under a cloud. When the War broke out, he wrote a series of articles which classed the British Imperialists with the German Junkers, and scoffed at the idea that regarding treaties as "scraps of paper" was at all unusual. He pictured the British Lion as only shamming sleep in order to tempt Germany to provocative action: "the Lion, with a mighty roar, sprang at last, and in a flash had his teeth and claws in the rival of England, and will not now let her go for all the pacifists or Socialists in the world until he is either killed or back on his Waterloo pedestal again." Shaw took off his hat to the noble old beast as he made his last charge, and applauded his splendid past and valiant breed; but in future, he added, "we must fight, not alone for England, but for the welfare of the world." To anyone versed in Shaw's hyperbolical manner and capable of penetrating to the real meaning lying behind his exaggerations, there was little in what he said to give offence,—but the British public was in no mood to make allowances and distinctions. Shaw's utterances were regarded as lending aid and comfort to the enemy—absurdly enough, for he was as far removed as the poles from pro-Germanism—and his licence as a popular entertainer was tacitly withdrawn. Many, even among his own followers, held him blameworthy in failing to respond to the national emotion and assuming an unseasonable attitude of detachment. It was a situation in which his keen intelligence did not make up for his lack of emotional sympathy. It is the fault of all his work up to this time—his characters talked about love, but they failed to give the impression of being in love, and their anger like their fear seemed to be put on from the outside. But the exhibition of this defect at a critical moment in the nation's history did not reasonably merit the bitter resentment it aroused, and calmer times brought back a juster appreciation of the offender's real genius, with a general return of his older successes to the stage.

'Playlets of the War' did not tend to conciliate public opinion, or indeed add to the author's reputation, and 'Heartbreak House' was a puzzle to most readers on its first publication. The preface, with its reference to Chekhov's 'The Cherry Orchard,' of which the play is an English transcription, was enlightening. "The same nice people, the same utter futility." When it was put on the stage by the Theatre Guild in New York, the play was surprisingly successful and had a good run, but it was less warmly welcomed on its reproduction in London. Probably English audiences were better able to realize the distance between Shaw's caricatures and the reality, and were in too serious a mood to be diverted by the satire. The American audiences took the play more objectively and were amused by its quick movement and intellectual extravagances, which they no doubt regarded as mere absurdities, without any relation to any society they knew. As a work of art it falls far short in delicacy and dramatic skill of 'The Cherry Orchard' on which it was modelled.

'Back to Methuselah' is a return, on an unprecedented scale for a drama, to Shaw's own manner. In a review of his dramatic activities in the preface he catalogues as subjects he has discussed, in a series of comedies of manners in the classic fashion, "slum landlordism, doctrinaire Free Love (pseudo-Ibsenism), prostitution, militarism, marriage, history, current politics, natural Christianity, national and individual character, paradoxes of conventional society, husband hunting, questions of conscience, professional delusions and impostures." 'Man and Superman' he had intended to make a dramatic parable of Creative Evolution, believing that this was the religion of which mankind stood in need; but "being then at the height of my invention and comedic talent, I decorated it too brilliantly and lavishly." Now, in his old age, he abandons the erotic associations of the Don Juan legend, and goes back to the legend of the Garden of Eden "without distractions and embellishments." The embellishments are not altogether lacking, fortunately for those who regard Shaw's decorations as more important than his Gospel. As presented by the Theatre Guild in New York in three instalments (and two of these lasted for nearly four hours), Shaw's version of the Garden of Eden legend proved quite entertaining, so long as it stayed in or near the Garden. When it wandered into the future—A.D. 2170, A.D. 3000, and A.D. 31,920—it was often tiresome; the central idea that man needs a longer life to enable him to solve the problems of existence was not sufficient to bear the strain put upon it, and the final solution in 'As Far as Thought can Reach' offered a view of human society which was singularly unattractive. As a critic of other people's isms, Shaw had shown extraordinary versatility and comic power; when he came to propound his own religion, he was less successful. Still,

the audiences responded sympathetically to the emotional
appeal of the final speech of the play:

"I am Lilith: I brought life into the whirlpool of force,
and compelled my enemy, Matter, to obey a living soul.
But in enslaving Life's enemy I made him Life's master;
for that is the end of all slavery; and now I shall see the
slave set free and the enemy reconciled, the whirlpool
become all life and no matter. And because these infants
that call themselves ancients are reaching out towards
that, I will have patience with them still; though I know
well that when they attain it they shall become one with
me and supersede me, and Lilith will be only a legend
and a lay that has lost its meaning. Of Life only is there
no end; and though of its million starry mansions many
are empty and many still unbuilt, and though its vast
domain is as yet unbearably desert, my seed shall one
day fill it and master its matter to its uttermost confines.
And for what may be beyond, the eyesight of Lilith is
too short. It is enough that there *is* a beyond."

The successful production of 'Back to Methuselah' by
the New York Theatre Guild cemented an alliance which
was of capital importance for both parties. Negotiations
had begun in June, 1920, when Shaw's reputation was still
under the cloud cast by his war pamphleteering, and
'Heartbreak House,' published in 1919, had not yet been
put on the stage. When St. John Ervine approached Shaw
with a view to its production by the Guild, Shaw expressed doubts whether there existed in New York a management "bold enough and clever enough to know that the
alternative to pleasing an audience for two hours is to
put the utmost strain upon their attention for three and
send them home exhausted but impressed." Ervine, who
had seen the work of the Guild during a visit to New
York, reassured him on this point, and he consented.

After the run of 'Heartbreak House' in the fall of 1920, the Guild asked permission to produce 'Back to Methuselah,' and Shaw replied, "You are quite mad, but go ahead." At the end of the run (February-April, 1922), the director of the Guild reported to Shaw a loss of $20,-000 on the production; unperturbed, he rejoined that inasmuch as the Guild had expected to lose $30,000, there had really been a clear profit of $10,000. But in recognition of the Guild's enterprise, Shaw gave them the first call upon his whole repertoire, including his new plays, and after a revival of 'The Devil's Disciple,' they gave, at the end of 1923, the first representation of 'St. Joan,' which had not yet been published or put on the stage.

The production was worthy of the occasion, which was a dramatic event of world-wide importance. In the following year the play was seen in London and in every other important dramatic centre in Europe, but no presentation exceeded in care and adequacy the original New York production. It was at once the height of Shaw's fame and of his dramatic achievement—the more remarkable that it was achieved at the age of 67; when he was seventy the award to him of the Nobel prize for literature set the seal of official approval on a distinction already indicated by popular applause at the productions of his plays all over the world. When, in May, 1925, Shaw, "in an unusual mood of modesty," reckoned the spectators of his plays and the readers of what he had written at "not less than a million people," the London 'Observer' pointed out that during the season there had been "a boom in Mr. Shaw," four of his plays having been produced or revived in London alone. The 'Observer' thought Shaw's estimate of a million far too low: "Seeing that his name has been a household word on the Continent for twenty-five years and in this country for ten; that it must be a poor week in which half-a-dozen of his plays are not running in one European town with another; that his published works number between thirty and forty; and that for many years he was a regular contributor to the daily and weekly Press, one might safely multiply the figure many times."

'St. Joan' was not an unworthy climax to a great career, pursued with unfaltering courage and devotion for nearly half a century, if we reckon only from Shaw's arrival in London at the age of twenty. What privations, vicissitudes, hardships, and disappointments he had gone through in the first half of that long struggle can scarcely be realized except by himself, but he arrived at an age when the creative power of most artists is exhausted, with undiminished fertility of wit and invention, and an added richness of emotional expression. Wal er Prichard Eaton, the leading American dramatic critic of the time, reviewing Shaw's dramatic activity the year before 'St. Joan' was produced, said of him: "Shaw has proved his easy mastery of the peculiar technique required to set imaginary characters on a stage and cause them to hold the interest of an audience. Indeed, his mastery is so easy that it makes the masters of the 'the well-made play' look like straining schoolboys. To this sheer theatrical skill he has added a pungent wit, a racy satire, and the driving force of a restless mind that questions, revolts, disturbs, harasses. It is a fact rather ignored by critics that his output of stage plays for the past quarter-century has been huge, considering their quality (about one a year for an average), and that their percentage of success in the popular theatre has been extraordinarily high. There is probably no other dramatist of our day whose works, over anything like an equal period of time, have seen so many performances. His reputation as an intellectual has obscured his solid success as a man of the theatre. But it is through the theatre that he has driven his ideas into the minds of his fellows; it is the theatre-goers who have made him the figure he is."

The historical figure of Joan of Arc doubtless suggested itself to Shaw because of its religious significance. His early outbursts against the popular conceptions of the Deity as an old gentleman with a white beard (something like Shaw himself in his old age) sitting upon a bank of clouds, were interpreted by some people as indicating a lack of the religious spirit, but there could not be a greater mistake. Shaw in his youth discarded the rather narrow evangelical Protestantism of his first environment, but he retained a good deal of its Puritan asceticism, being devoted, as he himself put it in 1924, to "a quiet and simple life, a vegetarian, a teetotaler, and non-smoker." He had also something of the Puritan *intransigeance*—not to say fanaticism—an uncompromising adherence to intellectual ideals and a rational view of life. He was, at the same time, something of a mystic, for his belief in the Life Force is obviously transcendental. There is a hint of this in 'You Never Can Tell' (written in 1896), and again in 'Cæsar and Cleopatra' (written in 1898), but it is first clearly brought out in the third act of 'Man and Superman' (written in 1901, and published in 1903); this act was omitted from stage performances of the play until 1925, when it was regarded as "skies higher in interest and power" than the brilliant and lavish dramatic setting Shaw had given to his parable of creative evolution, being at that time, as he put it "at the height of my invention and comedic talent." The fault was probably not so much that of the author as of the public, which, both in England and in the United States, needed another quarter of a century of training, by Shaw and others, before it was ready to lend, if not a sympathetic, at any rate a tolerant ear to Shaw's doctrine.

The subject of religion is dealt with, in one form or another in 'Major Barbara' (1905), 'The Doctor's Dilemma' (1906), 'Getting Married' (1908), and 'The Shewing-up of Blanco Posnet' (1909). In the first of these Andrew Undershaft acts under a "constant sense that he is only the instrument of a Will, or Life Force, which uses him for purposes wider than his own." "All genuinely religious people," Shaw adds, "have that consciousness." Louis Dubedat, the artist, has it, in 'The Doctor's Dilemma'; Mrs. George Collins has it, in 'Getting Married'; and it is the theme of 'The Shewing-up of Blanco Posnet,' which is "a sermon in crude melodrama —a religious tract in dramatic form." "God made me," says Blanco, "because he had a job for me. He let me run loose till the job was ready; and then I had to come along and do it." Not one of these characters is religious, or even moral, according to conventional standards; but each of them has the religious spirit, as Shaw understands it. Religion even creeps into that inspired pot-boiler 'Fanny's First Play.' It is the excitement of a religious revival that lands Margaret Knox in Holloway Gaol; and the incident moves her mother to express Shaw's view of popular religion: "We bring our children up just as we were brought up; and we go to church or chapel just as our parents did; and we say what everybody says; and it goes on all right until something out of the way happens: there's a family quarrel, or one of the children goes wrong, or a father takes to drink, or an aunt goes mad, or one of us finds ourselves doing something we never thought we'd want to do. And then you know what happens: complaints and quarrels and huff and offence and bad language and bad temper and regular bewilderment as if Satan possessed us all. We find out then that with all our respectability and piety, we've no real religion and no way of telling right from wrong. We've nothing but our habits; and when they're upset, where are we?"

Religion—and more especially the Christian religion—is the sole subject of 'Androcles and the Lion'—not only of the play but of a preface of over a hundred pages on The Prospects of Christianity. In the latter, he begins with the suggestion that Christianity as set forth by Jesus in the Gospels has never had a trial, summing up its doctrines as:

"The kingdom of God is within you.

"Get rid of your property by throwing it into the common stock.

"Get rid of judges and punishment and revenge.

"Get rid of your family entanglements."

In their application to modern life, these precepts of Jesus, according to Shaw's own view, mean simply Communism, the abolition of punitive imprisonment, and free divorce. In the play, however, indulging still his comedic talent and power of invention, he presents us with comic Christians, who joke and sing 'Onward Christian Soldiers' as they march to the arena, comic Romans, comic Gladiators, serving under a comic Editor, and above all a supremely comic Androcles and a still more comic Lion. At the end of the play Shaw explains that he is attempting, not to illustrate any doctrines, but a persecution like all other persecutions—"an attempt to suppress a propaganda that seemed to threaten the interests involved in the established law and order, organized and maintained in the name of religion and justice by politicians who are pure opportunist Have-and-Holders." The one serious character, Lavinia, presents—and that only incidentally—the author's point of view, accepting what is sincere in both paganism and Christianity and striving "for the coming of the God who is not yet."

It was not until after the War, in 'Back to Methuselah' (1921) that Shaw found an opportunity of presenting to the public his beginning of a Bible for Creative Evolution, and the effort, though made in full seriousness and at exhaustive length, was not particularly successful.

In his next play, 'St Joan,' Shaw made another and more successful attempt to embody his religious views in dramatic form. For him Joan of Arc is neither a hysterical patriot nor a military mascot, but a saint—one of those rare personalities who come into contact with unseen spiritual forces and endeavour to interpret them to their generation. He is not offended—as sceptical critics like Voltaire and Anatole France are—by her hearing of "voices"—to him these are merely the externalizations of the inner promptings of her own mind. She awakens the hostility of the ecclesiastical authorities because she brushes them aside to assert the direct contact between her soul and God. "What other judgment can I judge by but my own?" she asks, and so becomes for Shaw the exponent of the Protestant spirit of free inquiry and private judgment. Her miracles he explains as mere coincidences or lucky accidents, which impressed people as signs of the divine favour, for a miracle, according to the Archbishop's definition, is "an event which creates faith. That is the purpose and nature of miracles. They may seem very wonderful to the people who witness them, and very simple to those who perform them." Joan's miracles in the play are often simply examples of her courage or common sense.

Joan's Nationalism is of less interest to Shaw, except in so far as it helps to break down the power of the

Church and the Feudal System. Cauchon, Bishop of Beauvais, representing the former, and the Earl of Warwick, representing the latter, both strongly disapprove of it. Cauchon says Joan's Nationalism "is essentially anti-Catholic and anti-Christian; for the Catholic Church knows only one realm, and that is the realm of Christ's kingdom. Divide that kingdom into nations, and you dethrone Christ. Dethrone Christ, and who will stand between our throats and the sword? The world will perish in a welter of war." But the interpretations of Nationalism put into Joan's own mouth are much milder in tone. For Joan, the English also are servants of God, but they should serve God where God has put them—in their own country. What Joan wants is what all the saints have longed for—the kingdom of God on earth. That is the burden of her message to King Charles: "It is God's business we are here to do; not our own"; and that is the burden of her final prayer. "O God that madest this beautiful earth, when will it be ready to receive Thy saints? How long, O Lord, how long?"

Joan is the greatest and most original of Shaw's creations of character, apart from such triumphs in burlesque as the waiter in 'You Never Can Tell,' the dustman Doolittle in 'Pygmalion,' Cleopatra, and Androcles. Probably neither Winifred Lenihan, who played the part of Joan in New York, nor Sybil Thorndike, who played it in London, nor any of the Continental interpreters of the rôle, entirely realized Shaw's conception. Miss Lenihan was the young, self-confident, bluff country-girl, a thorough daughter of the soil in her peasant-like matter-of-factness and doggedness and her acceptance of great lords and kings and prelates as such without idolatry or snobbery, seeing at a glance how much they were individually good for; but Miss Lenihan did not always rise to the full spiritual and tragic significance of Shaw's conception of the character. This was better realized by Miss Thorndike's more mature art, but her representation necessarily lacked Miss Lenihan's youthful energy and go, her shrewd, practical common-sense, sexless attractiveness and masterfulness. In spite of the brilliance of the original New York production and the variety of the many European settings, it is a question whether the full meaning of the play is not better brought out by a quiet perusal with Shaw's preface and stage directions to help the attentive reader.

After a period of comparative quiescence, during which Shaw's predominance was kept before the public by numerous revivals of his earlier plays, and the publication of 'The Intelligent Woman's Guide to Socialism and Capitalism' (1928), Shaw came back to the English stage in 1929 at the Malvern Festival with the production of 'The Apple Cart,' which had been previously performed in a Polish version at Warsaw. It is a high-spirited extravaganza on modern democratic politics, set forward a few generations into a future in which Germany has become a chain of Soviet Republics extending from the North Sea to the Ural Mountains, France is an empire mainly African, with its capital at New Timgad, the Atlantic is controlled by the cosmopolitan fleet of the League of Nations, and the United States is ready to amalgamate with the British Empire (already threatened by the removal of its capital to Montreal or Melbourne) on condition that, like Ireland, it enjoys Dominion Home Rule under its own President. Great Britain still owes the United States its old War debt, but British capitalists have invested so heavily in American concerns that after the interest has been paid there are two thousand million dollars a year to be transmitted from New York to London to balance the account. England lives very comfortably by the exportation of chocolate creams, golf clubs, pottery, tapestry, racing motor boats, automobiles and other such popular luxuries. But the people's interests and recreations are as inane then as they are now; so long as they have high wages and cheap amusements, they do not care who owns the factories or runs the country. "There is not a single aristocrat left in politics, not a single member of the professions, not a single leading personage in big business or finance. They are richer than ever, more powerful than ever, more able and better educated than ever." But not one of them will touch the drudgery of public affairs, and government is left to ill-paid demagogues or politicians, many of them in the pay of big business and all of them under its thumb. The only safeguard of the democracy is the royal veto and the King's disinterested devotion to the public welfare. The politicians are as shortsighted, as crass, as quarrelsome, as conventionally oratorical and as absurdly blatant in the future as they are in the present.

All this might be regarded by the serious student of world politics as a very discouraging prognosis, but it is carried through with so much drollery, inventiveness, quick repartee, and high spirits, that in England especially, where every hit told, it was very well received; in the United States, where the local allusions were not so obvious, it was less welcome; and it is doubtful whether in Warsaw, where it was first produced, the Polish audience really understood what it was all about.

In 'Too True to be Good' (1932) Shaw returned to the subject of religion—not to set forth his own ideas, for he had evidently nothing new to say, but to exhibit the hopeless lack of the religious spirit in modern civilization: the title apparently indicates that an accurate view of the time could not be an encouraging one. The play was put on first at Boston at the end of February and at the beginning of April in New York by the Theatre Guild, but even their thousands of subscribers could not keep it going after May 21. In England, after trial performances at the Malvern Festival and at Birmingham in the summer, it had a London run in the autumn of six weeks only, whereas 'The Apple Cart' held the stage for ten months. The critics at all these dramatic centres were practically unanimous in disapproval or very faint and modified praise; no one showed any whole-hearted enthusiasm—not even the actors. At the end of the first act, one of the characters confessed: "The play is now virtually over, but the characters will discuss it at great length for two acts more." And so they do. The hero, if such he may be called, is a clergyman turned burglar, who induces a sweet young thing, whose pearls he is stealing, to elope with him to a Mediterranean pleasure resort and stage a pretended kidnapping as a means of obtaining more money for them to lead a gay life together. It is the clergyman-burglar who, at the end of the play, expounds its moral at inordinate length. In the course of his sermon he says: "It is clear to me that though they" (the present generation) "are dispersing quietly to do very ordinary things . . . yet they are all falling, falling, falling endlessly and hopelessly through a void in which they can find no footing. There is something fantastic about them, something unreal and perverse, something profoundly unsatisfactory . . . naked bodies no longer shock us, but the horror of the naked mind is still more than we can bear. . . .

"Swear; use dirty words; drink cocktails; kiss and caress and cuddle until girls who were like roses at eighteen are like battered demireps at twenty-two; in all these ways the bright young things of the victory have scandalized their pre-war elders and left nobody but their bright young selves a penny the worse. But how are we to bear this dreadful new nakedness? The iron lightning of war has burnt great rents in our angelic veils of ideal-isms, just as it has smashed great holes in our cathedral roofs and torn great gashes in our hillsides. Our souls go in rags now. . . .

"I stand midway between youth and age like a man who has missed his train: too late for the last one and too early for the next. . . . I am by nature and destiny a preacher. I am the new Ecclesiastes. But I have no Bible, no creed: the war has shot both out of my hands. . . . I am ignorant: I have lost my nerve and am intimi-dated; all I know is that I must find the way of life, for myself and all of us, or we shall surely perish. And meanwhile my gift has possession of me: I must preach and preach and preach, no matter how late the hour and how short the day, no matter whether I have nothing to say—"

It is no wonder that some of the critics were tempted to identify the preacher with the author, in spite of Shaw's protests against such an identification. Dr. J. W. Krutch takes the play to mean that Shaw has lost faith, not only in the future of Western civilization, but in his own remedies for its failures and corruptions. Even St. John Ervine, hitherto Shaw's steadfast admirer and disciple, reproaches the aged prophet for losing his once magnificent courage and becoming a counsellor of despair. It seems unnecessary to take so seriously what is obvi-ously a dramatic extravaganza—a satire on the de-pression and unfaith of the time. Shaw himself suggests as a sub-title for the play: 'A Collection of Stage Sermons by a Fellow of the Royal Society of Literature.' The

Royal Society of Literature is an organization which devotes itself to the defense of all that in literature is conventional and traditional: we may be sure that Shaw would never include himself in that category. That a large number of people in Great Britain are inclined to despair —clergymen among the rest—cannot be denied, but it would take stronger evidence than this to justify ranking Shaw among them. Besides, though he is seventy-six years of age, he has not yet said his last word.

BIBLIOGRAPHY

NOVELS

'Immaturity.' Written 1879. Published 1930 in 'Works of Bernard Shaw' (limited edition, Constable & Co., London).

'The Irrational Knot.' Written 1880. Serial publication 1885–7. American and English editions, 1905.

'Love among the Artists.' Written 1881. Serial publication 1887–8. American edition 1900. English edition 1914.

'Cashel Byron's Profession.' Written 1882. Serial publication 1885–6. English edition 1886.

'An Unsocial Socialist.' Written 1883. Serial publication 1884. English edition 1887.

SOCIALISM

1884　Fabian Tract No. 2, 'Manifesto.'

1885　Fabian Tract No. 3, 'Warning to provident Landlords and Capitalists.'

1887　Articles on Marxian Socialism in the 'Pall Mall Gazette' and 'National Reformer.'

1888　Address to the Economic Section of the British Association. Published as 'The Transition' with another chapter on the economic basis of Socialism in a volume of 'Fabian Essays' (1889) edited by Shaw.

1891　'The Legal Eight Hours Question.' A public debate with J. W. Foote.
'The Impossibilities of Anarchism.'

1892　'The Fabian Society; its Early History.'

1894　'Socialism and Superior Brains' (in 'Fortnightly Review' for May).

1896　'Socialism for Millionaires' (in 'Contemporary Review' for February. Published as a Fabian Tract, 1901).
'The Illusions of Socialism.'

1904　'Fabianism and the Fiscal Question.'
'The Common Sense of Municipal Trading.'

1913 'The Case for Equality.' An Address to the Political and Economic Circle of the National Liberal Club.

1928 'The Intelligent Woman's Guide to Socialism and Capitalism.'

CRITICISM

1891 'The Quintessence of Ibsenism.' New edition 'Now completed to the Death of Ibsen,' 1913.

1895 'A Degenerate's View of Nordau' in New York 'Liberty.' Published as 'The Sanity of Art: An Exposure of the current Nonsense about Artists being Degenerate,' revised, with new preface, 1908.

1898 'The Perfect Wagnerite.'

1906 'Dramatic Opinions and Essays,' selected from the 'Saturday Review' by James Huneker.

1930 'Our Theatres in the Nineties,' (being Criticisms to 'Saturday Review' 1895–1898), in 'Works of Bernard Shaw.'
'Music in London,' (Criticisms to 'The World,' 1890–1894) in 'Works of Bernard Shaw.'

PLAYS

1893 'Widowers' Houses' (Independent Theatre Series of Plays, No. 2), written 1885–92, produced 1892, first of three 'Unpleasant Plays' (1898) including also 'The Philanderer' (written 1893, produced 1907) and 'Mrs. Warren's Profession' (written 1894, produced 1902).

1898 'Arms and the Man' (written and produced 1894), published together with 'Candida' (written 1894, produced 1897), 'The Man of Destiny' (written 1895, produced 1897), and 'You Never Can Tell' (written 1896, produced 1899) as the second volume of 'Plays Pleasant and Unpleasant.'

1901 'Three Plays for Puritans':
'The Devil's Disciple,' written and produced 1897.
'Cæsar and Cleopatra,' written 1898, produced 1899.
'Captain Brassbound's Conversion,' written 1899, produced 1900.

1903 'Man and Superman,' written 1901–3, produced 1905.

1907 'John Bull's Other Island,' written and produced 1904.
      'Major Barbara,' written and produced 1905.
      'How he Lied to her Husband,' written and produced
        1904.

1909 'Press Cuttings.'

1911 'The Doctor's Dilemma,' written and produced 1906.
      'Getting Married,' written and produced 1908.
      'The Shewing-up of Blanco Posnet,' written and pro-
        duced 1909.

1914 'Misalliance,' written and produced 1910.
      'The Dark Lady of the Sonnets,' written and produced
        1910.
      'Fanny's First Play,' written and produced 1911.
      'Androcles and the Lion,' written 1912, produced 1913.
      'Over-ruled,' written and produced 1912.
      'Pygmalion,' written 1912, produced 1914.

1919 'Heartbreak House, Great Catherine and Playlets of the
        War.' The last-mentioned included 'O'Flaherty V. C.,'
        'The Inca of Perusalem' (produced 1917), 'Augustus
        does his Bit' (produced 1917), and 'Annajanska, the
        Bolshevik Empress' (produced 1918). 'Heartbreak
        House' was produced in New York in 1920.

1921 'Back to Methuselah,' produced, New York, 1922.

1924 'St. Joan,' produced New York 1923, London 1924.

1931 'The Apple Cart,' produced 1929.

1932 'Too True to be Good,' produced 1932.

There are books about Shaw by Holbrook Jackson (1906),
Renée M. Deacon (1910), G. K. Chesterton (1909), A. Hender-
son (1911, 1925, 1929, and 1932), Joseph McCabe (1914),
P. P. Howe (1915), John Palmer (1915), Richard E. Burton
(1916), Herbert Skimpole (1918), H. C. Duffin (1920), E. B.
Shanks (1924), Patrick Braybrooke (1925 and 1930), J. S.
Collis (1925), A. Brisner (1931), A. M. Ellehauge (1931),
H. L. Stewart (1931), Frank Harris (1931); in French, by
Charles Cestre (1912), and Augustin Hamon (1913), the latter translated by Eden and Cedar Paul (1916). The correspondence between Ellen Terry and Bernard Shaw was edited
by Christopher St. John, 1931. A bibliography of Shaw's works
and of literature concerning him, by C. L. and V. M. Broad,
was published in 1929.

CHAPTER IV

SHAW'S SUCCESSORS

SHAW's influence on the English drama was profound and extensive. He gave intellectual elevation to its tone and he immensely enlarged its range and variety of subject and treatment. But he founded no school, unless St. John Hankin and Granville-Barker may be regarded as his followers, and as an active playwright he outlived them both.

HARLEY GRANVILLE-BARKER (1877–   ), was better known as a producer of plays than as a writer for the stage, though he rendered distinguished service to the modern drama in both capacities. Early training as an actor and keen intellectual interests made him usefully active in the organization and management of the Stage Society, founded in 1898 to give private performances on Sunday evenings to plays which had failed to get a footing on commercial boards. Early in the twentieth century he helped in the production of several Shaw plays and put on for the Stage Society a comedy of his own, 'The Marrying of Ann Leete' (1902). It was highly praised, but many intelligent people—William Archer among them—professed themselves unable to understand it. Archer said: "It was written in a language not wholly unfamiliar to me; but the characters depicted, and the reasons for their sayings and doings, remained utterly enigmatic." It sets forth how Ann Leete, a charming young girl in the upper middle class, pressed to marry a suitor of her own station of life, finds a more congenial mate in her father's gardener; it is a situation not without precedent in English or American society, but it is not presented in the play in a manner that is convincing or even credible.

Granville-Barker in 1904 began the enterprise at the Royal Court Theatre, which, as has been narrated above, was the foundation of Shaw's rise to fame on the English commercial stage. With the production of his own plays, Granville-Barker was less successful, and had to be content with the more limited opportunities offered by the Stage Society, which put on his 'Voysey Inheritance' in November, 1905. Archer's verdict was one of emphatic approval. "I found," he wrote, "that I understood almost every word, one or two supersubtleties excepted; and at the end I realized that here was a great play, a play conceived and composed with original mastery, and presenting on its spacious canvas a greater wealth of observation, character, and essential drama than was to be found in any other play of our time."

The theme of the play is an original one—the problem presented to a young lawyer by the discovery, on his father's death, that the latter has been deliberately applying the money entrusted to the firm to his own private use. If young Edward Voysey rejects the family inheritance of debt and dishonour, he will not only blast his father's reputation, but he will ruin the creditors of the firm; he accepts the burden and continues his father's policy of using one client's money to pay another's interest in the hope of one day coming out clear; if a creditor presses him too hard, Edward tells him the truth, and he tells the truth to the girl he wishes to marry; she understands and approves, so that the play has a kind of happy ending.

But, first and last, it gives a bitter, satirical picture of human folly, hypocrisy, greed, and treachery, lightened only by the idealism of the two lovers.

'Waste,' Granville-Barker's next play, was written in 1906–7. It was stifled at its birth, by the English censor's refusal to allow its public performance on the ground that one of the main incidents of the plot was an illegal operation, which causes the death of the hero's mistress. He is a leading politician and his career is ruined. From an artistic point of view the great fault of the play is that it is overburdened with political intrigue and discussion, subjects of limited interest when they have to do with pressing national and international questions, and almost impossible to vitalize when the issues and the people concerned in them are imaginary.

'The Madras House,' written in 1909, acted in 1910, and published in 1911, is Granville-Barker's best-known play, and was produced on both sides of the Atlantic, with much applause from the critics and the intelligentzia generally, on account of its daring experimental technique. Act I introduces us to six Miss Huxtables, as like to each other as "one lead pencil and another, as these lie upon one's table after some six weeks' use." All are withering on the virgin thorn in a middle-class English suburb, and longing for an escape from the narrowness and monotony of a life which gives no opportunity to satisfy their desire for marriage, and no intelligent activity to substitute for it; they are nuns without vocation and without occupation, unwilling victims sacrificed to the convention of middle-class respectability. Such things were in 1910 in English suburbs, although for most families it ended with the War. Then we see another side of the repression and oppression of woman in the Madras House, in American parlance a department store with its

English attachments of living-in and enforced celibacy; the mannequins parade and an American capitalist discusses the possibilities of exploiting feminine and masculine susceptibilities by a succession of such exhibitions in department stores in the English provinces. The former proprietor of the Madras House (after seducing one of the girls in his employ) has become a Mohammedan and gone off to Mesopotamia to escape from the irresistible temptations which beset him in the English metropolis. Finally, we listen to an interminable conversation, between his intelligent son and the son's cultivated wife, as to how married life can be made tolerable under the conditions of contemporary English society. The conditions have changed a good deal since the play was written, and even at the time it was an extravagant satire rather than a faithful study of the position of woman in a society not yet liberated from Victorian convention. The play revolved around the woman question and presented its various phases instead of developing one side of the problem to a definite issue, and the end of the comedy left the subject—and most of the audience—up in the air. The satire, however, was pungent and near enough to what might happen in an extreme case to be not altogether fantastic. The treatment was novel, and the dialogue sometimes telling, though it had nothing like the briskness and point of the Shavian dialectic.

A later play 'The Secret Life' (published in 1923) did not reach the stage, and to understand it even by a careful and diligent perusal was no easy task. It presented the disillusion that followed the War, especially among the radical intellectuals, and the impossibility of honesty and frankness in political life, the despair of those devoted to high ideals of public service. It breathed the heavy atmosphere of disenchantment only too common in postwar England, and it was no wonder that it failed to attain a public—or even a private—performance. A later drama 'His Majesty' (published in 1928) seemed even less suitable for stage production. It seems strange that Granville-Barker, after his successful career as an actor and producer, should have wandered into what he himself described, in his book 'The Exemplary Theatre' (1922), as "that blind alley which leads to the play more fitted for the study than the stage—that yacht so perfectly adapted to lying in the harbour."

There is a general feeling that Granville-Barker somehow missed making the most of his undoubted talents. He was an excellent translator—his versions of Schnitzler's 'Anatol' and Sacha Guitry's 'Deburau' are models in that kind; and he wrote with Laurence Housman a charming little romantic play, 'Prunella,' which had a good run in New York in the earlier years of the century and was successfully revived after the War. He wrote essays on the performance of Shakespeare's plays—brilliantly illustrated by his own achievements in Shakespearean production—on a national theatre, and on the intellectual drama—all showing a vigorous and acute intelligence. But in the upshot he did more for the modern drama by the plays he produced at the Royal Court Theatre, the Savoy, and the Duke of York's Theatre in London, and by his notable productions in New York City than by anything he wrote for the stage.

ST. JOHN EMILE CLAVERING HANKIN (1860–1909) was, like Shaw, anti-romantic and a satirist of the upper middle class to which he belonged. His first publication, 'Three Plays with Happy Endings' (1907), evidently owes its title to Shaw's 'Three Plays for Puritans' published a few years before, and the endings are only "happy" in an ironical sense. The irony applies to the

subjects of the plays as well as to their titles: 'The Return
of the Prodigal' is an inversion of the traditional story,
for the prodigal son in the play makes himself so ob-
noxious to the family to which he has returned that he has
to be bribed by his father to go away again. 'The Charity
That Began at Home' illustrates the futility of promiscuous philanthropy and the folly of the woman who would
redeem a ne'er-do-well by marrying him. "The only real
way of helping people is to love them," says the romantic
Margery, "and if one loves people of course one should
marry them." "Surely, love is enough," she pleads to her
wastrel of a lover, and he retorts: "No. It isn't. Marriage
isn't a thing to be romantic about. It *lasts* too long. My
dear, it may last forty years. . . . Now what sort of a
life should we make of it together if we married, you and
I? Why, my dear, we've not an idea or a taste in common. Everything you say makes me laugh, and everything I think would make you blush. It's simply absurd
for a girl like you to marry a fellow like me. Let's say so
frankly and end it." So it is the villain who saves the virtuous heroine from her own romantic folly. 'The Cassilis
Engagement,' the third of the plays "with happy endings,"
ends with an engagement broken off by the wiles of the
hero's mother; the heroine-adventuress, who has been
outwitted by the mother's superior craft, later married an
aged lord and worried him into his grave in six months "so
that she also ended happily." There is the same anti-
romantic suggestion in the title of Hankin's other play
'The Last of the De Mullins.' Janet De Mullin is a girl
with an illegitimate child who has gone to London and
done very well as a fashionable milliner; far from being
ashamed of her "fall," she is proud of it. "It was so
splendid to find some one at last who really cared for me
as women should be cared for! Not to talk to because

I was clever or to play tennis with because I was strong, but to kiss me and to make love to me! Yes! To make love to me!" Nor is she afraid of the future. "Whatever happens, even if Johnny should come to hate me for what I did, I shall always be glad to have been his mother. At least I shall have lived. These poor women who go through life listless and dull, who have never felt the joys and the pains a mother feels, how they would envy me if they knew!" Next to Shaw, Galsworthy, and Granville-Barker himself, St. John Hankin was the most competent and original of the Court Theatre dramatists, and his work has hardly met with the recognition that it deserved.

Another anti-romantic of the time was GITHA SOW-ERBY (Mrs. John Kendall) whose 'Rutherford and Son,' with Norman McKinnel in the principal part, made a great hit on both sides of the Atlantic in 1912–13. It is a satirical study of a successful North of England "captain of industry," who tyrannizes over his family and his workpeople and sacrifices to his business interests every other consideration in life, until he is brought to book by his daughter-in-law, who triumphs over him through his one human weakness, his love for his only grandson.

Still another authoress of a single successful play was ELIZABETH BAKER (Mrs. J. E. Allaway) whose 'Chains' was put on at the Court Theatre in 1909. Though not without satiric touches, it was in the main a conscientious, realistic study of the life of a London clerk, bound to the wheel of business and the monotony of suburban life by an early marriage and economic conditions, from which his own weakness of character and limited outlook make it impossible for him to escape. Following the trail opened by the French Théâtre Libre and other Continental free theatres, this realistic drama of humble life was the forerunner of many others to be written by English and American dramatists during the next twenty years.

Of its immediate successors the most notable was ST. JOHN ERVINE'S 'Jane Clegg' (1913), which made a great impression in Manchester and London before its run in New York enriched the coffers of the Theatre Guild in the critical days of its early career. Ervine's first acted play was 'Mixed Marriage' (1911), dealing with religious intolerance and industrial disorder in Belfast, the North of Ireland city in which the author was born and grew up. In 1916 he was manager of the Abbey Theatre in Dublin, and after fighting in the Great War and visiting the United States, he settled down in London as a dramatic critic and wrote a very successful drawing-room comedy, 'The First Mrs. Fraser' (1929).

STANLEY HOUGHTON (1881–1913) was the most notable of the native dramatists who wrote for the Gaiety Theatre in Manchester, directed and subsidized by Miss A. E. F. Horniman, whose beneficence had put Shaw's 'Arms and the Man' on the London stage. His greatest achievement was 'Hindle Wakes' (1912), which within a year of its original production was acted two thousand times in Manchester, London, New York and Chicago. As to its artistic merits it is enough to quote the comment of William Archer upon the opening scene: "If Miss Horniman's enlightened public spirit had brought into being nothing but this one scene, it would not have been thrown away. The thing is absolutely real, not an unnatural word is spoken, and the sequence of incidents involves no departure from the normal and probable course of life. Yet you cannot but feel in the atmosphere of the dingy Lancashire sitting-room that strain of suspense, that throb of emotion, which was, is, and ever shall be the

central secret of the drama,—that which differentiates it
from all other arts and lends it such irresistible magic. A
better piece of drama than this opening scene was never
written. . . . It gives us a complex satisfaction, the
pleasure arising from a scene of intense and yet of absolutely truthful and natural emotion, and the pleasure
arising from the recognition that the artist is making the
best possible use of his medium, developing its highest
potentialities."

One other Manchester playwright must be mentioned,
ALLAN NOBLE MONKHOUSE, dramatic critic of the
'Manchester Guardian.' He wrote plays for Miss Horni-
man's company from the beginning of that remarkable
enterprise and for the repertory theatres of Liverpool and
Birmingham, which continued after the Manchester ven-
ture had come to an end. His style is at once more fan-
tastic and more ironical than the sober realism of St. John
Ervine and Stanley Houghton, and reveals the influence of
Shaw in its clever dialogue and extravagant paradoxes.

Of the dramatists who made their mark during or after
the War, mention should be made of A. A. MILNE, whose
best effort was 'The Truth about Blayds' (1921); of
C. K. MUNRO whose 'At Mrs. Beam's' (1921) gave an
amusing presentation of life in a London boarding house,
since deemed worthy of revival on both sides of the Atlantic; and of NOEL COWARD, whose extraordinary
versatility may be illustrated by his brilliantly cynical
society comedies, such as 'The Vortex' (1924), musical
entertainments, of which 'Bitter Sweet' (1929) was the
best, and spectacles such as 'Cavalcade' (1931), presenting scenes from the national history from the beginning
of the century to the present hour.

In poetic drama JOHN DRINKWATER'S 'Abraham
Lincoln,' first presented at the Birmingham Repertory

Theatre in October, 1918, came at a moment when America and Americans were still popular in Europe and was very favourably received; five years later JAMES ELROY FLECKER'S 'Hassan' had a prolonged run in London with its gorgeous oriental setting, ballets, and music. Both plays had poetic merits which would have deserved high esteem but would not have been likely to gain it without the adventitious circumstances which made them popular.

BIBLIOGRAPHY

(dates of production)

GRANVILLE BARKER

1902   'The Marrying of Ann Leete.'
1905   'The Voysey Inheritance.'
1906   'Prunella' (with Laurence Housman).
1907   'Waste.'
1910   'The Madras House.'
1911   'Anatol' (translated from Schnitzler).
1920   'Deburau' (translated from Sacha Guitry).
1923   (pub.) 'The Secret Life.'
1928   (pub.) 'His Majesty.'

ST. JOHN HANKIN

1905   'The Return of the Prodigal.'
1906   'The Charity that Began at Home.'
1907   'The Cassilis Engagement.'
1908   'The Last of the De Mullins.'

CHAPTER V

THE IRISH RENAISSANCE

THE Irish Literary Revival was carefully organized and its history is well documented. During the last decade of the nineteenth century there were founded, both in London and in Dublin, Irish literary clubs and societies, which published joint manifestoes under the title 'The Revival of Irish Literature.' As early as 1894 W. P. Ryan issued a volume called 'The Irish Literary Revival, its History, Pioneers, and Possibilities.' About the same time Stopford Brooke submitted to the London Society a definite programme. Taking it for granted that the work already done to preserve and edit old Irish manuscripts would be continued, he urged: (1) that the pieces of finest quality should be accurately translated "with as much of a poetic movement as is compatible with fine prose, and done by men who have the love of noble form and the power of shaping it"; (2) that Irishmen of formative genius should take, one by one, the various cycles of Irish tales, and grouping each of them round one central figure, supply to each a dominant human interest to which every event in the whole should converge, after the manner of Malory's 'Morte d'Arthur'; (3) that suitable episodes in these imaginative tales should be treated in verse, retaining the colour and spirit of the original; (4) that the folk-stories of Ireland should be collected. Douglas Hyde's 'Beside the Fire,' which had appeared in 1890, was mentioned as exactly the thing that ought to be done for the folk-tales of all Ireland, and it is possible that Stopford Brooke realized what Dr. Hyde had already accomplished or was on the way to accomplish—the discovery of a new literary idiom, Hibernian English or Anglo-Irish. It is not the literal translation of Gaelic, but the adoption of Irish idioms, "of the kind used all over Ireland, the kind the people themselves use," which rest ultimately, no doubt, upon translation from that Irish which was the language of the speaker's father, grandfather, or great-grandfather, and have perpetuated themselves, "even in districts where you will scarce find a trace of an Irish word." Hyde continued and successfully developed the experiment in 'Love Songs of Connacht' (1893) and the Movement found itself endowed with the priceless boon of a medium of expression which had the charm of literary freshness and the ease and naturalness of a spoken tongue.

WILLIAM BUTLER YEATS (1865–   )

Of the third kind of work to be done on the Irish cycles —the rendering of selected episodes in modern verse— Stopford Brooke gave as one of the two best examples he had seen 'The Wanderings of Oisin' by William Butler Yeats, a young and then little-known poet who had been actively connected with both the London and the Dublin Societies. Born in Dublin of a Sligo Protestant family in 1865, Yeats had spent his childhood and the most impressionable years of his youth in Ireland, with the exception of some five years in England at school. He had written poetry when he was 16 and began to publish before he was 20 in Irish magazines and newspapers. He was an ardent patriot, read old Irish literature "in bad translations" (there were at that time very few good ones), and gathered folk lore from the lips of the Connaught peasantry by their turf fires. He had edited 'Poems and Ballads of Young Ireland' and 'Fairy and Folk Tales of the Irish Peasantry' in 1888, 'Stories from Carleton' in 1889, and two volumes of 'Representative Irish Tales' in 1890. The early poems included in 'The Wanderings of Oisin' volume (1889) bear marks of the influence of Spenser and Shelley, Morris and Rossetti; several of them were suppressed, and others severely revised by their author, who had already discovered his individual bent and very soon perfected his style. He had dabbled in theosophy with a wandering Brahmin who came to Dublin, and in 1893 completed a three-volume edition of Blake. He read all this mystical lore into the peasant tales he gathered, being "at no pains to separate my own beliefs from those of the peasantry" ('The Celtic Twilight,' 1893). Similarly in his poetry, Yeats found the way to express his mysticism by means of the mythology which old Irish literature had in common with the traditional superstitions of the Irish peasant. Contact with a mass of material so long unused for literary purposes that it had been almost forgotten gave his work freshness of appeal, his devotion not merely to Ireland as a nation, but to the Irish spirit as he interpreted it gave him sincerity and authority of utterance, and his philosophy, though it was one of escape from life rather than a resolute attempt to face its problems and agitations, was not unwelcome to a generation world-weary and somewhat oppressed with a sense of its own meaningless materialism. Yeats had a genuine lyrical gift and his inspiration was supplemented by conscientious and skilful craftsmanship. The volume of 'Poems' he published in

1895 established not merely his own reputation, but the position of the literary movement of which he now became the protagonist, and won a hearing for his friend and fellow mystic "A. E." (George William Russell), whose 'Homeward Songs by the Way' (1894–5) and 'The Earth Breath' (1897) gained wide acceptance. Probably few of the English readers of either poet paid much attention to the mystical doctrine involved in the new mythology, but both Yeats and "A. E." were fully and keenly conscious of the use to which they were putting the Old Irish legends. In an essay on 'The Literary Movement in Ireland' (1901) Yeats wrote: "Irish literature may prolong its first inspiration without renouncing the complexity of ideas and emotions which is the inheritance of cultivated men, for it will have learned from the discoveries of modern learning that the common people, wherever civilization has not driven its plough too deep, keep a watch over the roots of all religion and all romance. Their poetry trembles upon the verge of incoherence with a passion all but unknown among modern poets, and their sense of beauty exhausts itself in countless legends and in metaphors that seem to mirror the energies of nature. . . . It may be that poetry is the utterance of desires that we can only satisfy in dreams, and that if all our dreams were satisfied there would be no more poetry. Dreams pass from us in childhood, because we are so often told they can never come true, and because we are taught with so much labour to admire the paler beauty of the world. The children of the poor and simple learn from their unbroken religious faith, and from their traditional beliefs, that this world is nothing, and that a spiritual world, where all dreams come true, is everything; and therefore the poor and simple are that imperfection whose perfection is genius."

"A. E." defended the modern interpretation of the Old Irish myths on similar grounds: "They have crept through veil after veil of the manifold nature of man, and now each dream, heroism, or beauty has laid itself nigh the divine power it represents, the suggestion of which made it first beloved; and they are ready for the use of the spirit, a speech of which every word has a significance beyond itself, and Deirdre is like Helen, a symbol of eternal beauty, and Cuchulain represents as much as Prometheus the heroic spirit, the redeemer in man." Yeats, passing under the influence of the French Symbolist School, became even more explicit and avowed his intention to use the heroes of Irish mythology "more as principles of the mind than as actual personages." Thus Hanrahan is "fire blown by the wind," and Aedh "fire burning by itself." "To put it in a different way, Hanrahan is the simplicity of an imagination too changeable to gather permanent possessions, or the adoration of the shepherds; and Michael Robartes is the pride of the imagination brooding upon the greatness of its possessions, or the adoration of the Magi; while Aedh is the myrrh and frankincense that the imagination offers continually before all that it loves."

Even in his early publications, Yeats had shown some inclination towards the dramatic form, though his "dramatic" poems of the eighties are in reality lyric. 'The Countless Cathleen,' in the form in which it was originally published in 1892, falls into the same category, and two years later W. P. Ryan could say without offence: "As the Irish revival expands in new directions, will not some one take heart and attempt something for Irish dramatic literature? The real Irish drama is a thing unknown." Yeats's short lyric drama 'The Land of Heart's Desire' was produced at the Avenue Theatre in London the same year

(1894) and had no great success, but he did not relinquish his dream of an Irish literary theatre, and in 1898, in talk with Lady Gregory, the project took definite shape. Their first plans were simple and modest—the performance by English actors of Yeats's 'The Countess Cathleen' and of Edward Martyn's 'The Heather Field' at the Antient Concert Rooms, Dublin, on May 8 and 9, 1899. George Moore, who had looked after the rehearsals in England, has given in 'Ave' an amusing account of the performance of 'The Countess Cathleen,' which met with a hostile reception on account of supposed heretical implications, but the success of the venture was sufficient to secure the repetition of the experiment in February, 1900, when 'The Bending of the Bough' by George Moore, 'The Last Feast of the Fianna' by Alice Milligan, and 'Maeve' by Edward Martyn were given, and in October, 1901, when 'Diarmuid and Grania' by W. B. Yeats and George Moore was presented by English actors, and 'The Twisting of the Rope' by Douglas Hyde in Gaelic by an Irish company. It was during the rehearsals of the Gaelic play that the brothers Fay conceived the idea of an Irish amateur company for plays in English, encouraged thereto by the enterprise of Ole Bull at the Norwegian National Theatre. Accordingly, in April, 1902, the Irish National Dramatic Company produced 'Deirdre' by "A. E." and 'Cathleen ni Houlihan,' a short play symbolic of Irish patriotism, by W. B. Yeats.

JOHN MILLINGTON SYNGE (1871–1909)

The production of 'In the Shadow of the Glen' on October 8, 1903, marks the accession of a new creative force, J. M. Synge, who had been discovered by Yeats at

Paris in 1899, and sent to the Aran Islands in search of native material and a native style. Ernest A. Boyd in his 'Ireland's Literary Renaissance' well says that the great "event" in the history of the Irish theatre was "the discovery and universal recognition of the genius of J. M. Synge." The timely help of Miss Horniman, who restored and endowed the Abbey Theatre for the Company, secured the necessary material opportunity, but what really won the attention of the English-speaking world on both sides of the Atlantic was the dramatic power of Synge's plays, aided no doubt by the simplicity and naturalness of the gestures and speech of the actors, and the quiet appropriateness of costumes and scenery. When Yeats, with Lady Gregory's help, had projected the Irish Literary Theatre in 1899, he had called for plays "that will make the theatre a place of intellectual excitement," and had added: "Such plays will require, both in writers and audiences, a stronger feeling for beautiful and appropriate language than one finds in the ordinary theatre." Synge's plays satisfied both demands, but not in the way that Yeats expected, for it is evident that what the latter had in mind was lyric drama, though his one permanently successful play on the stage, 'Cathleen ni Houlihan,' is in prose. Synge found the heroes and fairies of Old Irish legend "too far away from life to appease his mood," as Yeats puts it, and he forsook "sweet Angus, Maeve and Fand" for the poachers and topers of the countryside. The plot of 'In the Shadow of the Glen,' Synge took from a story he picked up during his wanderings in Aran from old "Pat Dirane," just as he took the story of 'The Tinker's Wedding' from a herd he met at a Wicklow fair. Whence did he gain the "beautiful and appropriate" language, which Yeats described, and which forms one of the great charms of Synge's plays? The discovery of the

Anglo-Irish idiom is rightly ascribed to Douglas Hyde, with whose 'Love Songs of Connacht' Synge was well acquainted; indeed he borrows from it a phrase or two. Synge also acknowledged indebtedness to Lady Gregory's 'Cuchulain of Muirthemne,' a rendering of Irish legends in the Anglo-Irish of Kiltartan, which was published the year before his first play was produced, and which he had doubtless seen before it was printed. But both Dr. Hyde and Lady Gregory drew from a common source—the spoken language of the Irish peasant—with which Synge himself was in direct contact. He says in the preface to 'The Playboy of the Western World' that in all his plays he used only one or two words he had not heard among the country people of Ireland. "When I was writing 'The Shadow of the Glen,' some years ago, I got more aid than any learning could have given me, from a chink in the floor of the old Wicklow house where I was staying, that let me hear what was being said by the servant girls in the kitchen. This matter, I think, is of importance, for in countries where the imagination of the people, and the language they use, is rich and living, it is possible for a writer to be rich and copious in his words, and at the same time to give the reality, which is the root of all poetry, in a comprehensive and natural form."

In another passage Synge speaks of his achievement of striking and beautiful phrases as a collaboration with the Irish peasantry; and so no doubt it was, but it was a collaboration in which his genius was predominant. In Dr. Hyde or Lady Gregory one gets an occasional poetic phrase or alluring turn of Gaelicized syntax; but no one except Synge (and besides these two predecessors he has had numerous followers) has been able to use the Anglo-Irish idiom so that (to use his own phrase) "every speech should be as fully flavoured as a nut or apple." The discovery of the idiom was no doubt a lucky chance for Synge, who was acquainted not only with Anglo-Irish but with Gaelic; but the power to use it was his own, partly natural gift, but cultivated by his long studies of French literature and his years of residence in Paris. He came of an old Anglo-Irish family and was educated at Trinity College, but it was neither from Protestant nor from Catholic Ireland, but from modern France that he won his attitude of ironical detachment, which was so alien to Irish sentiment that his plays repeatedly aroused violent protest in Dublin and elsewhere. In 'The Shadow of the Glen,' Synge cancels the ending of the old folk tale in which the faithless wife and her lover meet condign punishment, and allows his heroine to go off by her own choice with the tramp, while her husband sits down to drink with the man who a few minutes before was ready to fill his shoes. The Catholic Church, which has so strong a hold on the affections of the Irish peasantry, furnishes Synge with dramatic machinery, as in 'The Well of the Saints,' or with opportunity for frank ridicule, as in 'The Tinker's Wedding.' As to the latter play, Synge said: "In the greater part of Ireland the whole people, from the tinkers to the clergy, have still a life, and view of life, that are rich and genial and humorous. I do not think that these country people, who have so much humour them-selves, will mind being laughed at without malice, as the people in every country have been laughed at in their own comedies."

So far as 'The Tinker's Wedding' is concerned, the directors of the Abbey Theatre have not ventured to put Synge's high estimate of the tolerant humour of the Irish public to the test, and in view of the stormy reception given to 'The Playboy of the Western World,' they were well-advised in not running the risk. Except in that gem of sheer pathos, 'The Riders to the Sea,' it must be confessed that Synge's picture of the Irish peasantry is neither complimentary nor sympathetic. It has humour; it answers Synge's own test of giving "the nourishment, not very easy to define, on which our imaginations live"; his "drama, like the symphony, does not teach or prove anything." It appeals, not to any sense of nationality, but to our sense of humanity and our sense of beauty. If it is regarded from a narrower point of view, the judgment passed on it in a recently recorded conversation between two Irishmen is not wholly unjustified:

" 'They do be putting quare plays on in Dublin nowadays!' I replied, 'Ah!' with encouraging intimation.

'Yes' he continued, 'very quare plays. They do be putting on plays where a boy from the country kills his da!'

'That seems wrong.'

'Yes. And they make us out to be nothing but cutthroats, and murderers, and dijinirates.'

'What on earth do they mean by doing that?'

'They calls it—ART.' "

It is art, and art of a very rare and fine quality; but whether one may reasonably expect the Irish peasantry to be proud to be the vehicle of it, is an open question. It seems a good deal to expect from them a higher degree of tolerant intelligence than the townspeople of Tarascon gave to Daudet, or the inhabitants of the Five Towns to Arnold Bennett.

Whether or no the Irish peasant should be grateful to Synge, Synge's literary reputation is under deep indebtedness to the Irish peasant, who gave him not merely an idiom he could turn to beauty, but a way of thinking he could turn to dramatic effect. The idiom proved much less effective in 'Deirdre,' and the way of thinking, which remains much the same, seems less suited to an age of primitive romance, far removed in time, than to the primitive moderns, sufficiently removed in space to allow the imagination play, but endowed with actuality by Synge's realistic genius. Whether he would have succeeded with the Dublin slum drama he was meditating at his untimely death, can only be conjectured. His Irish peasant drama remains a unique achievement, for though there are other plays written for the Abbey Theatre which have literary interest or achieved popular success, no others seem likely to win for themselves the abiding place in literary history to which Synge's work is clearly entitled.

GEORGE MOORE (1852–1933)

George Moore was in the Irish movement, but he was never really of it. Born in County Mayo in 1852, he had passed most of his youth and early manhood in Paris and London, and before the Movement really began, he had established his place in literature by his book on 'Modern Painting' and his realistic novel 'Esther Waters.' It was when he was engaged on these works in 1894 that Edward Martyn said to him: "I wish I knew enough Irish to write my plays in Irish," and he replied, "I thought nobody did anything in Irish except bring turf from the bog and say prayers." Then he learnt that a new literature was springing up in Irish, and he thought what a wonderful thing it would be to write a book in a new language or in an old language revived and sharpened to literary usage for the first time. Five years later, Yeats and Martyn came to Moore to interest him in the project of an Irish Literary Theatre in Dublin, and going to Ireland at their

invitation he yielded to the fatal charms of Cathleen ni
Houlihan. This, at least, is one of the explanations he
gives, for there are many to choose from. "The Englishman that was in me, (he that wrote 'Esther Waters'), had
been overtaken and captured by the Irishman." After
the Boer war, he turned from England in horror; "it became so beastly." Also there was "Stella," who, after
receiving two telegrams asking her to come, two telling
her not to come, and the last one just in time, met him
on the boat. At Lady Gregory's house he undertook to
write 'Diarmuid and Grania' with Yeats, who took him
aback to begin with by remarking that "the first act of
every good play is horizontal, the second perpendicular."
"And the third, I suppose, circular?" Moore retorted, and
Yeats agreed. He agreed also with Moore's casual suggestion that he preferred to write the play in French
rather than in Yeats's vocabulary. "Lady Gregory will
translate your text into English. Taidgh O'Donohue will
translate the English text into Irish, and Lady Gregory
will translate the Irish text back into English." Moore
gives us in 'Ave' the French text of the first scene of the
second act as the only way of convincing the reader "that
two such literary lunatics as Yeats and myself existed,
contemporaneously, and in Ireland, too, a country not
distinguished for its love of letters." Moore left Ireland
for France, as a French atmosphere was necessary for
French composition, and returned home to England, but
a divine revelation convinced him that "the Messiah Ireland was waiting for was in me and not in another." He
had some difficulty in convincing "A. E.," who was experienced in such matters, of the genuineness of the vision,
but he stuck to it, and made the acquaintance of all the
leading figures in the Irish Movement. Familiarity
brought him to the conclusion that the Irish Renaissance

was "but a bubble," but he had a second revelation—"that no Catholic had written a book worth reading since the Reformation." Born into a Catholic family and still an agnostic, he determined to become a Protestant, to the no small embarrassment of the Church of Ireland clergy. "My belief never faltered that I was an instrument in the hands of the gods, and that their mighty purpose was the liberation of my country from priestcraft." He knew he was not a preacher, and strove to fashion first a story, then a play, but "the artist in me could not be suborned." Davitt came with a project for a newspaper, but he died. Moore was beginning to lose hope when the form which the book should take was revealed to him—an autobiography—an unusual form for a sacred book he reflected, until the example of St. Paul occurred to him.

This is Moore's own account of 'Hail and Farewell'—the three volumes in which he said 'Ave,' 'Salve,' and 'Vale' to Ireland and the Irish Movement. The Renaissance was well provided with fairies of the serious sort, but had no knavish elves, and Moore took upon himself the part of Puck in the disguise of a literary historian. It is the most entertaining account of the Irish Renaissance, and would be the most authoritative if one could only believe half of what is told. But when Moore ascribes to Edward Martyn the remark to himself: "I never believed that your life is anything but pure; it is only your mind that is indecent," we detect invention, as in the definition put in the mouth of "A. E.": "A literary movement consists of five or six people, who live in the same town and hate each other cordially." It was a good thing that Moore said "Farewell" to Ireland in the last volume, for he could certainly not have returned to it, and it is a wonder that the British Isles remained large enough to contain himself and the victims of his malicious wit. 'Hail and Farewell' is and is likely to be a unique literary achievement, for the combination of impish skill and thoroughgoing disregard of the feelings of one's most intimate literary associates and friends is fortunately rare.

LORD DUNSANY (1878–)

Edward John Moreton Drax Plunkett, Lord Dunsany, educated at Eton and the English Military School at Sandhurst, may be regarded as a by-product of the Irish literary movement, for he owed his first inspiration to W. B. Yeats and his early plays were put on at the Abbey Theatre, though his reputation as a maker of romantic one-act dramas was achieved in England and America. Yeats rejected Matthew Arnold's theory of literature as "a criticism of life" and was in favour of romance as "a revelation of a hidden life" or even as an escape from life as it is lived today. Dunsany not only accepted Yeats's recommendation of romance, but his prescription for a one-act romantic play: "Surprise, and the more Surprise, and that is all." As to the need for romance, Dunsany wrote: "Something must be wrong with an age whose drama deserts romance. Romance is so inseparable from life that all we need to obtain romantic drama is for the dramatist to find any age and any country where life is not too thickly veiled and cloaked with puzzles and conventions, in fact to find a people that is not in the agonies of self-consciousness. For myself, I think that it is simpler to imagine such a people, as it saves the trouble of reading to find a romantic age, or the trouble of making a journey to lands where there is no press."

Dunsany chose as his medium, according to his own

account, simple stories, but stories with an inevitable meaning, though the dramatist himself may be unconscious, at the time of composition, of any deliberate spiritual intention. He takes as an instance his first London success 'The Gods of the Mountain' (1911). The true gods are seven images of jade squatting in the mountain far off from the city. Seven beggars sit at the gates of the city impersonating the gods for their personal gain; they get the offerings they desire, but the gods in their wrath come to the city and turn the beggars to stone. "That is the kind of way that man does get hit by destiny." But the stone images of the beggars are accepted as divine by all the citizens, who thus get the gods they deserve and desire.

Dunsany made this type of play his own and wrote some twenty examples of the type, all of them very popular until the public taste turned another way. He had great versatility in the invention of a thrilling situation and in investing it with an atmosphere of astonishment or horror which made it for the moment almost—and for some altogether—credible; but the imagination of the audience had to go a long way to meet that of the dramatist.

SEAN O'CASEY (1884–   )

The drama of Dublin slum life projected by Synge was actually accomplished by a slum-dweller whose last job as a bricklayer's labourer was done on a dwelling adjacent to the Abbey Theatre. To an interviewer who saw him when he was still living in a Dublin tenement, Sean O'Casey confessed that he had had a hard life: his father died when he was three, and his mother brought the family up. For nine years he was half-starved: "We had dry bread and a drink of tea in the morning, and that again at night if we were lucky." He taught himself to read when he was fourteen, and from fifteen to thirty earned his living as a navvy and day labourer. "You can see from the way my plays are written I never went to school. The first book I bought was Shakespeare. Shakespeare was my education. I learned to read by Shakespeare and used to act scenes from the plays in my room. When I was seventeen I could recite whole passages from 'Hamlet,' 'Macbeth,' and 'Julius Cæsar' by heart." He did not regret missing the sort of primary and secondary education in force in Ireland in his childhood, believing that kind of education to be "a terrible drawback to a dramatist,"— and therein agreeing with Bernard Shaw, who also congratulated himself on his escape from the influence of a conventional schooling.

O'Casey showed his ingenuous modesty in the admission that he had no technique beyond what he had learnt from Shakespeare; and certainly no one since Shakespeare has accomplished such daring combinations of the tragic and the humorous. In his first acted play, 'The Shadow of a Gunman' (1923), the contrast is already to be noted, but it is not so marked; the humour is less rich and the pathos less profound, being mainly confined to the catastrophe at the end of the play.

'Juno and the Paycock' (1924) is a more elaborate effort, both in the construction of its plot and the delineation of its characters. "The Paycock" is so called on account of his flashy manners and consequential bearing, his love of hearing himself talk, and his general uselessness and idleness; he is addressed as "Captain" Boyle because of a single voyage he made as a common seaman from Dublin to Liverpool. Juno is his wife, and has received that name from her husband because she "was born an' christened in June. I met her in June; we were married in June, an' Johnny was born in June." Under favourable conditions she would have been a handsome, active, and clever woman, but living with the shiftless Paycock has worn down her face into "a look of listless monotony and harassed anxiety blending with an expression of mechanical resistance." The other members of the family are the daughter, Mary, a good-looking girl of twenty-two, and the son Johnny, a delicate, nervous boy, who has been wounded in the rebellion of Easter Week, 1916, and has later lost an arm in the internecine strife between the troops of the newly established Free State and the Die-Hard Republicans. A hint is given that Johnny has been guilty of treachery to his comrades, but most of the first act is taken up with the humour of the Paycock and his boon companion Joxer, and their efforts to avoid work and consume all the food and drink they can without arousing the wrath of the ever-watchful Juno. The only other characters from outside the two tenement rooms occupied by the Boyle family—bedroom and bed-sittingroom—are Mary's two suitors—a tradeunion organizer whom she has discarded, and his successor, a schoolteacher and law student, who brings word that through his good offices with a relative of the Boyle family, the Paycock has come in for a handsome legacy. In the next act we see the two rooms absurdly adorned with borrowings from the neighbours on the strength of the expected good fortune, and the neighbours themselves rejoicing with the family, but in the last Act the comedy is changed to tragedy. Through the law student's carelessness in drawing up the will, the legacy is lost, neighbours and tradesmen call to recover their property or collect their bills, Mary is deserted with an illegitimate child in prospect, and Johnny forfeits his life

to the vengeance of his comrades. There is a moving scene
in which Juno laments her son's death: "Mother o' God,
Mother o' God, have pity on us all! Blessed Virgin, where
were you when me darlin' son was riddled with bullets?
. . . Sacred heart o' Jesus, take away our hearts o' stone,
and give us hearts o' flesh! Take away this murdherin'
hate, and give us Thine own eternal love!" But the last
word of the play is spoken by the drunken Paycock, be-
moaning the "terrible state of chassis" (presumably
"chaos") to which the world has been reduced.

The third play dealing with Irish political struggles
was 'The Plough and the Stars' (1926), acted, like its
predecessors, at the Abbey Theatre and the occasion for
a formidable riot. The subject of the play is the Easter
Rebellion of 1916, and offence was taken by the audience
—or part of it—because the dramatist—although he himself had served in the Citizen Army—had chosen to show
the Rising in its humorous as well as in its tragic aspects.
The scene is again one of those fine eighteenth century
houses which has become a tenement in a Dublin slum.
The array of odd characters is more varied than in either
of O'Casey's previous efforts. The principal grotesque
is the drunken and loquacious carpenter, Fluther Good,
whom we see when the curtain goes up, admiring a door
he has repaired "openin' and shuttin' now with a well-
mannered motion, like a door of a select bar in a high-
class pub." He is well matched by the sharp-tongued
Mrs. Gogan, another tenement dweller who introduces us
to the heroine of the play, the young wife, Nora Clitheroe,
who is too modern and uppish in her notions to please
Mrs. Gogan. "Her skirts are a little too short for a married woman. An' to see her sometimes of an evenin' in her
glad-neck gown would make a body's blood run cold."
But Nora is a good housekeeper and does well out of her

two lodgers. "An' she has th' life frightened out o' them; washin' their face, combin' their hair, wipin' their feet, brushin' their clothes, thrimmin' their nails, cleanin' their teeth—God Almighty, you'd think th' poor men were undergoin' penal servitude." One of the lodgers, Nora's uncle Peter Flynn, is having difficulty in getting himself into white whipcord breeches and a boiled shirt for a patriotic procession, and is the butt, not only for Mrs. Gogan's ridicule, but for the more maddening scorn of his Socialist fellow lodger, young Covey. Mrs. Gogan describes him as "like somethin' you'd pick off a Christmas Tree. . . . When he's dressed up in his canonicals, you'd wondher where he'd been got. God forgive me, when I see him in them, I always think he must ha' had a Mormon for a father." Covey tells him he looks "like the illegitimate son of an illegitimate child of a corporal in th' Mexican army." Peter Flynn chases him with his sword, and the uproar is increased by a quarrel between Nora Clitheroe and the top-storey tenant, Bessie Burgess. Nora's husband comes home, and a charming love scene between them is interrupted by the news that he has been appointed a Commandant in the Citizen Army and is to lead the eighth battalion that very night. In the second Act we see the troops assembling and hear the orators addressing them, but we hear them from the vantage ground of a neighbouring bar parlour, where, leaning over the counter, a girl of the streets, Rosie Redmond, is in conversation with the Barman—"Nothin' much doin' in your line tonight, Rosie," says he, and she replies: "Curse o' God on th' haporth, hardly, Tom. There isn't much notice taken of a pretty petticoat of a night like this. . . . They're all in a holy mood. Th' solemn-looking dials on th' whole o' them an' they marchin' to th' meetin'. You'd think they were th' glorious company of th' saints an' th'

noble army of martyrs thrampin' through the sthreets of
paradise. They're all thinkin' of higher things than a
girl's garters." It was at this point that at the first performance the riot occurred. In Act III we see the Easter
Rising and the part the tenement dwellers played in it—
looting the stores and bringing home characteristic spoil
—Fluther laden with jars of whiskey, and the women
with gorgeous finery which they propose to wear after
lifting "th' bodices up a bit higher, so as to shake th'
shame out o' them, an' make them fit for women that
hasn't lost themselves in th' nakedness o' th' times." But
in the shooting that follows Nora's husband is killed, and
she goes out of her mind in the strain of a premature confinement brought on by the disaster. The final Act, which
shows us the tenement raided by British soldiers in search
of snipers, mingles humour and tragedy in O'Casey's most
effective manner.

All these plays were produced at the Abbey Theatre,
Dublin, before being put on in London and New York.
But with O'Casey's next tragi-comedy, 'The Silver Tassie,'
there came a regrettable clash of opinion between the
author and the management. Though the characters in the
play are still Irish, the subject, the scenes and the setting
have all to do with the Great War. O'Casey not only combines tragedy with comedy, but supplements his traditional realistic method with modern impressionism. The
first Act introduces us to the "eating, sitting and part
sleeping" room of the Heegan family in an Irish seaport,
presumably Dublin; Harry Heegan, the son, is a famous
football player and has just carried off a silver cup for the
local club by scoring the winning goal; his parents, his
admiring comrades, and no less admiring girls are seeing
him off to the front on the expiry of his last day of leave.
The women are concerned about getting the men off, for

they do not want to lose the government pay and the high wages they earn in munition work; Heegan's mother exclaims when he is at last induced to go: "Thanks be to Christ that we're after managin' to get the three of them away safely." So far, everything is in O'Casey's familiar style and manner. But with the second Act the scene shifts to the war zone, with a shell-rent monastery in the background, barbed wire, ruined houses, and spiky stumps of trees, and a gun emplacement in the foreground. The dialogue is no longer the racy Irish brogue, but literary and stylized, sometimes in rhymed lines, sometimes in blank verse, sometimes in the prose of the Authorized Version of the Old Testament. The characters are no longer individuals, but types, common soldiers without names, a corporal, a "brass hat," a visitor, stretcher-bearers and wounded, brought together at last for a chant of adoration to the gun with a refrain sung in chorus: "We believe in God and we believe in thee." Bernard Shaw thought it wonderful, "the work of a genius—a climax of sheer war imagery." But Lennox Robinson, then manager for the Irish players, was doubtful about the new method, and especially about the mixture in the third and fourth Acts of the two manners—the realism of of the first Act and the unrealism of the second. In these doubts he was upheld by W. B. Yeats, who was dissatisfied not only with the manner but with the theme of the play, which was ultimately refused by the Abbey Theatre. It was first put on the stage in London by the great English producer, C. B. Cochran, who spent (and lost) a good deal of money on it, the war scene of the second Act being magnificently designed by Augustus John, the great English painter. The hospital ward scene of Act III and the dance hall of the Avondale Football Club in Act IV were equally impressive. Harry Heegan, now paralyzed and propelling himself in a wheeled chair, sees his sweetheart carried off by a comrade, with whom he has a terrible quarrel. The play ends with a tango song:

> Let him sigh with the shadows of men
> For men shall just reap as they sow.
> A kiss may breed sorrow, and then
> Sorrow may spring from a blow.
> Time to look sad when we know,
> So let us be merry again.
> He is gone, we remain, and so
> Let him wrap himself up in his woe—
> For he is a life on the ebb,
> We a full life on the flow.

It is an original treatment of a strange theme, and perhaps Yeats was right in his view that O'Casey was not sufficiently moved and excited by his subject to make the play dramatically effective. He was thwarted by the "mere greatness of the World War," which overpowers all personal interest and makes the fate of Harry Heegan appear insignificant.

BIBLIOGRAPHY

WILLIAM BUTLER YEATS

POEMS

1886 'Mosada. A Dramatic Poem.'
1889 'The Wanderings of Oisin, and other Poems.'
1895 'Poems' (including Lyrics published with 'The Countess
      Cathleen' (1892).
1899 'The Wind among the Reeds.'
1906 'Poems, 1899–1905.'
1914 'Responsibilities.'
1917 'The Wild Swans at Coole, other Verses and a Play in
      Verse' ('At the Hawk's Well,' a "Noh" play, per-
      formed privately in 1916 by the Japanese dancer Ito
      and others).
1928 'The Tower.'

PLAYS

1892 'The Countess Cathleen' (acted 1899).
1894 'The Land of Heart's Desire.'
1900 'The Shadowy Waters' (acted 1904).
1902 'Cathleen ni Houlihan.'
1903 'The Hour Glass.'
      'On Baile's Strand' (acted 1904).
1904 'The King's Threshold' (acted 1903).
      'The Pot of Broth' (acted 1902).
1907 'Deirdre' (acted 1906).
1910 'The Green Helmet.'
1911 'Plays for an Irish Theatre,' containing all the above
      except the first two.
1921 'Four Plays for Dancers' (including the "Noh" play
      mentioned above).
1924 'Plays and Controversies.'

PROSE

1893	'The Celtic Twilight.'
1897	'The Secret Rose.'
1903	'Ideas of Good and Evil.'
1907	'Discoveries: A Volume of Essays.'
1912	'The Cutting of an Agate.'
1915	'Reveries over Childhood and Youth.'
1918	'Per Amica Silentia Lunæ.'
1921	'Four Years' (1887–1891).

George Moore

1878	'Flowers of Passion.'
1881	'Pagan Poems.'
1883	'A Modern Lover.'
1885	'A Mummer's Wife.'
1886	'A Drama in Muslin.'
1888	'Confessions of a Young Man.'
1893	'Modern Painting.'
1894	'Esther Waters.'
1898	'Evelyn Innes.'
1900	'The Bending of the Bough.'
1901	'Sister Teresa.'
1903	'The Untilled Field.'
1911	'Ave.'
1912	'Salve.'
1914	'Vale.'
1916	'The Brook Kerith.'
1919	'Avowals.'
1921	'Héloïse and Abelard.'
1930	'Aphrodite in Aulis.'
	Bibliography by Iolo A. Williams (1921).

John Millington Synge

DATES OF PRODUCTION

1903	'In the Shadow of the Glen.'
1904	'Riders to the Sea.'
1905	'The Well of the Saints.'

1907   'The Playboy of the Western World.'
1908   'The Tinker's Wedding' (pub. 1907).
1910   'Deirdre of the Sorrows.'
    The four volumes of Synge's Works (1911) included 'The
Aran Islands' (1907) and 'Poems and Translations' (1909), in
addition to the dramas listed above, which are collected also
in the one-volume edition of his 'Dramatic Works' (1915).

LORD DUNSANY

1909   'The Glittering Gate.'
1911   'King Argimenes and the Unknown Warrior.'
       'The Gods of the Mountain.'
1912   'The Golden Doom.'
1913   'The Lost Silk Hat.'
1914   'The Tents of the Arabs.'
1916   'A Night at an Inn.'
       'The Queen's Enemies.'
1918   'The Prince of Stamboul.'
       'Fame and the Poet.'
1919   'The Laughter of the Gods.'
       'The Murderers.'
1920   'The Compromise of the King of the Golden Isles.'
       'A Good Bargain.'
       'If Shakespeare Lived Today.'
1921   'Cheezo.'
       'If.'
1922   'The Flight of the Queen.'
1925   'The Amusements of Khan Kharuda.'
       'Old King's Tale.'
       'Alexander.'

SEAN O'CASEY

1923   'The Shadow of a Gunman.'
1924   'Juno and the Paycock.'
1926   'The Plough and the Stars.'
1929   'The Silver Tassie.'

CHAPTER VI

JOSEPH CONRAD (1857–1924)

ROMANCE, to which the genius of Scott had given vitality by his power to tell an exciting story and to create human characters, had sunk, in the hands of his English imitators in the nineteenth century, to be merely a literary tradition or a process of manufacture. R. L. Stevenson galvanized the genre to a temporary revival by his gifts of style and personal charm, but even in his hands it was still a tradition and a process, springing rather from literature than from life, with which, indeed, Stevenson's acquaintance was very limited; he was a student and a stylist, with no experience of the life of adventure, and not a great deal of the adventure of life, for he had been, almost from birth to death, nursed and shielded from harsh and violent contacts because of his weak physical condition. It was left, therefore, for Conrad to create a romance founded on experience of the haunts of adventure, remote from Western civilization, vitalized by keen analysis of human character and motive, and embodied in a style distinguished by sensitive beauty, elasticity, and power.

It was not by accident that Conrad underwent, without any thought of turning them to literary account, the adventures he was afterwards to narrate. Brought up in Poland, the most inland of the great countries of Europe, of an aristocratic family, whose adventures had been entirely political, he had, while he was still a boy, made up his mind to go to sea, and putting his finger on the central region of the map of Africa, marked as "Unexplored," he had said, "When I grow up I shall go there." The natural inclination of his Polish relatives (his parents had died in exile) was to regard this as a mere boyish fancy, but their objections were overcome by his persistence, and at the age of seventeen, instead of matriculating at the University of Cracow, he shipped on a French sailing vessel out of Marseilles. He had spoken French from infancy and made two voyages to the West Indies under the French flag as a cabin boy; that he should have become an officer in the French merchant service and even a French writer of note would not have been without precedent; but that Joseph Theodor Konrad Nalecz Korzeniowski, who at nineteen knew not a word of English, should have become a captain in the British Mercantile Marine, and one of the foremost writers in the English language, seems little short of a miracle. It was in 1878 that he landed at Lowestoft with the set purpose of becoming a British seaman; in 1885 he was naturalized as a British subject and admitted to the rank of Master Mariner in the British merchant service. How this miraculous change was accomplished has been best explained in the words of Conrad's personal friend, Sir Hugh Clifford: "At Lowestoft he made the casual acquaintance of an old fellow named Captain Cook who for untold years had been in command of a collier which plied regularly between that port and Cardiff. He was by then well stricken in years, but it was popularly reported of him that during the whole course of his sea service he had never been out of sight of land—a fact which, combined with the historic name he bore, caused him to be commonly known as 'The Great Circumnavigator.' By this old man was young Conrad befriended, and it was on board his collier that the latter, first as a common hand and later as an able seaman, made a succession of voyages between Lowestoft and Cardiff. . . . Meanwhile, during the long, uneventful days afloat, old Captain Cook, who had taken a fancy to the lad, coached him in navigation and seamanship, and when he believed his pupil to be ripe for the experiment sent him up to London to sit for his examination for his second mate's certificate.

"Conrad must have been not quite twenty-one years of age when he sailed to the East as the second mate on board the Judea, and thereafter for nearly thirteen years he knocked about the world, mostly on sailing ships and steam tramps. In turn he visited all the principal ports of both hemispheres, unconsciously accumulating memories which he subsequently put to such stupendous use; and during all this time, he told me, though he read voraciously in French and English, he hardly ever put pen to paper, and very rarely even wrote to his uncle in Cracow. Toward the end of that time he, for a space, lay ill for some weeks in the hospital at Singapore, but even then the inclination to write did not assert itself.

"He had worked hard, however, for many years wrestling with the sea, and of a sudden he felt himself to be weary and in need of rest. He told his friends that he had decided to give himself a holiday and to spend a year ashore—out of sight of the sea. He chose for this purpose lodgings in Bessborough Gardens, a dismal place in Pimlico off the Vauxhall Bridge Road; and he presently made the discovery that living in this unlovely locality amid a wilderness of strangers, even though it were out of sight of the sea, was one of the roughest jobs to which he had set his hand. Yet he was loth to acknowledge himself defeated—to return to the sea in spite of his resolve and his proclamation of his intentions to his friends; and thus it was, as it were in self-defence and because idleness was foreign to his nature, that he began, as one might say by accident, to write."

Between Conrad's arrival at Lowestoft and the publication of his first novel over twenty years elapsed. 'Almayer's Folly' was begun in Pimlico in 1889, and Conrad took the unfinished manuscript with him on his return to the sea. "It went with him to Poland," says Sir Hugh Clifford, "during the first visit he had paid to his native land for a decade and a half, it went with him to West Africa and up the Congo, where he commanded for a short time a river steamboat; and never once, I think, during all the time that he was engaged in working at it was anything in the nature of literary ambition present to his consciousness." He showed it only to a young Cambridge man named Jacques whom he met when he was first mate of the sailing ship Torrens in 1892. "Is it worth finishing?" asked Conrad when Jacques had read it through. "Distinctly," answered the young Englishman with native terseness. "Were you much interested?— Very much." "Is the story quite clear to you as it stands? —Yes? Perfectly." That was all the conversation and they never spoke of it again. Nor did Conrad speak of it to John Galsworthy, who was a passenger on the boat, although they had long talks together during Conrad's off hours. It was only when ill health forced Conrad in 1894 to give up his intention of returning to sea life, that he wrote the last three chapters of 'Almayer's Folly' and sent the manuscript to Fisher Unwin, a publisher chosen almost at a venture. Unwin's reader was a young man named Edward Garnett, son of the well-known scholar, Dr. Garnett, of the British Museum. He was greatly impressed by the qualities of the story, which was immediately accepted and published in the spring of the following year. Under the stimulus of Garnett's appreciation and encouragement, Conrad was induced to write a second story, 'An Outcast of the Islands,' which appeared in 1896. Most of the characters of both were taken from life, and were encountered by Conrad during his voyages on the Borneo Coast in 1887–8. Conrad's first novel tells the story of the moral disintegration of Almayer through his marriage for the sake of money to a Malay girl whom Captain Lingard had rescued from pirates and wished to provide for. Conrad had a strong sense of human solidarity, but he believed also that a man should be true to his own racial tradition. Almayer loses not only the respect of other white men but his own self-respect; the half-caste daughter who is his one tie to life deserts him and runs off with a Malay: he sinks into complete degradation and utter disregard for the good opinion of his fellows.

Conrad's second novel, 'An Outcast of the Islands,' is also a story of the Malay Peninsula and has a somewhat similar theme—the tragic downfall of a man disloyal to his European tradition and guilty of treachery in his dealings with the natives. 'The Nigger of the Narcissus' is a sea story, and attracted the attention of the critics by its power of description as well as its analysis of character. The preface to this story showed, moreover, that by this time (1897) Conrad had given considerable thought to the romantic novel as a literary form and was fully conscious of his artistic purpose and of the methods to be used for its attainment. Fiction, so far as it is an art, he writes, is an appeal to temperament—"to our capacity for delight and wonder, to the sense of mystery surrounding our lives, to our sense of pity, and beauty, and pain. Such an appeal, to be effective, must be an impression conveyed through the senses; and in fact, it cannot be made in any other way, because temperament, whether individual or collective, is not amenable to persuasion. All art, therefore, appeals primarily to the senses, and the artistic aim when expressing itself in written words must also make its appeal through the senses, if its high desire is to reach the secret spring of responsive emotions. It must strenuously aspire to the plasticity of sculpture, to the colour of painting, and to the magic suggestiveness of music—which is the art of arts. And it is only through complete unswerving devotion to the perfect blending of form and substance; it is only through an unremitting, never-discouraged care for the shape and ring of sentences that an approach can be made to plasticity, to colour; and the light of magic suggestiveness may be brought to play for an evanescent instant over the commonplace surface of words: of the old, old words, worn thin, defaced by ages of careless usage.

"The sincere endeavour to accomplish that creative task, to go as far on that road as his strength will carry him, to go undeterred by faltering, weariness, or reproach, is the only valid justification for the worker in prose. And if his conscience is clear, his answer to those who, in the fulness of a wisdom that looks for immediate profit, demand specifically to be edified, consoled, amused; who demand to be promptly improved or encouraged, or frightened, or shocked, or charmed, must run thus: My task which I am trying to achieve is, by the power of the written word, to make you hear, to make you feel—it is, before all, to make you *see*. That—and no more, and it is everything. If I succeed, you shall find there according to your deserts: encouragement, consolation, fear, charm—all you demand, and, perhaps, also that glimpse of truth for which you have forgotten to ask."

In all of these three novels Conrad told a straightforward tale, using the time-honoured convention that the novelist has complete knowledge of the fortunes and motives of the characters he creates. In 'Lord Jim' he used for the first time the intermediary of a narrator—imagining not only the story but the man who tells it, so that the narrator's knowledge of character and incident must be confined to what he has seen, heard, or guessed from hearsay or accidental contacts. The intermediary invented by Conrad for the purpose of this story is Captain Marlow, a seafaring man of wide experience and keen psychological insight, whom Conrad was to use again in later work; he is, as a matter of fact, very like Conrad himself, so that the author's problem was reduced to revealing in his story only such facts and fancies as might have come to him in the contacts of everyday life. The method implies a gain, no doubt, in verisimilitude, but it involves something of a strain on the powers of the novelist, who must show us not merely his characters as they are figured forth by his own imagination, but as they would have appeared to an observer, if they had really existed. Jim, the hero of the story, is the first officer of a tramp steamer, a romantic young man whose mind is "full of valorous deeds; he loved these dreams and the success of his imaginary achievements. They were the best parts of life, its secret truth, its hidden reality. They had a gorgeous virility, the charm of vagueness, they passed before him with a heroic tread; they carried his soul away with them and made it drunk with the divine philtre of an unbounded confidence in itself. There was nothing he could not face." Yet when a sudden emergency springs upon them, Jim, with the other officers, deserts the ship and leaves the native pilgrims, who are its passengers, to drown. They do not drown because the ship does not sink; and the result is that Jim is tried for dereliction of duty and disgraced. The analysis of his state of mind and of the process of his recovery to confidence in himself and the esteem of his fellows—though it is at the sacrifice of his life—makes a story of absorbing interest, distinctly in advance of anything Conrad had yet done.

His next novel 'Nostromo' is an extraordinary achievement as a piece of exciting narrative. It sets before us the life of a South American mining port—with which indeed Conrad had only a passing acquaintance—with remarkable vividness and power of invention. We see them all—Indians and Europeans, American business men and local politicians, scheming and plotting, loving and hating, all involved in a complex of contending interests and passions which resolves itself in a magnificent climax and tragic conclusion. It illustrates perhaps more clearly and directly than any other novel the malign power of human greed for material wealth, which, to Conrad's thinking, was the greatest impediment to the natural solidarity of mankind and the most potent source of evil in human experience.

His two novels following, 'The Secret Agent' and 'Under Western Eyes,' dealt with the anarchistic agitation which was about that time troubling the peace of Europe, and did not add particularly to his fame. But with 'Chance' (1914) and 'Victory' (1915) he rose suddenly to the height of popular approval. Hitherto, although he had been highly praised by the critics and his fellow novelists, the response of the public had been feeble; his first three books showed a loss in the publisher's ledger for many years, and the return to the author was necessarily small. Conrad had in consequence worked under adverse conditions of serious ill-health and an insufficient income. After the publication of 'Chance' there was a change for the better—unfortunately too late, for Conrad was now nearly sixty years of age, his health was permanently broken down, and his spirit was embittered by prolonged hardship and disappointment. 'Chance' employed as intermediaries two principal narrators beside subordinates, and thereby won from Henry James the high praise for Conrad of choosing the "way to do a thing that shall undergo most doing." For those who can appreciate the difficulties of this elaborate technique, Conrad's triumph was a conspicuous proof of his genius, and as his method implies difficulties for the reader as well as for the writer, it is to the credit of the public taste that the sale of 'Chance' was greater than that of any previous Conrad novel. Its subject and treatment are more psychological than romantic, for the characters are English people living under the conditions of modern commercialism. The villain of the story is one of those exploiters of modern gullibility who prey upon the desire of the mob to make easy money, and who succeed—for a time—by the simple plan of paying high interest to their earlier victims out of the money subscribed by later investors for schemes which, if not deliberately fraudulent, have no real prospect of producing profits for anyone except the promoters. De Barral, Conrad's example of this recurring type of swindler, is a self-deceiver who protests to the day of his death that he is the victim of a conspiracy and that he would have paid everything if he had been allowed more time. The interest of the story, however, centres about his young daughter, who, innocent herself, believes in her father's innocence, and to afford him a refuge after his release from prison marries a Quixotic sea-captain who had fallen in love with her desolate maidenhood. The romantic element of the story lies in the relations between "the damsel" and "the knight" and their ultimate reconciliation by mutual understanding of each other's character and motive. Chance, which has brought them together, apparently to their own undoing, in the end gives them happiness through their steadfast devotion to their own sense of honour, for "the science of life consists in seizing every chance that presents itself." This "gospel truth," proclaimed at the end of the story, chimes in with the quotation from Sir Thomas Browne with which it opens: "Those that hold that all things are governed by Fortune had not erred, had they not persisted there." The philosophy of the story, as well as its method of presentation, was probably above the heads of the majority of the readers of 'Chance,' who may have been induced to read it by the critics' admiration for this and earlier novels by Conrad. As a romance, it is of less enthralling interest than 'Victory,' in which a misanthropic Swedish philosopher, Axel Heyst, on his lonely island of Samburan, offers a refuge to the pathetically friendless Lena from the persecutions of the lustful Schomberg, in whose hotel she has been employed as a musician. Schomberg takes a terrible revenge, but Lena is able to save Heyst's life by the sacrifice of her own and thus to gain a final victory for love and loyalty over human treachery and greed. It is in some ways the most original and the most romantic of Conrad's novels.

'The Arrow of Gold' (1919) and 'The Rover' (1923) are again romances of European political history in which Conrad does not seem at his best; but with 'The Rescue' (1920) he returned to Melanesia and his Malay warriors. As early as 1896 in 'An Outcast of the Islands,' Conrad listed as the first of the exploits of Captain Tom Lingard his "successful fight with the sea robbers, when he rescued, as rumour had it, the yacht of some bigwig from home, somewhere down Carimata way." The scene and the cen-

tral situation are those of 'The Rescue' and it is clear that
Conrad had the main outlines of the story in mind at that
time. By 1898 it was far advanced, but he laid it aside
for twenty years, because he felt that he had not yet
command "of the proper formula of expression, and the
only formula that would suit"; in reality, he says, it was
"the doubt of my prose, the doubt of its adequacy."
There can be no doubt of the adequacy of the prose in
which the work was completed, or of Conrad's entire
command over his medium. In style, in characterization,
in dramatic movement, in psychological analysis we have
Conrad at his best, and above all we have that brooding
quality which Professor H. S. Canby has singled out as
the quality distinguishing Conrad from all other English
writers of fiction—a quality of the Slav rather than of the
Anglo-Saxon mind.

Beside Captain Tom Lingard and the Europeans he
rescued, we have native characters of more than usual interest—Lingard's friends, Rajah Hassim and his sister
Immada; the faithful runner, Jaffir; the mysterious chief-
tain Belarab and his subordinates, Malays who have kept
to the end "their love of liberty, their fanatical devotion
to their chiefs, their blind fidelity in friendship and hate
—all their lawful and unlawful instincts." Romance for
Conrad consists not in remoteness of scene or sensational
incident, but in people who have "that responsive sensitiveness to the shadowy appeals made by life and death,
which is the groundwork of a chivalrous character."
Such is Tom Lingard, torn by the conflict between his
devotion to his friends and his passion for the woman
who betrays and deserts him. Lingard is romantic above
all in his affection for his brig, the one thing left to him
at the end of the story. "To him she was always precious
—like old love; always desirable—like a strange woman;

always tender, like a mother; always faithful—like the favourite daughter of a man's heart." The woman who bewitches Lingard, Edith Travers, is herself romantic by nature, but her native impulses have been overcome by her contact with the selfishness and conventionality of the fashionable world. "As a young girl, often reproved for her romantic ideas, she had dreams where the sincerity of a great passion appeared like the ideal fulfilment and the only truth of life. Entering the world she discovered that ideal to be unattainable because the world is too prudent to be sincere. Then she hoped that she could find the truth of life in ambition which she understood as a lifelong devotion to some unselfish ideal. Mr. Travers's name was on men's lips; he seemed capable of enthusiasm and of devotion; he impressed her imagination by his impenetrability. She married him, found him enthusiastically devoted to the nursing of his own career, and had nothing to hope for now." Her romantic impulses are momentarily revived by contact with Lingard's passionate ardour and generosity, but in the end she is guilty of an act of treachery which brings all his plans to naught and leaves him, for the time at least, a broken and embittered man. It is not surprising that Conrad found the relations between characters so violently contrasted too difficult for his 'prentice hand, and that for twenty years he left the novel unfinished; but the conclusion he finally achieved is a masterpiece. The closing chapters which for so long a time he felt unable to write proved to be the triumph of his mature art. He had done nothing better during his previous career; and he did nothing equal to them during the few years of life that were left to him.

BIBLIOGRAPHY

NOVELS

1895 'Almayer's Folly.'
1896 'An Outcast of the Islands.'
1897 'The Nigger of the Narcissus.'
1900 'Lord Jim.'
1903 'Nostromo.'
1907 'The Secret Agent.'
1911 'Under Western Eyes.'
1914 'Chance.'
1915 'Victory.'
1917 'The Shadow Line: A Confession.'
1919 'The Arrow of Gold.'
1920 'The Rescue.'
1923 'The Rover.'
1925 'Suspense.' (Unfinished.)

IN COLLABORATION WITH FORD MADOX HUEFFER

1901 'The Inheritors: An Extravagant Story.'
1903 'Romance: A Novel.'

TALES AND SHORT STORIES

1898 'Tales of Unrest.'
1902 'Youth: A Narrative; and two other Stories.'
1903 'Typhoon, and other Stories.'
1908 'A Set of Six.'
1912 ' 'Twixt Land and Sea.'
1916 'Within the Tides.'
1924 'Shorter Tales.'

ESSAYS AND AUTOBIOGRAPHY

1906 'The Mirror of the Sea: Memories and Impressions.'
1912 'A Personal Record.' (Published in England as 'Some Reminiscences.')

1921   'Notes on Life and Letters.'
1926   'Last Essays.'

DRAMA

Several of Conrad's novels were dramatized by other hands. One, 'The Secret Agent,' he himself made into a drama under the same title. It was acted at the Ambassadors Theatre, London, on November 2, 1922.

BIOGRAPHICAL AND CRITICAL

Richard Curle, 'Joseph Conrad: A Study,' 1914.
Hugh Walpole, 'Joseph Conrad,' 1916. (New Edition, 1924.)
Jessie Conrad, 'Joseph Conrad as I knew Him,' 1926.
G. Jean-Aubry, 'The Life and Letters of Joseph Conrad,' 1927.
Edward Garnett, 'Letters from Joseph Conrad, 1895–1924,' 1928.
Richard Curle, 'The Last Twelve Years of Joseph Conrad,' 1928.
Gustav Morf, 'The Polish Heritage of Joseph Conrad,' 1930.
V. Walpole, 'Conrad's Method,' 1930.
R. L. Mégroz, 'Joseph Conrad's Mind and Method,' 1931.
   Bibliography by Thomas J. Wise (London, 1920), in Ruth M. Stauffer, 'Joseph Conrad and his Romantic Realism' (Boston, 1922).

CHAPTER VII

HERBERT GEORGE WELLS (1866–   )

IF, as many think, sociological fiction is the characteristic literary product of the time, H. G. Wells has a fair claim to be considered its most representative writer, on account not merely of the extent and variety of his contacts with current thought but of the power with which he has brought vague popular discontents to clear and artistic expression. He sprang from the lowest scale of the middle class—barely divided in his birth and upbringing from the working class which during his youth and early manhood came into educational opportunity and political power. One of his grandfathers was head gardener at Penshurst, the other an innkeeper at Midhurst, his father a professional cricketer and small shopkeeper at Bromley, Kent. His earliest recollections are thus recorded in 'First and Last Things': "I recall an underground kitchen with a drawered table, a window looking up at a grating, a back yard in which, growing out by a dustbin, was a grape-vine; a red-papered room with a bookcase, over my father's shop, the dusty aisles and fixtures, the regiments of wine-glasses and tumblers, the rows of hanging mugs and jugs, the towering edifices of jam-pots, the tea and dinner and toilet sets in that emporium, its brighter side of cricket goods, of pads and balls and stumps. Out of the window one peeped at the more exterior world, the High Street in front, the tailor's garden, the butcher's yard, the churchyard and Bromley church tower behind; and one was taken upon expeditions to fields and open places. This limited world was peopled with certain familiar presences, mother and father, two brothers, the evasive but interesting cat, and by intermittent people of a livelier and more transient interest, customers and callers."

Upper-class life he saw (from the point of view of the servants' hall) when owing to family misfortune, his mother in 1880 became housekeeper in the family in which she had formerly been lady's maid at Up Park near Petersfield, the "Bladesover" of 'Tono-Bungay,' which also enshrines some early experiences in the chemist's shop (drug-store) at Midhurst. He had a bitter struggle, both for livelihood and for education, beginning work as a draper's assistant (dry goods clerk) at the age of 13 and experiencing in his own person some of the humiliations he has described in 'Kipps.' Striving to educate himself, he took a humble post as assistant-master in an obscure school, and from this in turn he escaped with the aid of a Government Scholarship to the Royal College of Science, South Kensington. It was his good fortune to come under Huxley, the leading exponent of the new science of biology and one of the most stirring spirits in the intellectual unrest of the time. Economically and socially the immediate gain for Wells was the London B.Sc. degree with first class honours in zoölogy; upon his mental development, the effects were far-reaching. It is really of himself under the name of Oswald that Wells speaks in 'Joan and Peter': "Those were the great days when Huxley lectured on zoölogy at South Kensington, and to him Oswald went. Oswald did indeed find science consoling and inspiring. Scientific studies were at once rarer and more touched by enthusiasm a quarter of a century ago than they are

now, and he was soon a passionate naturalist, consumed
by the insatiable craving to know how. That little, long
upper laboratory in the Normal School of Science, as the
place was then called, with the preparations and diagrams
along one side, the sinks and windows along the other, the
row of small tables down the windows, and the ever-
present vague mixed smell of methylated spirit, Canada
balsam, and a sweetish decay, opened vast new horizons to
him. To the world of the eighteen-eighties the story of life,
of the origin and branching out of species, of the making
of continents, was still the most inspiring of new romances.
Comparative anatomy in particular was then a great and
philosophical 'new learning,' a mighty training of the
mind; the drift of biological teaching towards specializa-
tion was still to come."

For the time being, however, Wells had to work hard
for a living as a university coach—so hard that in 1893
his health broke down. He had already published a textbook on biology and had written for the 'University Correspondent,' the 'Educational Review' and the 'Fortnightly.' He now abandoned teaching and adventured
boldly on journalism in the 'Pall Mall Gazette,' 'Saturday Review' and 'Nature.' By 1895 he had published
his first romance and his first volumes of essays and of
short stories, and was fairly launched on a literary career.

His early stories were a curious amalgam of scientific
knowledge and riotous romance which he has himself
compared to the "monstrous experimental imaginings" of
children. The verve and technical skill with which they
were written won for them a wide popularity, but it was
inevitable that Wells should soon be discontented with the
themes he was treating and the public to which he was
appealing. Between 'The Time Machine' (1895) and
'When the Sleeper Wakes' (1899) he had reduced the

scope of his imaginative flight from 30 million years to a mere matter of a century ahead, and as early as 1896 he had begun to turn his glance from the far future to the present. 'The Wheels of Chance' (1896), recounting the adventures, amorous and other, of a draper's assistant on a holiday, is slight, but it is a well-told story of contemporary life. 'Love and Mr. Lewisham' (1900) marks a distinct advance in the same direction, and was written with great care and toil, an earnest striving after fidelity to life, with "entire seriousness in treatment and outlook."

In spite of severe overwork and continued ill-health, the turn of the country found Wells on the highroad to success—" 'ammer, 'ammer, 'ammer, on the 'ard 'igh road," as he put it in a letter to a friend, but with a sense of confidence and security. He had made the difficult transition from the slavery of journalism to the comparative freedom of the man of letters. He had built himself a comfortable house on the south-east coast between Folkestone and Sandgate, where he could work in peace. He had been married, divorced, and married again; and his second venture into matrimony was entirely satisfactory. In 'The Book of Catherine Wells' (1928) he pays the following tribute to the partner of thirty years of successful effort: "I do not know what I should have been without her. She stabilized my life. She gave it a home and dignity. She preserved its continuity. Not without incessant watchfulness and toil. I have a hundred memories of an indefatigable typist carrying on her work in spite of a back-ache; of a grave judicial proof-reader in a garden shelter, determined that no slovenliness should escape her; of a resolute little person, clear-headed but untrained in business method, battling steadfastly with the perplexities of our accumulating accounts and keeping her grips on them." He had many friends in the literary world, including George Gissing, who in 'The Private Papers of Henry Ryecroft' (1903) painted a wistful picture of his younger comrade's triumphant well-being. "He is happy with his wife and children; the thought of all the comforts and pleasures he is able to give them must be a constant joy to him; were he to die, his family is safe from want. He has friends and acquaintances as many as he desires; congenial folk gather at his table; he is welcome in pleasant houses near and far; his praise is upon the lips of all whose praise is worth having. With all this, he has the good sense to avoid manifest dangers; he has not abandoned his privacy, and he seems to be in no danger of being spoilt by good fortune. His work is more to him than a means of earning money; he talks about a book he has in hand almost as freshly and keenly as in the old days, when his annual income was barely a couple of hundred."

With the future of scientific invention still in his mind, Wells began to get into shape his ideas about a great many other things, and embodied them in a book entitled 'Anticipations of the Reaction of Mechanical and Scientific Progress upon Human Life and Thought' (1901). While still at college he had become interested in socialism, which to him meant not absolute equality, but equality of opportunity, to be realized by the abolition of inheritance and the restriction of property to that earned by individual exertion. So, while 'Anticipations' promised to be merely a more sober, scientific view of the future than the romances, it was intended as an authoritative statement of the author's opinions on burning questions of politics, morals, and religious faith. It was indeed something of both of these. Wells foretold some of the developments, advantageous and disadvantageous, that

have since resulted from the automobile, the telephone,
and other mechanical inventions which were then still
novelties engaging public interest; and at the same time
he drew attention to the displacement of the landed aristocracy, with its sense of responsibility, by a new share-
holding class with only one specific characteristic—"the
possession of property and the potentialities property en-
tails, with a total lack of function with regard to that
property. . . . The shareholder owns the world *de jure*,
by the common recognition of the rights of property; and
the incumbency of knowledge, management, and toil falls
entirely to others. He toils not, neither does he spin; he
is mechanically released from the penalty of the Fall; he
reaps in a still sinful world all the practical benefits of a
millennium—without any of its moral limitations." This
absorption of irresponsible wealth by the idle rich is balanced at the other end of the scale by the "submerged"
portion of the social body—"a leaderless, aimless multitude, a multitude of people drifting down towards the
abyss. Essentially it consists of people who have failed
to 'catch on' to the altered necessities the development
of mechanism has brought about; they are people thrown
out of employment by machinery, thrown out of employment by the escape of industries along some newly opened
line of communication to some remote part of the world,
or born under circumstances that give them no opportunity
of entering the world of active work. Into this welter of
machine-superseded toil there topples the non-adaptable
residue of every changing trade; its members marry and
are given in marriage, and it is recruited by the spend-
thrifts, weaklings, and failures of every superior class."

Wells had no less revolutionary things to say on morals
and religion, especially on the subject of sex, but the
reading public did not appear to be at all disconcerted.

'Anticipations' went into eight editions within a year, and Wells was recognized as a conspicuous leader of the forward movement. The Shaws and the Webbs were already among his friends, and the latter persuaded him to join the Fabian Society. But there was a temperamental difference between the doctrinaire and bureaucratic socialists led by Bernard Shaw and Sidney Webb on the one hand and the more romantic and positive idealists like Wells on the other; there was a battle royal as to principles and policy between Shaw and Wells, in which the older debater won all the engagements, and Wells withdrew to go his own way. His way was not to be content with small advantages in municipal administration, but to effect by education a fundamental change in the public mind as to religion, sex, property, and half a dozen other crucial issues. To this end he published several prose treatises, such as 'Mankind in the Making,' 'A Modern Utopia,' 'First and Last Things,' and 'Social Forces in England and America'—the last in 1914—and he devoted to the same end his skill in the writing of fiction. Early in the century he worked off two scientific romances, 'The First Men in the Moon,' and 'The Food of the Gods,' and then definitely committed himself to the sociological novel of contemporary life in 'Kipps' (1905). The misadventures and successes of the suddenly-enriched draper's apprentice are told with a humorous kindliness which is in itself a delight, but the novelist never loses sight of the social significance of his hero's vain endeavours to accommodate himself to the conventional requirements of a society to which he comes too late. It is a mere chance that he comes to it at all; but if by another chance he had come to it earlier he would have found his way perfectly smooth.

'In the Days of the Comet' (1906) is a partial return

to Wells's older manner, but even in it the main interest is sociological, and the romantic science is merely an ill-fitting patch upon the presentation of the serious questions which were then occupying the writer's mind. The resulting combination is unsuccessful alike as a romance and as a novel.

In 'Tono-Bungay' (1909) the scientific element is less prominent and much less fantastic; if the flight of the hero in an airplane across the Channel was at the time of composition not very probable, it was only a step or two in advance of actuality. The career of the patent medicine promoter, in spite of some grotesque elements, was characteristic of the time (being, indeed, founded on the exploits of some recent commercial adventurers) and it gave Wells the opportunity to reveal both the powers and limitations of his genius as a novelist. The story is told with sustained sweep and vitality; the three main characters are originally conceived and finely drawn. The minor characters are less successful, especially Beatrice, who never has the touch of life, least of all in the love scenes. This appears to be due, not so much to lack of social experience on the part of the novelist, as to temperamental defect. The little stenographer with whom the hero comes so quickly to an understanding is real enough, but this affair can hardly be called romantic. It is when Wells tries to convey passion purified by its own fire that he fails most dismally. The lower forms of sex attraction he represents faithfully and sympathetically; for the portrayal of real passion in its higher, intenser moods he has no gift.

This is often exemplified in the novels, in none more clearly than in 'Ann Veronica,' which is a study of sex and of the efforts of an intelligent girl to free herself from the trammels of conventional surroundings. The novelist's picture of Ann's struggles to gain economic independence is not any more encouraging than Brieux's treatment of a somewhat similar situation in 'La Femme Seule.' In both, man is represented as a predatory animal controlling economic opportunity and exercising that control to satisfy his sensual desires. The War changed the economic situation of women for the better in both England and France, and it may be doubted whether at any time in the United States a capable woman eager to earn her own living would have found the path of virtue so difficult as Ann did. The solution in her particular case, under an appearance of unconventionality, is thoroughly in accord with conventional opinion. Only the existence of a discarded wife prevents Capes from marrying Ann in the first instance, and as soon as he is free, he does marry her. They settle down to the conventional felicity of the hearth and the cradle, and Ann's conventional relatives recognize that her rebellion is condoned by her ultimate submission. There is no sympathy wasted by the author on the more extreme emancipators of her sex with whom Ann comes in contact during her struggle for freedom; they are frankly ridiculed. Take for instance this scrap of Miss Minifer's conversation: " 'We do not want the men, we do not want them, with their sneers and loud laughter. Empty, silly, coarse brutes. Brutes! They are the brute still with us! Science some day may teach us a way to do without them. It is only the women matter. It is not every sort of creature needs—these males. Some have no males.'

" 'There's green-fly' admitted Ann Veronica. 'And even then—'

"The conversation hung for a thoughtful moment. Ann Veronica readjusted her chin on her hand. 'I wonder which of us is right?' she said. 'I haven't a scrap—of this sort of aversion.' "

'The History of Mr. Polly' recounts with humour and

sympathy the misadventures of a small tradesman, cursed with indigestion, an unsuccessful business, and a shrewish wife, but blessed with a mild romantic imaginativeness which lends his character a certain charm. A much more ambitious effort from the sociological point of view is 'The New Machiavelli,' which opens with a searching analysis of social conditions in the later Victorian period, and proceeds to present, not without personal feeling, the clash between public ambition and irregular passion. There are amusing, if somewhat malicious, portraits of contemporary personalities, and some acute reflections on contemporary political tendencies, but the development of the novel, as not infrequently happens with Wells, fails to bear out the promise of its beginning, partly because of the author's inability, already noted, to convey adequately the overmastering passion which is the centre of the story.

'Marriage' deals again with a particular phase of the sex question—the conflict between sexual attraction and devotion to science. The young scientist and his somewhat conventional bride are amusingly and not unsympathetically drawn in their earlier difficulties of courtship and housekeeping, but when they get out into the wilds of Labrador to discuss sex relations in the abstract, they cease to be either natural or entertaining, and their disquisitions on matrimony cannot be said to add anything new to a subject already well-worn.

'The Passionate Friends' is still another treatment of the same theme; in this case, romance is kept alive by enforced separation, but the resulting love letters have neither the accent of passion nor the stimulus of intellectual inspiration. The didactic element is again overemphasized in 'The World Set Free,' 'The Wife of Sir Isaac Harman,' and 'The Research Magnificent,' and in none of these did the theme sufficiently stir the author's imagination to enable him to write more than a readable story, with occasional lapses into philosophical dulness.

'Bealby' is a mere extravaganza, and 'Mr. Boon,' (at first only half acknowledged), is simply a fling at some contemporaries Wells disliked but apparently did not care to attack openly. The Great War, however, really fired the novelist's imagination, and 'Mr. Britling Sees it Through' is by far the best of contemporary accounts of the social and intellectual conditions of the English middle class immediately before and immediately after the opening of the new epoch. Britling, apart from being endowed with unnecessarily numerous amours before the story opens, is treated with that humorous sympathy which is one of the author's best gifts, and his searchings of heart are vitalized by the sudden change affecting his life, as it did millions of others at the same time. The widespread popularity of the story was not undeserved, for its sincerity of utterance gave it a universal appeal, and it will remain an invaluable and moving record of a mind sensitive to spiritual change in a great crisis of the world's history.

It was a pity that Wells did not leave this incursion into the spiritual field to stand by itself. 'The Soul of a Bishop,' with its superfluous potion, was as unhappy a venture into the domain of religion as 'God the Invisible King,' published about the same time, which had not even the novelist's narrative power to relieve its ineffectiveness. All that Wells did as a theologian was to present ancient heresies with the surprised air of a modern conjurer.

Wells made large claims for the modern novel and he did his best to occupy the wide territory he sketched out as its proper field. He wrote in an article on 'The Contemporary Novel' (1911): "It is to be the social mediator, the vehicle of understanding, the instrument of self-

examination, the parade of morals and the exchange of
manners, the factory of customs, the criticism of laws
and institutions and of social dogmas and ideas. It is to
be the home confessional, the initiator of knowledge, the
seed of fruitful self-questioning. Let me be very clear
here, I do not mean for a moment that the novelist is going to set up as a teacher, as a sort of priest with a pen,
who will make men and women believe and do this and
that. The novel is not a new sort of pulpit; humanity is
passing out of the phase when men sit under preachers
and dogmatize influences. But the novelist is going to be
the most potent of artists, because he is going to present
conduct, devise beautiful conduct, discuss conduct, analyse
conduct, suggest conduct, illuminate it through and
through. He will not teach, but discuss, point out, plead
and display. And this being my view, you will be prepared for the demand I am now about to make for an absolutely free hand for the novelist in his choice of topic
and incident and in his method of treatment; or rather,
if I may presume to speak for other novelists, I would say
it is not so much a demand we make as an intention we
proclaim. We are going to write, subject only to our own
limitations, about the whole of human life. We are going
to deal with political questions and religious questions
and social questions. We cannot present people unless
we have this free hand, this unrestricted field. What is
the good of telling stories about people's lives if one may
not deal freely with the religious beliefs and organizations
that have controlled or failed to control them? What is
the good of pretending to write about love and the loyalties and treacheries and quarrels of men and women, if
one must not glance at those varieties of physical temperament and organic quality, those deeply passionate
needs and distresses from which half the storms of human

life are brewed? We mean to deal with all these things,
and it will need very much more than influential people in
London, the scurrility of the 'Spectator,' and the deep and
obstinate silences of the 'Westminster Gazette,' to stop
the incoming tide of aggressive novel-writing. We are
going to write about it all. We are going to write about
business and finance and politics and precedence and
pretentiousness and decorum and indecorum, until a thousand pretences and ten thousand impostures shrivel in the
cold, clear air of our elucidations. We are going to write
of wasted opportunities and latent beauties until a thousand new ways of living open to men and women. We
are going to appeal to the young and the hopeful and the
curious, against the established, the dignified, and de-
fensive. Before we have done, we will have all life within
the scope of the novel."

Wells did his best work in the novel before his removal
in 1912 to Easton Glebe, Dunmow, Essex, where the most
prosperous years of his life were spent. The enormous
circulation, first of 'Mr. Britling Sees it Through,' and
then of the 'Outline of History,' made him rich beyond
all he could ever have dreamt of, but he continued to
write with unabated industry, though his work no longer
had the spontaneity and verve of his middle years. After
the War his novels continued to be heavily weighted with
the subject—philosophical, religious, economic, or social
—that happened at the time of writing to be engaging his
attention. 'Joan and Peter, The Story of an Education'
(1918) can hardly be called a novel, for it has barely
enough thread of story to hold it together and the characterization is slight. Joan and Peter are any two young
people growing up to womanhood and manhood, and
Oswald is any guardian (as it might be Wells himself)
with an inquiring mind and a sense of responsibility for

the future of the Empire and of the world. The dons and schoolmasters Oswald interviews are types in the sense that they have no individuality—one hopes that they are not typical—and they say the kind of thing Wells wants them to say to bring out the points of his argument, not the kind of thing human beings would say—for schoolmasters are still human—if confronted by such a persistent questioner of all established principles as Wells is and Oswald is set out to be. A paper by Wells in the 'Fortnightly Review' of the previous year (April, 1917), 'The Case against the Classical Languages,' gives his view more clearly and concisely without the impression that he is setting up men of straw for the pleasure of bowling them over. He says: "I want . . . to see my country and my English-speaking race thinking more massively than it does at present, thinking more strongly and clearly. I want to see the hundred and fifty millions of English-speakers as one great unifying mind finding itself in expression. I do not want to see what should be the best thing in our university life, the philosophical teaching in the universities, the teaching that attracts the best intelligences of the country, perpetually cut off from the market-place because it is reading Greek, thinking partly in Greek and partly in English, with a partition between, and writing its thoughts sloppily and confusedly in an Anglo-Greek jargon. . . . These Greek monopolists have to get their trade and their prejudices and privileges out of the way of our sons and our people and our public services. It is their share in the sacrifices of these creative days."

In the United States the Greek monopolists have got out of the way—or rather they have been pushed into a corner—and still the educational problem is not solved. For the rest, besides English and philosophy, Wells wants to have biology, physiology, hygiene, sociology, and history taught—all of which has been done already in many American schools. The advanced educationalist in the United States of today would find Wells's educational programme quite conservative. In one point, however, he is radical enough; he wants a new race of teachers. Those encountered by Joan and Peter "seemed to be for the most part little-spirited, gossiping men. They had also an effect of being underpaid; they had been caught early by the machinery of prize and scholarship, bred, as they say at the Zoölogical Gardens, 'in the menagerie'; they were men who knew nothing of the world outside, nothing of effort and adventure, nothing of sin and repentance." One wonders how the teachers Wells has in mind would find time to acquire knowledge, seeing that personal experience of "those graver and larger sins that really distress and mar mankind" makes heavy demands on health and energy. Hardly in this way could the problem be solved of "making the teacher of youth an inspiring figure," and under the present system it has not been found so insoluble as Wells seems to think.

Wells is too much of an artist not to relieve his dissertation by many lively and amusing passages of description and narration, and when in the course of some 500 pages he has got his young people educated—as well as he could, though not at all to his own satisfaction— just in time for the outbreak of the War, he turns to an account of the state of English society in 1914 almost as good as the sketch of later Victorian England at the beginning of 'The New Machiavelli'—not quite so good, for the author's personal feeling comes more into play and distorts the picture. But the restless excitement of the years before the War is vividly portrayed in its various manifestations; feminism, trades unionism, socialism, the

Irish question are presented concretely, and there follows a graphic review of the various phases of public feeling and opinion as the great struggle proceeds. Intermixed with this there is inevitable philosophizing, and some theology—more modest in tone than Wells's first incursion into this field. Peter arrives at "a new conception, the conception of Man taking hold of the world, unassisted by God but with the acquiescence of God, and in fulfilment of some remote, incomprehensible planning on the part of God." At this point, however, Wells adds the saving clause: "Probably Peter in thinking this was following one of the most ancient and well-beaten of speculative paths, but it seemed to him that it was a new way of thinking." The book ends with Oswald's 'Valediction,' a discourse on things in general with education as its kernel, given to us in two versions, first as Oswald devised it in bed, and then as he actually delivered it with the interruptions of Peter, which are so considerable that it takes an entirely different shape—the mind of Wells in its last phase, Oswald's midnight reverie representing the one before the last. Friendship with America, the League of Nations, yes, but for what? Not merely for peace, not for democracy, but for progress, "for the adventure of mankind." And this brings us back to education—"the State explaining itself to and incorporating the will of the individual" so as to fulfil the will of God.

In 1922 Wells announced to the students of Glasgow University that he was "seriously thinking" of writing no more novels. A captious critic might have retorted that he had written none for some years, for 'The Undying Fire' and 'The Secret Places of the Heart' were really treatises with an all too thin envelope of fiction. Admirers of Wells's extraordinary verve and skill in imaginative narration could not but regret the diversion of his genius to current issues of fact and opinion. His visits to Russia and to Washington during the Conference of 1921 produced excellent journalism, but the interest in such work is necessarily evanescent. 'The Salvaging of Civilization,' embodying the content of lectures Wells was prevented by illness from delivering in the United States, is of more permanent value, especially the first part, with its vivid and fresh presentation of world problems and its ardent expression of the author's desire for a world order of peace and progress. He makes a suggestive contrast between the United States, an essentially modern nation extending its boundaries by the steamboat and the railway, and the older countries of the European Continent, whose limits were set by the horse and the highroad. The size of the latter has made them impossible of defence against modern explosives and hampered them by restrictions of commerce and communication in time of peace. The British Empire might be described as not a railway but a steamship nation, but its communications and food supplies are subject to attack by sea and air. The United States, on the other hand, in addition to its enormous natural resources, has the advantage of being practically safe from external aggression.

The 'Outline of History,' undertaken at the suggestion of a gathering of English and American writers and professors in London at the end of the War, presents not merely the author's view of human evolution, but his main interest in a world order towards which the Babylonian, Persian, Greek, and Roman Empires, Christianity, Mohammedanism, the ambitions of Napoleon and the German Emperor, the British Empire and the United States are mere ineffectual beginnings. The book has been violently criticized by some professional historians for alleged errors in detail, but when all allowance is made for these and for some personal bias, it remains a most remarkable achievement in virtue of the skill shown in the arrangement and presentation of an unwieldly mass of material and the narrative power which carries the reader from century to century and gives him a clear and consistent view of human development and achievement.

In 1922 Wells was further diverted from his natural bent towards imaginative fiction by his candidacy for the Rectorship of Glasgow University, in the course of which he made the announcement mentioned above, and by standing as Labour candidate for the University of London at the parliamentary election. On both occasions he was unsuccessful, and to many of the admirers of his work his failure was not altogether a disappointment. He was not a good speaker, and one cannot believe that he would have submitted patiently to the tedium of debate and committee work in the House of Commons, to say nothing of the other labours incidental to any real achievement in constructive legislation.

He went back to his desk and added materially to the body of his work, but little to his reputation. The course of events was not such as to give either satisfaction or stimulation to any radical thinker. He went to Russia and met Lenin, to the disappointment of both. "What a bourgeois! What a Philistine!" was Lenin's verdict on Wells, and the impression made on Wells by the Bolshevists was unfavourable. The League of Nations, for which Wells had worked wholeheartedly in the last year of the War, turned out to be merely "a league of Allied imperialisms"; it seemed to him that the War "ended nothing, began nothing, and settled nothing"—it was a huge waste of life, and wealth, and energy. He was not pleased with the performances of the Labour Party after they got into office; the Labour Government appeared to him lacking in courage and initiative. Somewhat wearily —for he was now nearly sixty, and he had never been physically robust—he turned to a recapitulation of his main ideas in the form of fiction, "The World of William Clissold"—an enormous work which the public found hard to absorb, the dose of propaganda being so much heavier than the capsule of fiction. He lost his wife and gave up the Essex estate to live in London or on the Riviera. In the last years he returned to editorial journalism, superintending the preparation of an encyclopedic volume (for which the work was done mainly by his son, G. P. Wells, and Professor Julian Huxley) entitled 'The Science of Life' (1930). It is mankind regarded biologically, as the 'Outline' was man regarded historically; it was succeeded by another huge volume dealing with man regarded economically—'The Work, Wealth, and Happiness of Mankind' (1931). Both were well done and were educationally useful; but they gave no sufficient scope for the originality and verve of Wells at his best.

In 'The Bulpington of Blup' (1933), Wells returned to the earlier and better manner of 'Kipps.' There is more story and less propaganda than in any of his other novels since the War. There is still a good deal of argument, but it is kept within bounds and firmly embedded in the substance of the story. In the hero's youth he and his friends discuss the subjects that interest Wells—religion, education, capitalism, socialism, and the rest; but each side gets a fair show. The Communist view is set forth in these terms: "The Capitalist system is becoming more and more top-heavy. It keeps on saving and reinvesting instead of distributing all its production. Fresh capital accumulates, more dividends have to be produced, and the workers are economized upon, impoverished, expropriated and enslaved. More and more top-heavy. Capitalism therefore had a beginning and it will have an end, it will pile up debt on the workers until there is a crash." The hero visits the London slums but he can see no sign of the coming Revolution. "The crowds went about their work, they went to it and came back from it, they bought their dismal and inartistic commodities in their ugly and tawdry shops, they got drunk, the more wretched sold matches, crooned songs at the pavement edge or begged frankly, and the less wretched jostled. There was nothing there, nothing at all, to liken to the Giant Proletarian, that vast potent simpleton, pure in heart and mightily just, of Bern-stein's Marxist cartoons. Theodore felt it in his bones that the sordid poor—and the glittering rich also—were going on for an interminable time, that in a hundred years' time or so, though fashions and traffic might change, and buildings come and go, the contrasts of the great town would still be there, a different but not very different rich on the frontages, and a still drab, dull, drifting and congested multitude, the slaves of circumstances, beneath and behind. His mind could not imagine it fundamentally different. At the bottom of his heart, he believed that the appearances of the present were invincible."

Apart from these stirrings of the youthful mind, the story is that of a young man, Theodore Bulpington, who manufactures for himself in his childhood a secondary personality "The Bulpington of Blup" (Blup is a fanciful transversion of his native town, Blayport) as an escape from the humdrum or humiliating experiences of his real self. "The Bulpington of Blup" has romantic adventures which compensate for the very mediocre achievements of Theodore in actual life; but in memory the two become fused, until Theodore comes to persuade himself that he has really thought, said, and done things that have only occurred to his imaginary double. Thus he carries him-

self through disappointments in love, sensual degrada-
tions, failure and cowardice in the War, and a host of
minor humiliations by investing them in his mind with an
aura of fictitious glory and magnificence which entirely
transmogrifies the painful or disgusting facts. In the rout
of the British Fifth Army in 1918 he had really run with
the best—in fact, so far outrun his own Company as to
escape court-martial only by a fluke; but ten years afterwards, when well warmed with wine, he can tell tall
stories, wholly imaginary, of how he stemmed for a
while the British retreat and afterwards captured the
Kaiser, whom he personally conducted into Holland under secret instructions from the British Government.
This last is somewhat extravagant fooling, but it is
amusing enough, and Wells, while making his hero abun-
dantly ridiculous, never allows him to become entirely con-
temptible. There is something human and sympathetic
about Theodore in all his humiliations and extravagances,
for have we not all of us, consciously or unconsciously,
a secondary romantic personality who helps us to reconcile ourselves to the necessarily imperfect achievements of
actual life?

For real imaginative power we must turn to the novels
of Wells's prime. Careful consideration of his work as a
whole justifies the central position in twentieth century
literature ascribed to him at the beginning of this chapter.
He widened the scope of the novel, and reflected powerfully many characteristic tendencies of the thought of his
time. His direct contributions to that thought are stimulating and suggestive; and if they are not always consistent with each other, the variations often indicate changes
in public opinion. He is something more than a good
story-teller; and when the historian in a future age wishes
to discover what were the material and spiritual dis-

contents, the misgivings and aspirations of the more restless thinkers in England during the years immediately before and after the War, he will find them more adequately and vividly expressed in the works of Wells than in those of any other writer.

BIBLIOGRAPHY

ROMANCES

1895 'The Time Machine.'
1896 'The Island of Dr. Moreau.'
1897 'The Invisible Man.'
1898 'The War of the Worlds.'
1899 'When the Sleeper Wakes.'
1901 'The First Men in the Moon.'
1904 'The Food of the Gods.'
1906 'In the Days of the Comet.'
1908 'The War in the Air.'

SOCIOLOGICAL AND HISTORICAL ESSAYS

1901 'Anticipations of the Reaction of Mechanical and Scientific Progress upon Human Life and Thought.'
1903 'Mankind in the Making.'
1905 'A Modern Utopia.'
1906 'The Future in America.'
1907 'This Misery of Boots.'
1908 'New Worlds for Old.'
      'First and Last Things.' (Revised and enlarged in 1917.)
1914 'Social Forces in England and America.' (Published in England as 'An Englishman looks at the World.')
1916 'What is Coming?'
1917 'God the Invisible King.'
1921 'The Salvaging of Civilisation.'
      'Outline of History.'
1922 'A Short History of the World.'
1928 'The Way the World is Going.'
1930 'The Science of Life.'
1931 'The Work, Wealth, and Happiness of Mankind.'

NOVELS

1896 'The Wheels of Chance.'
1900 'Love and Mr. Lewisham.'

1905 'Kipps.'
1909 'Tono-Bungay.'
      'Ann Veronica.'
1910 'The History of Mr. Polly.'
1911 'The New Machiavelli.'
1912 'Marriage.'
1913 'The Passionate Friends.'
1914 'The World Set Free.'
      'The Wife of Sir Isaac Harman.'
1915 'Bealby.'
      'The Research Magnificent.'
1916 'Mr. Britling Sees it Through.'
1917 'The Soul of a Bishop.'
1918 'Joan and Peter.'
1919 'The Undying Fire.'
1922 'The Secret Places of the Heart.'
1923 'Men like Gods and Air like Wine.'
1924 'The Dream.'
1925 'Christina Alberta's Father.'
1926 'The World of William Clissold.'
1927 'Meanwhile.'
1928 'Mr. Blettsworthy on Rampole Island.'
1930 'Autocracy of Mr. Parham.'
1933 'The Bulpington of Blup.'

BIOGRAPHICAL AND CRITICAL

Alexander H. Crawford, 'The Religion of H. G. Wells,' 1909.
J. D. Beresford, 'H. G. Wells, A Biography and a Critical Estimate of his Work,' 1915.
Van Wyck Brooks, 'The World of H. G. Wells,' 1915.
Edouard Guyot, 'H. G. Wells,' Paris, 1920.
Sidney Dark, 'An Outline of Wells,' 1922.
R. Thurston Hopkins, 'H. G. Wells: Personality—Character—Topography,' 1922.
I. J. C. Brown, 'H. G. Wells,' 1924.
F. H. Doughty, 'H. G. Wells: Educationist,' 1927.
Patrick Braybrooke, 'Some Aspects of H. G. Wells,' 1928.
Geoffrey West, 'H. G. Wells,' 1930.

There are bibliographies by F. A. Chappell (Chicago, 1924), and by G. H. Wells (1926); also a dictionary (of characters and scenes up to 1924) by Georges Connes (1925).

CHAPTER VIII

JOHN GALSWORTHY (1867–1933)

GALSWORTHY has not Wells's narrative power or infectious enthusiasm for ideas or first-hand knowledge of the lowest middle class. The qualities which give him a permanent place in the literature of the period are a very real sympathy for the lowest working class—the oppressed and outcast—and skill in analysis of character and emotion, especially of amorous passion in people. of intelligence and refinement.

The son of a leading London lawyer, born in Surrey and educated at Harrow and Oxford, a briefless barrister who completed his education by extensive travel, Galsworthy at early manhood had acquired an intimate knowledge of the habits and prejudices of the English upper middle class and a superficial acquaintance with various foreign types met in the course of his globe-trotting. It was unfortunately with the latter that he chose to deal in his first published work, which shows a curious immaturity and uncertainty. 'From the Four Winds,' printed when he was thirty, is a collection of sensational foreign adventures which give no promise of the power of analysis and criticism he developed later. 'Jocelyn' and 'Villa Rubein,' which followed, conduct love-stories of no special interest to happy endings; in each case the attempt is made to depict and analyse overmastering passion, but without success, for the characters have little grip on reality. The foreign settings and the foreign English used in the dialogue—the Americans talk a selection of slang apparently culled from every State in the Union—add to the impression of artificiality. In 'The Island Pharisees' the women are still shadowy, but the two men—the hero Shelton and the French vagabond, Louis Ferrand—are firmly drawn. It is a pardonable impertinence to identify Shelton—well-born, educated at Eton and Oxford, travelled and detached from the cultivated society to which he belongs—with the author, whose point of view he obviously presents. He and Ferrand—both greatly enriched and developed—were later taken over into 'The Pigeon' —Shelton as Wellwyn and Ferrand under his own name. In the novel they produce a continuous stream of social criticism—almost the only part of the book of any real value—but it lacks the balance, subtlety and sympathy of Galsworthy's later work.

It was in 'The Man of Property,' published when Galsworthy was nearly forty, that the novelist first showed complete mastery of his material and of his art. Soames Forsyte, though he is not an agreeable character, is represented not as a criminal (as are some of his typical predecessors), but as a victim of his own nature, his education and his environment. He is the embodiment of middle class prejudices, limitations and virtues; he regards everything—including his wife—from the point of view of possession; he has no sense of beauty, no real affection. With individual differences which are very subtly indicated, the whole Forsyte family has the same point of view. The women, though still not very profoundly realized, are more lifelike than the passionate heroines Galsworthy had hitherto attempted; and the men are admirably differentiated from each other; old Jolyon Forsyte, whose business capacity does not prevent him from remaining thoroughly human—he uses his money to indulge the domestic affections by which he really lives—is a masterpiece. The young architect who stands for love and beauty but has no financial sense, is beaten by the power of money as the woman he loves is undone by the lack of it, and the novel ends with "the man of property" in absolute control of the situation. The spirit of the story is one of bitter irony, and young Jolyon, who has rebelled against his class but is still part of it, sets forth openly and directly on behalf of the author the view which the whole story is intended to illustrate: "The Forsytes are the middle-men, the commercials, the pillars of society, the cornerstones of convention, everything that is admirable! ! The great majority of architects, painters, or writers have no principles, like any other Forsytes. Art, literature, religion, survive by virtue of the few cranks who already believe in such things, and the many Forsytes who make a commercial use of them. . . . They are magnificently represented in religion; in the House of Commons perhaps more numerous than anywhere; the aristocracy speaks for itself. . . . My people are not very extreme, and they have their own private peculiarities, like every other family, but they possess in a remarkable degree those two qualities which are the real tests of a Forsyte —the power of never being able to give yourself up to anything soul and body, and the 'sense of property.' "

Galsworthy was well advised in continuing 'The Man of Property' more than ten years later in a charming sketch of the old age of Jolyon Forsyte entitled 'Indian Summer of a Forsyte.' Two novels, 'In Chancery' and 'To Let,' recount the further adventures and misfortunes of Soames Forsyte, with an intervening sketch, 'Awakening,' devoted to the childhood of a Forsyte of the next generation. The three novels with the two interludes make up 'The Forsyte

Saga,' published in 1922 with a special preface and an elaborate family tree of the Forsytes, extending from 1741 to the present day. The whole constitutes Galsworthy's most substantial claim for endurance as a writer of fiction, and is an important contribution to the social history of the English upper middle class during the period which ended with the War.

In 'The Country House,' which followed 'The Man of Property' in order of composition and publication, the author's satire is directed against the characteristic limitations of country house life. "They're crass," says Mr. Paramor, who defines 'Pendycitis' as young Jolyon in the previous novel made "the diagnosis of a Forsyte": "they do things but they do them the wrong way! They muddle through with the greatest possible amount of unnecessary labour and suffering. It's part of the hereditary principle." This "crassness," the author says in another passage, "common to all men in this strange world, and in the Squire intensified, was rather a process than a quality —obedience to an instinctive dread of what was foreign to himself, an instinctive fear of seeing another's point of view, an instinctive belief in precedent." This crass unintelligent traditionalism, adhered to with invincible obstinacy, embroils old Pendyce—a much less sympathetic figure than his parallel, old Jolyon Forsyte—with his tenants, his wife, his son. When the son breaks the tradition by falling in love with a married woman and meets obstinacy with obstinacy, stupidity with stupidity, all that his father can think of is that he wishes he had sent George to Harrow instead of Eton! This, the author comments, was his simple creed: "I believe in my father, and his father, and his father's father, the makers and keepers of my estate; and I believe in myself, and my son, and my son's son. And I believe that we have made the country, and shall keep the country what it is. And I believe in the Public Schools and especially the Public School that I was at. And I believe in my social equals and the country house, and in things as they are, for ever and ever. Amen."

His son, equally unintelligent and unattractive, ruins himself for a worthless woman, and his single redeeming virtue, that of constancy, becomes a blind, unreasoning jealousy. Seldom has Galsworthy drawn father and son so wholly self-centred and disagreeable. With Mrs. Pendyce, who is not a Pendyce at all, but a Totteridge—not a provincial but a true aristocrat—a gentle soul, the author deals gently, almost lovingly—most lovingly of all with Mr. Pendyce's other devotee, the spaniel John. All these are strongly conceived and firmly drawn. The appendages of the country house and the outsiders—Gregory Vigil with his quixotic romance and his absurd philanthropic organization—have hardly—except perhaps the Rector—the breath of life.

From the "crassness" of country house life, Galsworthy turned the arrows of his satire on the artificiality of London artistic and philanthropic circles in 'Fraternity.' The title is of course ironical, the novelist's view being that no fellow-feeling is possible among classes so profoundly separated by education, habit, and convention. The note of division is struck in the account of 'Bianca's Day' with which the story opens, and the climax is reached when Hilary Dallison, estranged from his wife and attracted by the "little model," finds he has not the courage to run away with her. To begin with, her nails were not clean, and when she kissed him "the touch of her lips was moist and hot. The scent of stale violet powder came from her warmed by her humanity. It penetrated to Hilary's heart. He started back in sheer physical revolt."

'The Patrician' offers us the most winning family group Galsworthy has yet drawn, from the fascinating little Ann to her no less charming great-grandmother. Lord Miltoun is hardly the characteristic English aristocrat, and his father, who comes much nearer the modern type, plays a secondary rôle. The story suffers from a shift of central interest from Lord Miltoun in the first half to Lady Barbara in the second, and there is no real suspense in either case, as it is obvious from the beginning that both will remain true to the traditions of their class; but both characters are subtly analysed and powerfully as well as skillfully portrayed. The complete passivity of Mrs. Noel leaves her too much in the background to be distinctly realized, and Courtier never becomes altogether lifelike. In spite of much excellent craftsmanship, the novel won only a *succès d'estime*.

In 'The Dark Flower' Galsworthy concentrated on his strongest gift—the analysis of romantic passion. Besides the hero's affection for the gentle Sylvia whom he marries and to whom he constantly returns, he suffers the bitter experiences of disillusion with an older woman in his youth, of blighting tragedy in middle life, and of difficult renunciation in the years when his senses make their last effort to overcome his brain, his conscience and his will. Throughout he retains our sympathy and respect because of his essential humanity and refinement. The book suffers somewhat both from its division into three parts, each with its own heroine, and from dwelling continuously on the same note of passion, but it is originally conceived and powerfully as well as delicately executed.

'The Freelands' brings us back to the discussion of one of the most important social questions of the day—the question of the land and of the social tyranny exercised by landowners. The Freeland brothers are some-what artificially set off against each other—Felix stands for intellectualism against officialism and industrialism, John for officialism against industrialism and intellectual-ism, Stanley for industrialism against officialism and intellectualism. But this is merely the setting for the conflict waged by the young rebels, Derek and Sheila Freelands, against the tyranny of Sir Gerald and Lady Malloring, the model landlords. The rebellion is, of course, a failure, and the arch rebel, Derek, gives up the unequal contest, but the story offers Galsworthy the op-portunity of saying with feeling and emphasis much that he had in his heart. The contrast that he draws between the life of the landlord and that of the ordinary farm labourer will serve as an example: "Your Malloring is called with a cup of tea, at, say, seven o'clock, out of a nice, clean, warm bed; he gets into a bath that has been got ready for him; into clothes and boots that have been brushed for him; and goes down to a room where there's a fire burning already if it's a cold day, writes a few letters, perhaps, before eating a breakfast of exactly what he likes, nicely prepared for him, and reading the news-paper that best comforts his soul; when he has eaten and read, he lights his cigar or his pipe and attends to his digestion in the most sanitary and comfortable fashion; then in his study he sits down to steady direction of other people, either by interview or by writing letters, or what not. In this way, between directing people and eating what he likes, he passes the whole day except that for two or three hours, sometimes indeed seven or eight hours, he attends to his physique by riding, motoring, playing a game or indulging in a sport that he has chosen for himself. And, at the end of all that, he probably has another bath that has been made ready for him, goes down to a good dinner that has been cooked for him, smokes, reads, learns and inwardly digests, or else plays cards, billiards and acts host till he is sleepy, and so to bed in a clean, warm bed, in a clean, fresh room.

"Now, to take the life of a Gaunt. He gets up summer and winter much earlier out of a bed that he cannot afford time and money to keep too clean or warm, in a small room that probably has not a large enough window; into clothes stiff with work and boots stiff with clay; makes something hot for himself, very likely brings some of it to his wife and children; goes out, attending to his digestion crudely and without comfort; works with his hands and feet from half-past six or seven in the morning till past five at night, except that twice he stops for an hour or so and eats simple things that he would not altogether have chosen to eat if he could have had his will. He goes home to a tea that has been got ready for him, and has a clean-up without assistance, smokes a pipe of shag, reads a newspaper perhaps two days old, and goes out again to work for his own good, in his vegetable patch, or to sit on a wooden bench in an atmosphere of beer and 'baccy.' And so, dead tired, but not from directing other people, he drowses himself to early lying again in his doubtful bed.

"Candidly, which of those two lives demands more of the virtues on which human life is founded—courage and patience, hardihood and self-sacrifice? And which of two men who have lived those two lives well has most right to the word 'superior'?"

'Beyond'—still the analysis of passionate love, this time from the woman's side—was coldly received by a public, which in 1917 was intent on more important matters. 'Saint's Progress' (1919) was an effort to combine a love story with war psychology and had only a temporary interest—and not very much even of that. It was at this point that Galsworthy turned to the completion of 'The Forsyte Saga' by the composition 'In Chancery' (1920) and 'To Let' (1921). These rounded out the saga, and exhibited the bankruptcy of the Forsyte conception of life. After all, "the man of property" had not triumphed; in the clash between the idea of possession, embodied in Soames, and the idea of beauty, embodied in Irene, Soames had not won in the end; he had lost Irene and he had lost his own soul. At the end of the saga he meditates: " 'To Let'—the Forsyte age and way of life, when a man owned his soul, his investments, and his woman, without check or question. And now the State had, or would have, his investments, his woman had herself, and God knew who had his soul. 'To Let'—that sane and simple creed!

"Athwart the Victorian dykes the waters were rolling on property, manners, and morals, on melody and the old forms of art—waters bringing to his mouth a salt taste as of blood, lapping at the foot of this Highgate Hill where Victorianism lay buried. And sitting there, high up on its most individual spot, Soames—like the figure of Investment—refused their restless sounds. Instinctively he would not fight them—there was in him too much primeval wisdom, of Man the possessive animal. They would quiet down when they had fulfilled their tidal fever of dispossessing and destroying; when the creations and the properties of others were sufficiently broken and dejected—they would lapse and ebb, and fresh forms would rise based on an instinct older than the fever of change—the instinct of Home."

The instinct of home—of family life—on which Soames based his hope for the future did not afford him any great consolation in the sequel which Galsworthy brought

to a conclusion during the next seven years, and entitled
'A Modern Comedy' (1929). It consists of three novels,
'The White Monkey,' 'The Silver Spoon,' and 'Swan
Song,' with two connecting links or "interludes," as in
'The Forsyte Saga.' The real bond of interest is Soames,
whose disposition becomes mellower, gentler, and more
sympathetic with the oncoming years. When Soames
saw that he had finally lost Irene, he attempted to fill her
place with a second wife, who betrayed him but left him
with one child, the wayward and self-indulgent Fleur—
the principal character of the 'Modern Comedy' and
the representative of the new generation. Defeated in
her passion for Irene's son, young Jon Forsyte, Fleur
marries for money and position a man whom she does not
love, and endeavours to find satisfaction in social success. Disappointed and disillusioned, she makes love to
Jon Forsyte—who has meanwhile married an American
girl—and momentarily takes possession of him—but only
for a moment of bewildering passion, after which he
casts her off and returns to his wife. Soames suffers intensely through Fleur's evident unhappiness and misbe-
haviour, and she is only brought to a sense of her
obligations by his death. 'A Modern Comedy' covers a
period of only four years (from 1922 to 1926)—much
shorter than that of 'The Forsyte Saga,' of which the
action begins in 1886 and ends in 1920. The 'Comedy' is
a much less massive construction and much inferior in
interest, though it contains a great deal of artistic and
conscientious work. Galsworthy was not really in sympathy with the young people of after-war England, and his
satire has more than a touch of malice; in contrast with
them, Soames, with his uprightness of character, sense of
responsibility, and deep family affection appears a dignified and honourable figure, and make a very different

impression from that of his youthful domineering acquisitiveness in 'The Man of Property.' It seems as if Galsworthy had conceived a more favourable opinion of the Victorians—and even of Victorian standards—when he got further away from them and became acquainted with their successors.

Two later novels, 'Maid in Waiting' (1931) and 'Flowering Wilderness' (1932), keep us still in touch with Fleur —not much improved by her misfortunes, for she is still hard and selfish, with a keen eye for material considerations. Both novels are cases of conscience in conflict with love—the first ending in the union of the lovers, the second in their separation. In the first, a young officer has behaved badly on an exploring expedition, in the second a young poet in the Far East has professed conversion to Mohammedanism under the pressure of a pistol held to his head by a fanatical Arab. The problem is something like that of Conrad's 'Lord Jim,' except that Galsworthy makes the failure of his heroes less serious and complicates the issue by having very nice English girls fall in love with them. The result is to render the problem less real and to drive the reader to ask himself sometimes what all the pother is about. Galsworthy himself seems to be not unconscious of this possibility, for in 'Flowering Wilderness,' after a passionate and melancholy scene between the hero and heroine, as they stand in the street "looking deeply at each other," they are interrupted by a seller of matches "without the money to indulge in spiritual troubles." Their troubles are, indeed, not so much spiritual as conventional. The young poet who has preferred a profession of Mohammedanism to sudden death has done nothing irreparable; most people would say he had merely shown common sense. The noble family to which the heroine belongs condemn him for having shown the white feather and drive him away from England and his beloved. Galsworthy fails to make it seem probable that they would do so, or that the hero would go, or that the heroine would let him go; but the final question to be asked is, "After all, does it really matter whether he goes or not?"

Until the success of 'The Forsyte Saga' was well established, there were many people who held that Galsworthy was more gifted as a playwright than as a novelist; it was an exceptionally shrewd critic who suggested that his apparent superiority on the stage was mainly due to the fact that good plays were rarer than good novels. There was also to be taken into account the consideration that the more concentrated and more plastic medium gave scope for Galsworthy's powers of character-analysis and dialogue and supplemented his besetting weakness—a certain flatness in the minor personages, who were rounded out by the skill of the actors he had the good fortune to secure for the interpretation of his dramatic successes alike in Manchester, London and New York.

His first play, 'The Silver Box,' was produced in the same year that his best novel 'The Man of Property' was published (1906). The play deliberately attempts a formal symmetry which is one of Galsworthy's favourite dramatic devices and may be remarked even in his latest plays. Jones, an "out-of-work," has stolen in a drunken fit of resentment from Jack Borthwick, the idle son of a wealthy Liberal M. P., a purse of crimson silk which Jack in a drunken fit of resentment has stolen from "an unknown lady, from beyond." Jones has taken also the silver cigarette box, and adds to the complications of his own case by assaulting the police. Jack gets a scolding from an indulgent father;

Jones gets a month's hard labour. Jones is removed from the dock shouting: "Call this justice? What about 'im? 'E got drunk! 'E took the purse—'e took the purse, but it's *'is money* got *'im* off—Justice!"

There are additional (and perhaps unnecessary) touches of pathos in the crying of Jones's child outside the Borthwick's house and the disposal of two forsaken little girls by the police magistrate before Jones's case comes on; but the real effect of the play consists in the contrast between the Borthwick household, purseproud and pampered, and the Jones family, driven to desperation by poverty. Mrs. Jones, who furnishes the connection between the two by acting as charwoman in the Borthwick house, is an admirable character study, very effective on the stage.

Passing by 'Joy,' which is merely a dramatization of the psychological gulf which stretches between two generations, "a play on the letter 'I,'" we have a similar contrast in 'Strife'; the issue is a strike at the Trenartha Tin-Plate works, whose chairman, John Anthony, is balanced against the workmen's leader, David Roberts, the Directors against the Workmen's Committee, the Manager against the Trades Union Official. Anthony and Roberts are both fighting to win, regardless of consequences, and both men are broken by the determination of their supporters to end the struggle by compromise— on the very terms that were suggested when the strike began. So far Galsworthy holds the balance even between Capital and Labour, but it is obvious that his sympathies are on the side of Labour, though he makes the capitalist's son and daughter full of kindly eagerness to do what they can for the workpeople. The real interest of the play lies in the conflict between the two masterful characters, Anthony and Roberts, who are both splendidly realized, the former with very few words, the latter with burning eloquence about the wrongs of his class.

'Justice' is a protest against the denial of the privilege of divorce to the poor and against the severity of English prison administration, which, indeed, it did something to ameliorate. It was preceded in order of composition—though not of production—by 'The Eldest Son' (written 1909, produced 1912), which transfers to the stage the atmosphere and principal characters of 'The Country House,' though the illicit tie formed by the son is not now with a married woman of his own class, but with his mother's maid. On the stage, father and son take on more humanity—they are more living people and less types than in the novel, and the father's determination is stiffened by previous severity to a keeper on his own estate who has been guilty of a similar offence; but the point insisted on is the same—the "crassness" of country house life, its immovable adherence to caste and tradition.

One other play of Galsworthy's belonging to the pre-war group seems to call for comment on account of its social significance, 'The Pigeon.' Wellwyn is our old friend Shelton of 'The Island Pharisees,' richly humanized and provided with a sensible daughter. The Frenchman Ferrand is taken over under the same name without change, and is the spokesman of the outcasts for whom the drama makes an impassioned plea. By the side of these three,—the vagabond Frenchman, the broken-down cabman, and the loose-living flower-girl—the Professor, the Magistrate and the Clergyman are mere mechanical figures stuck into the play to prove the foolishness of the attempt "to make wild birds tame":

"*Ferrand.* They do a good work while they attend with their theories to the sick, and the tame old, and the good unfortunate deserving. Above all to the little children. But, Monsieur, when all is done there are always us hopeless ones. What can they do with me, Monsieur, with that girl, or with that old man? Ah! Monsieur, we, too, 'ave our qualities, we others—it wants you courage to undertake a career like mine, or a life like that young girl's. We wild ones—we know a thousand times more of life than ever will those sirs. They waste their time trying to make rooks white. Be kind to us if you will, or let us alone like Mees Ann, but do not try to change our skins. Leave us to live, or leave us to die when we like in the free air. If you do not wish of us, you have but to shut your pockets and your doors—we shall die the faster.

Wellwyn (with agitation). But that, you know—we can't do—now can we?

Ferrand. If you cannot, how is it our fault? The harm we do to others—is it so much? If I am criminal, dangerous—shut me up! I would not pity myself, nevare. But we in whom something moves—like that flame, Monsieur, that *cannot* keep still—we others—we are not many—that must have motion in our lives, do not let them make us prisoners with their theories because we are not like them—it is life itself they would enclose."

During and after the War Galsworthy produced and published a number of plays, some of which did not meet with the approval either of the critics or of the public. Of these it is enough to say, in the words of St. John Ervine, that they belong to "the class of work done by a distinguished man on a wet day when he is rather tired." The list of comparative failures was, however, broken by two remarkable successes—'The Skin Game' and 'Loyalties.' The former sets forth the havoc wrought by the incursion of a pushing northern manufacturer into a county society, which succeeds in driving him out, but only at the sacrifice of every delicacy of feeling which makes an aristocracy worth its salt. The "Hillcrists" and the "Hornblowers" are admirably characterized and contrasted (perhaps with a little extra sympathy for the aristocratic side), and Galsworthy shows unusually clever stagecraft in the management of material which at times demanded very delicate treatment.

'Loyalties' is an even better play, with an exciting plot, which would have turned to melodrama but for the deftness of the handling. It revolves round the theft in a country house of £1000 from the bedroom of a young Jewish guest who makes himself sufficiently disagreeable to alienate the sympathies of his fellow-guests—and of the audience. He suspects a wild young officer who occupies the next room, and as, in spite of the social pressure brought to bear upon him, he does not keep his suspicions to himself, the matter becomes one for the club of which both are members and is ultimately the subject of an action for slander. In the middle of the action the young D. S. O.'s solicitor and counsel receive privately convincing proof of his guilt, and withdraw from the case. The young officer finds the only solution in suicide. The theme of the play is indicated by its title, but is not unduly stressed in the action, which brings out, subtly and naturally, the clashing loyalties of the various characters —loyalty to one's race, to one's caste, to one's friends, to one's profession, to one's regiment, to one's club, and so on.

Both these plays illustrate the theory of the drama which Galsworthy sets forth in one of his best essays. He says, "A drama must be shaped so as to have a spire of meaning. Every grouping of life and character has its inherent moral; and the business of the dramatist is so to pose the group as to bring that moral poignantly to the light of day." In this matter of the moral, there are three courses open to the serious dramatist: (1) He may set forth popular and accepted views. (2) He may set forth his own views, "the more effectively if they are the opposite of what the public wishes to have placed before it, presenting them so that the audience may swallow them like powder in a spoonful of jam." (3) He may set before the public "no cut-and-dried codes, but the phenomena of life and character, selected and combined, but not distorted by the dramatist's outlook, set down without fear, favour or prejudice, leaving the public to draw such poor moral as nature may afford." Obviously this third method is the one Galsworthy himself prefers —it requires detachment, sympathy, the far view, and it depends mainly on the interpretation of character.

"The dramatist's licence, in fact, ends with his design. In conception alone he is free. He may take what character or group of characters he chooses, see them with what eyes, knit them with what idea, within the limits of his temperament; but once taken, seen, and knitted, he is bound to treat them like a gentleman, with the tenderest consideration of their mainsprings. Take care of character; action and dialogue will take care of themselves."

It is not surprising to find that Galsworthy despises plot construction; but his frequent neglect of this element of drama has two resulting weaknesses. In the first place, his characters often fail to develop within the action of the play; the vast majority are the same at the end as they were at the beginning, the impression conveyed is that of a dramatic situation, not of the ever-moving current of life. In the second place, Galsworthy is inclined, for lack of a well-constructed plot, to build up his characters symmetrically, one balanced against the other, as in 'Strife,' 'The Pigeon,' and 'The Skin Game'—and this adds to one's sense of artificiality. He is not a born story-teller or dramatist, and though he always writes well—his style is a never-failing pleasure—one has often a consciousness of thinness in his imaginative work. The beauty of his prose and his artistic sincerity may save much of his work from oblivion when that of more successful competitors is forgotten, but it seems likely to be treasured by the few who can appreciate delicacy and subtlety and do not ask either for the excitement of a stirring action or for the intellectual stimulus of brilliant paradox. He has no 'ism to offer as a cure for all human ills. He sees men bound by class limitations—the poor by actual want, the rich by ignorance and prejudice—and he found no remedy except understanding and sympathy.

There are times when Galsworthy's sympathy slips over the line into sentimentality. St. John Ervine says: "His pity often becomes undiscerning sentimentality that has no relation to any real thing and is extraordinarily irritating to those who are as compassionate as he, but are eager not to bog themselves in a morass of emotion." Patrick Thompson pronounced him "at heart a sentimentalist," and Max Beerbohm accused him of selling his artistic birthright for "a pot of message." His novels written after the completion of his two great series, and (among the plays done after the War) 'Windows,' 'The Show,' and 'Exiled' exhibit this characteristic weakness. Even 'Escape' (1926), though very successful on the stage, is not free from sentimentality; at the first performance a lady in the audience protested against the display of so much sympathy for escaped convicts and asked for more consideration of their victims. The fact is that though Galsworthy criticized very severely and acutely some Victorian points of view, he retained something of Victorian sentiment. This was probably what H. G. Wells meant when he said that it was no wonder that Galsworthy described the Forsytes well; he *was* a Forsyte. It was with the same thought in mind that Wells said of himself that he was not a gentleman. A thorough gentleman Galsworthy undoubtedly was, and he exhibited the limitations as well as the excellences of the English form of that ideal. When, towards the end of Galsworthy's career, the characteristic virtues of the English upper class seemed on the point of disappearance, he invested their setting with a tender glow of sentiment. But he had no less pity for the victims of poverty and oppression, though he saw no way of escape for them, no remedy for their wrongs. He was not, like Wells, a propagandist of social reform and an advocate of international organization to secure the peace and welfare of the world. The P.E.N. Club, of which he was the moving spirit, was the vaguest and most innocuous of international efforts, aiming merely at the "exchange of international thought" as the only possible salvation of the world. Galsworthy was nothing of an organizer, nothing of a politician—always an idealist and an artist.

His eminence was recognized by his appointment to the Order of Merit on the death of Thomas Hardy in 1928 and by the award of the Nobel Prize in 1932. These distinctions he accepted gladly. He had previously declined a knighthood, which was almost thrust upon him at the end of the War. His refusal was doubtless due to his desire to keep his war services for the wounded, in France and England, as free from public recognition as when they were given. Essentially modest and reserved, he shrank from notoriety and made no attempt to exploit his literary fame, though he had a natural pleasure in official acknowledgment by competent authorities of the excellence of the literary work he had done. Of the group of novelists and playwrights who attracted attention during the first quarter of the century there was none who established himself more firmly in the affections of the public on both sides of the Atlantic.

BIBLIOGRAPHY

NOVELS

1898 'Jocelyn.'
1900 'Villa Rubein.'
1904 'The Island Pharisees.'
1906 'The Man of Property.'
1907 'The Country House.'
1909 'Fraternity.'
1911 'The Patrician.'
1913 'The Dark Flower.'
1915 'The Freelands.'
1917 'Beyond.'
1919 'Saint's Progress.'
1920 'In Chancery.'
1921 'To Let.'
1922 'The Forsyte Saga.'
1923 'The Burning Spear' (published anonymously, 1919).
1924 'The White Monkey.'
1926 'The Silver Spoon.'
1928 'Swan Song.'
1931 'Maid in Waiting.'
1932 'Flowering Wilderness.'

ESSAYS AND STORIES

1897 'From the Four Winds.'
1901 'A Man of Devon.'
1908 'A Commentary.'
1910 'A Motley.'
1912 'The Inn of Tranquillity.'
1915 'The Little Man and other Satires.'
1916 'A Sheaf.'
1917 'Indian Summer of a Forsyte.'
1918 'Five Tales.'
1919 'Another Sheaf.'

1920 'Tatterdemalion.'
      'Awakening.'
1923 'Captures.'
1925 'Caravan.'
1927 'Castles in Spain.'
1930 'On Forsyte Change.'

PLAYS

(Dates of Production)

1906 'The Silver Box.'
1907 'Joy.'
1909 'Strife.'
1910 'Justice.'
1911 'The Little Dream.'
1912 'The Pigeon.'
      'The Eldest Son.'
1913 'The Fugitive.'
1914 'The Mob.'
1915 'A Bit o' Love.'
1917 'The Foundations.'
1920 'The Skin Game.'
1921 'A Family Man.'
1922 'Loyalties.'
      'Windows.'
1924 'The Forest.'
      'Old English.'
1925 'The Show.'
1926 'Escape.'
1929 'Exiled.'
      'The Roof.'

POEMS

1912 'Moods, Songs and Doggerels.'
1921 'The Bells of Peace.'
1926 'Verses New and Old.'

BIOGRAPHICAL AND CRITICAL

Sheila Kaye-Smith, 'John Galsworthy,' 1916.
L. Schalit, 'John Galsworthy,' 1929.
Bibliography (up to 1927) by H. V. Marrot, 1928.

CHAPTER IX

ARNOLD BENNETT (1867–1931)

THE greatest obstacle to the permanence of Arnold
Bennett's literary reputation is the mass of commonplace
production which threatens to distract attention from his
few masterpieces. One may pass an idle hour pleasantly
enough with what Bennett calls 'fantasies,' 'frolics,'
'melodramas,' 'idyllic diversions' (and some of the books
he calls novels really belong to the same class), but
what has the student of literature to do with such pre-
tentious pot-boilers (Bennett applied the word indis-
criminately to his own work and George Meredith's
novels) as 'How to Live on Twenty-four Hours a Day,'
'The Reasonable Life,' 'Friendship and Happiness,' 'The
Married Life,' etc., which the author classed under
'Belles-Lettres,' and which his publishers (not, one hopes,
himself) heralded as containing "big, strong, vital, thinking"? The danger is that this over-advertised deadweight
of platitudes will overwhelm Bennett's reputation as a
conscientious artist and hinder appreciation of his really
significant work. To those who are acquainted with both
it must be an astonishment that the author of these
cheap popular essays should also be the novelist of 'The
Old Wives' Tale' and the 'Clayhanger' trilogy.

The key to the enigma is supplied by Arnold Bennett
himself. In 'The Truth about an Author,' originally published anonymously in the columns of the 'Academy,'

and reprinted years afterwards under the author's name, Bennett gives an unblushingly veracious account of his early struggles and successes. He was born near Hanley, the 'Hanbridge' of the Five Towns which his novels were to launch into literary fame, and received a somewhat limited education at the neighbouring 'Middle School' of Newcastle, his highest scholastic achievement being the passing of the London University Matriculation Examination. Some youthful adventurers in journalism were perhaps significant of latent power and literary inclination, but a small provincial newspaper offers no great encouragement to youthful ambition, and Enoch Arnold Bennett (as he was then called) made his way at twenty-one as a solicitor's clerk to London, where he was soon earning a modest livelihood by "a natural gift for the preparation of bills of costs for taxation." He had never "wanted to write" (except for money) and had read almost nothing of Scott, Jane Austen, Dickens, Thackeray, the Brontës, and George Eliot, though he had devoured Ouida, boys' books and serials. His first real interest in a book was "not as an instrument for obtaining information or emotion, but as a *book,* printed at such a place in such a year by so-and-so, bound by so-and-so, and carrying colophons, registers, water-marks, and *fautes d'impression.*" It was when he showed a rare copy of 'Manon Lescaut' to an artist and the latter remarked that it was one of the ugliest books he had ever seen, that Bennett, now in his early twenties, first became aware of the appreciation of beauty. He won twenty guineas in a competition, conducted by a popular weekly, for a humorous condensation of a sensational serial, being assured that this was "art," and the same paper paid him a few shillings for a short article on 'How a bill of costs is drawn up'; in 1895 he had a story in the 'Yellow

Brok.' Meanwhile he was "gorging" on English and French literature, his chief idols being Flaubert, the brothers de Goncourt, Maupassant, and Turgenef. He was quickly conscious of the new current of influence, chiefly French, which began to affect the English novel about the middle of the last decade of the nineteenth century. An entry in his 'Journal' in January, 1898, records his impression that up to that time none of the great masters of English fiction cared much for form or treatment, that they had no interest in the science of construction, what the pictorial artists call *Composition;* "as regards fiction," he writes, "it seems to me that only within the last few years have we absorbed from France that passion for the artistic shapely presentation of truth, and that feeling for words as words, which animated Flaubert, the Goncourts, and Maupassant." Young Bennett learnt the lessons of these masters well, and practised their precepts with the utmost assiduity, observing current life with constant care and remarkable insight, and recording his impressions in his diary in meticulous detail. He was encouraged by the success of Eden Phillpotts, a disciple of Hardy, who was assistant editor of 'Black and White,' and earned a comfortable living by writing stories and novels about Dartmoor in his days and hours of leisure, spent in a comfortable villa, with a garden to potter about in. After paying a visit to Phillpotts at Torquay, Bennett left full of "a desire to live in the country in a large house with plenty of servants, not working too hard, but working when and how one likes, at good rates." Bennett was convinced that he could write, and he determined to adopt the vocation of letters. After a humiliating period of free-lancing in Fleet Street, he became assistant editor and later editor of 'Woman.' He was only thirty when his first novel, 'A

Man from the North,' was published. Believing that
popular fiction was his best way to prosperity he confided
to his 'Journal' under date September 12, 1898, the resolution that up to the end of 1899 he would give himself
absolutely to writing "the sort of fiction that sells itself.
My serious novel, 'Anna Tellwright', with which I had
made some progress, is put aside indefinitely—or rather
until I have seen what I can do. To write popular fiction
is offensive to me, but it is far more agreeable than being
tied daily to an office and editing a lady's paper; and
perhaps it is less ignoble, and less of a strain on the
conscience. To edit a lady's paper, even a relatively
advanced one, is to foster conventionality and hinder
progress regularly once a week. Moreover, I think that
fiction will pay better, and in order to be happy I must
have a fair supply of money." This good resolution he
kept so effectively that at the end of 1899 he could write
in his diary: "This year I have written 335,340 words,
grand total; 224 articles and stories and four instalments
of a serial called 'The Gates of Wrath' have actually been
published, also my book of plays, 'Polite Farces.' My
work included six or eight short stories not yet published,
also the greater part of a 55,000 word serial 'Love and
Life' for Tillotsons, and the whole draft, 80,000 words,
of my Staffordshire novel 'Anna Tellwright.' "

This last was not published in book form till 1902
under the title of 'Anna of the Five Towns'; but in the
ten years that had elapsed since he came to London, Bennett had risen from a clerk at six dollars a week to be a
successful "editor, novelist, dramatist, critic, connoisseur
of all arts" with a comfortable suburban residence, at
which he held a party of twenty-six people on the tenth
anniversary of his arrival, to celebrate his success. Still
he was not satisfied; he was weary of journalism and

the tyranny of his Board of Directors. He threw up his editorial post, with its certain income, and retired first to the country and then to a cottage at Les Sablons on the edge of the Forest of Fontainebleau, to devote himself to literature. At this stage of his career Bennett admitted that he was still a Philistine. "Preserve me," he prayed, "from all peculiar people, high self-conscious people, vainly *earnest* people." He himself was very much in earnest, but not vainly. He described himself, at the beginning of the twentieth century, as "a writer, an artist pure and simple, yet with strong mercantile instincts." His family tradition and his business training (he had worked in his father's law-office at Burslem as well as in London) impelled him to assure his financial position by means of newspaper fiction and polite farces before he ventured on undertaking a "big novel."

In the autumn of 1903, when Bennett used to dine frequently in a Paris restaurant, it happened that a fat old woman came in who aroused almost universal merriment by her eccentric behaviour. The novelist reflected: "This woman was once young, slim, perhaps beautiful; certainly free from these ridiculous mannerisms. Very probably she is unconscious of her singularities. Her case is a tragedy. One ought to be able to make a heart-rending novel out of a woman such as she." The idea then occurred to him of writing the book which afterwards became 'The Old Wives' Tale,' and in order to go one better than Guy de Maupassant's 'Une Vie' he determined to make it the life-history of two women instead of one. Constance, the more ordinary sister, was the original heroine; Sophia, the more independent and attractive one, was created "out of bravado." The project occupied Bennett's mind for some years, during which he produced five or six novels of smaller scope, but in the autumn of 1907 he began to write 'The Old Wives' Tale' and finished it in July, 1908. It was published the same autumn, and though its immediate reception was not encouraging, before the winter was over it was recognized both in England and America as a work of genius. The novelist's reputation was upheld, if not increased, by the publication of 'Clayhanger' in 1910, and in June, 1911, the most conservative of American critical authorities, the 'New York Post' could pronounce judgment in these terms: "Mr. Bennett's Bursley is not merely one single stupid English provincial town. His Baineses and Clayhangers are not simply average middle class provincials foredoomed to humdrum and the drab shadows of experience. His Bursley is every provincial town, his Baineses are all townspeople whatsoever under the sun. He professes nothing of the kind; but with quiet smiling patience, with a multitude of impalpable touches, clothes his scene and its humble figures in an atmosphere of pity and understanding. These little people, he seems to say, are as important to themselves as you are to yourself, or as I am to myself. Their strength and weakness are ours; their lives, like ours, are rounded with a sleep. And because they stand in their fashion for all human character and experience, there is even a sort of beauty in them if you will but look for it."

The appreciation is a just one, and suggests the further elucidation of a side of Bennett's art which is often misunderstood. He is often regarded as the unsparing critic of provincialism; he is really its apostle. It is not because he dislikes and despises the life of the Five Towns that he describes it with such minute care, it is because he loves it. This is in accord with a well-established principle which Bennett has himself very clearly set forth: "The sense of beauty [is] indispensable to the creative artist. Every creative artist has it, in his degree. He is an artist because he has it. An artist works under the stress of instinct. No man's instinct can draw him towards material which repels him—the fact is obvious. Obviously, whatever kind of life the novelist writes about, he has been charmed and seduced by it, he is under its spell—that is, he has seen beauty in it. He could have no other reason for writing about it. He may see a strange sort of beauty; he may—indeed he does—see a sort of beauty that nobody has quite seen before; he may see a sort of beauty that none save a few odd spirits ever will or can be made to see. But he does see beauty." ('The Author's Craft.')

As early as 1897 Bennett set down in his 'Journal' his consciousness of the beauty of Burslem—the "Bursley" of his five towns. "It thrills and reverberates with the romance of machinery and manufacture, the romance of our fight against nature, of the gradual taming of the earth's secret forces. And surrounding the town on every side are the long straight smoke and steam wreaths, the dull red flames, and all the visible evidences of the immense secular struggle for existence, the continual striving towards a higher standard of comfort." It is a complete misapprehension to suppose that the novelist, who was born and spent his youth in the Five Towns and made his own literary reputation at the same time as he made theirs, regarded them with the superficial condescension of the ordinary London journalist. Bennett put his feelings of admiration and sympathy for his home town and native tradition very clearly on record. "It seems to me," he wrote in 1907, "the most English piece of England that I ever came across. With extraordinary clearness I see it as absurdly, ridiculously, splendidly English! All the English characteristics are, quite remarkably, exaggerated in the Potteries." To anyone who knows English provincial life, this is an obvious truth, and the fact that Bennett makes kindly fun of the oddities and limitations of his provincial characters says nothing to the contrary. Constance and Sophia are provincial heroines—but they are heroines. Unintelligent, self-centred, eccentric, if you like, but full of honesty and courage, of practical ability and sincere affection. Take, for instance, the first "Good Night" of the two sisters after their long years of separation: "They looked at each other again, with timid affectionateness. They did not kiss. The thought in both their minds was: 'We couldn't keep on kissing every day.' But there was a vast amount of quiet, restrained affection, of mutual confidence and respect, even of tenderness in their tones." Above all, they have common sense, the knowledge how to live. When Madame Foucault makes her confession, Sophia thinks "What a fool you have been!" not, "What a sinner!" "If I couldn't have made a better courtesan than this pitiable woman I would have drowned myself." It is character that saves Sophia from the treachery of Gerald Scales and that makes her repulse Chirac. "The instinct which repulsed him was not within her control. Just as a shy man will obstinately refuse an invitation which he is hungering to accept, so, though not from shyness, she was compelled to repulse Chirac." It is an inherited and traditional instinct for decency and order. It is the same instinct that makes Sophia shrink from the dust in the corners of Madame Foucault's room, and the showiness of the furniture. "Nothing in it, she found, was 'good.' And in St. Luke's Square 'goodness' meant honest workmanship, permanence, the absence of pretence."

It is the same fundamental solidity of character which saves Hilda Lessways from the consequences of her own waywardness and enables her to make a success of life with Edwin Clayhanger in the old-fashioned provincial way of material advancement and family affection. The Orgreaves in the same series of novels are a model—almost an ideal—family, for they have, in addition to the everyday virtues, a keener sense of beauty than Bennett claims for the ordinary Five Towns families. He says in 'The Truth about an Author,' speaking of his own youth: "I had lived in a world where beauty was not mentioned, seldom thought of. I believe I had scarcely heard the adjective 'beautiful' applied to anything whatever, save confections like Gounod's 'There is a green hill far away.' Modern oak sideboards were called handsome, and Christmas cards were called pretty, and that was about all." So, among the provincial characters of 'What the Public Wants,' only John Worgan is described as "highly educated," "with very artistic tastes," but we are told that "all these people are fundamentally 'decent' and sagacious," and it is their point of view that is upheld, despite their queer clothes, food and manners.

Substantially their point of view is Arnold Bennett's own point of view, and it is no wonder that his treatment of them is sympathetic, for he remained a thorough provincial at heart. He admires their qualities of faithfulness and endurance, and is never tired of insisting on the essential wholesomeness and rightness of English provincial life, though he is not blind to its æsthetic shortcomings. Of its shortcomings on another side—its narrowness of vision and lack of spirituality—he is only half conscious. Religion plays a curiously small part in any of his books, and the great political and social questions of the period he describes find only a faint echo now and then, almost always on their mechanical or material side. We learn in 'The Old Wives' Tale' about such changes as the introduction of public baths, free libraries, municipal parks, telephones, and electric tramcars and automobiles, and in 'Clayhanger,' we have references to parliamentary elections, strikes, and religious revivals, but the reader would hardly gather that in the period covered by these two novels the intellectual, social and political life of England had undergone revolution.

There is the same defect in Bennett's novel dealing with the earlier years of the War, 'The Pretty Lady.' It is noteworthy that he chooses to see the great struggle through the eyes of a Parisian courtesan, flung upon Leicester Square by the tide of the Belgian invasion, and of a London man about town, sobered to serious work as a member of a war committee and carrying into his amours the systematic punctuality of business. G. J. Hoape may have acquired some London polish, but he was surely born in one of the Five Towns. The solid painting of this character contrasts with the sketchiness of the portraits of the neurotic London ladies who seek in war charities a new form of excitement. The "pretty lady" herself is somewhat dimly realized; perhaps she would be more convincing if she were allowed to talk French, for the literal translation of her terms of endearment fails as a literary device to give any touch of actuality; but in any case it would be hard to away with her mysticism, which is twice associated with purely accidental coincidence. That she should obey the unuttered summons of a lover who happens, all unknown to her, to be in the next street might be tolerated, but that she should again hear his voice when he is not there and thus by an evil chance wrongly convince her regular protector, who happens to be looking out of his club window at the time, of her faithlessness, is too much. The external features of London in 1916–17 are vividly presented—

the dark streets and the Zeppelin raids, committee meet-
ings and war charities feverishly alternating with revues
and night clubs—but apart from these incidental interests
the story is unsatisfactory either as a rendering of the
English mind at a period of crisis or as a study of particular persons under the strain of deep emotion.

'The Roll Call' is a combination, not altogether successful, of the war interest with the fortunes of a minor
character in the Clayhanger series, George Cannon, now
a young architect in London, his mother (more familiar
to us as Hilda Lessways) and her husband, Edwin Clayhanger, being introduced only incidentally towards the
end of the book. It is almost the end, too, before Bennett
catches up with the subject of the novel as indicated by
the title, for George Cannon has only just got into the
Army and is still in England when the story come to an
abrupt close.

Instead of continuing the adventures of George Cannon,
public and publishers being, at that time, alike weary of
war novels, Bennett, with his usual flair for a subject of
current interest, took up in 'Mr. Prohack' the contrast
between the "new rich" and the "new poor" after the
War. If the hero had made a fortune by profiteering, the
reader's sympathies would have been alienated, and Bennett would have been embarrassed, for he never lost the
"Five Towns" admiration for worldly success. So he
ascribes Mr. Prohack's sudden accession to wealth to a
windfall in the shape of a totally unexpected legacy. The
social adventures of the hero, his wife, his son and his
daughter are recounted with a good deal of verve and
kindly humour, and we get a glimpse of the mad rush
for pleasure and excitement that took place in certain
circles in London after the War. As social documents,
this novel and the two preceding it may have some value;

as works of art, they are not worthy to rank with the studies of provincial life before the War on which the permanent fame of the author seems likely to rest.

Bennett married a French lady in 1907, and for some years they resided alternately in France and in England. After the remarkable success of 'Milestones,' a comedy he made in 1912 in collaboration with Edward Knoblauch, Bennett and his wife settled down on an estate in Essex (with a flat in London) until 1921, when they separated. The intervening period was one of great prosperity, in spite of the energy with which he threw himself into the task of organizing the publicity department of the British Government during the War; his income amounted to about a hundred thousand dollars a year, and he was able to indulge himself in a yacht and to go out a great deal into society.

The weekly column of literary chat Bennett wrote for a London paper during the last few years of his life obtained an almost unprecedented authority; he could make the fortune of a new novelist or ruin the reputation of an old one. His original work continued to be of very varied merit. His comedy 'The Bright Island' (1925) was described as "the worst play written by a celebrated man for a long time past." It became a critical common-place in the London press that there were three grades of Bennett as of butter: (1) Prime Bennett—good novels for those who like literature; (2) Pure Bennett, novels for those who read fiction; and (3) Just Bennett, for those who read anything. Not much of Bennett's work after the War can be rated Grade 1; but in this category should certainly be placed 'Riceyman Steps' (1923). The scene of the novel is one of the most sordid districts in London—unrelieved even by the romance of vice: its inhabitants are the "ignobly decent," as Gissing called them. But Gissing hated and despised them: he saw no beauty in their lives. Bennett loves them and reveals the beauty of their love and devotion. We have a love affair—two love affairs—but of the most humdrum character, the lovers being quite ordinary people between forty and fifty: an old bachelor of a second-hand bookseller and a widow who keeps a small and dreary confectioner's shop opposite; their charwoman and her shell-shocked soldier-lover. By way of a wedding present to her new husband, the widow has the old bookshop vacuum-cleaned. He gives her a safe. He is a miser: the programme for the honeymoon is a dinner at a cheap restaurant which costs two dollars; a visit to Madame Tussaud's waxworks, and a movie-show (cinema) at night. But he cannot bear to spend his money so foolishly, and pleading fatigue after the waxworks he takes his wife home. There is no provision for the evening meal; but Elsie, the charwoman, promoted to be maid, gives them a wedding cake. "The cake was a danger to existence. It had the consistency of marble, the richness of molasses, the mysteriousness of the enigma of the universe. It seemed unconquerable. It seemed more fatal than daggers and gelignite. But they attacked it. Fortunately neither of them knew the inner meaning of indigestion." But they learn it. The continuous lack of nutritious food brings both to death, the husband from cancer, the wife from a fibroid tumor. The real heroine of the story, however, is the oppressed and half-starved maid, Elsie, a figure suggested by a servant girl whose courtship Bennett had noted ten years before at a corner of a London street.

Bennett was popular in London society on account of his generosity to young authors and his genial, though somewhat reserved, manner. At his death he left a fortune of half a million dollars—said to be the largest on record for any English author up to that time. His 'Journals' (from 1896 almost up to the date of his death) is an enormous work, although it offers only a selection from the entries in the diary Bennett actually kept. The interest is remarkably sustained in view of the reticence displayed as to Bennett's private life, though he is frank enough about his literary ambitions and general views. The story of his engagement to an American girl in 1906 is told in half a dozen lines: "Friday, June 15. At 5 P.M. on this day in the Forest of Fontainebleau, I became engaged to marry Eleanora.—Friday, August 3. At eleven A.M. on this day, at Caniel, my engagement to Eleanora was broken off." That is all, although Mrs. Dorothy Cheston Bennett, the companion of his last years, adds a note: "The breaking of this engagement was a hurt he bore marks of to the end of his life."

BIBLIOGRAPHY

NOVELS

1898 'A Man from the North.'
1902 'Anna of the Five Towns.'
1903 'Leonora.'
1904 'A Great Man.'
1905 'Sacred and Profane Love.' (Revised edition, U. S.
        1911: 'The Book of Carlotta.')
1906 'Whom God hath Joined.'
1908 'Buried Alive.'
     'The Old Wives' Tale.'
1910 'Clayhanger.'
1911 'The Card.' (U. S.: 'Denry the Audacious.')
     'Hilda Lessways.'
1913 'The Regent.'
1914 'The Price of Love.'
1916 'These Twain.'
1918 'The Pretty Lady.'
1919 'The Roll-Call.'
1922 'Mr. Prohack.'
     'Lilian.'
1923 'Riceyman Steps.'
1927 'The Vanguard.'
1930 'Imperial Palace.'
1932 'Dream of Destiny' (unfinished); and 'Venus Rising
        from the Sea.'

SHORT STORIES

1905 'Tales of the Five Towns.'
1907 'The Grim Smile of the Five Towns.'
1912 'The Matador of the Five Towns.'
1924 'Elsie and the Child.'
     'The Woman who Stole Everything.'

PLAYS

1908   'Cupid and Commonsense.'
1909   'What the Public Wants.'
1912   'Milestones.' (With Edward Knoblauch.)
       'The Honeymoon.'
1913   'The Great Adventure.'
1918   'The Title.'
1919   'Judith.'
       'Sacred and Profane Love.'
1922   'The Love Match.'
       'Body and Soul.'
1923   'Don Juan de Marana.'
1925   'The Bright Island.'

BELLES LETTRES

1903   'The Truth about an Author.'
1912   'Those United States.' (U. S.: 'Your United States.')
1914   'The Author's Craft.'

There is a little book about Arnold Bennett by F. J. Harvey Darton, in the 'Writers of the Day' series, a biography by his wife, 'My Arnold Bennett' (1931), and a sketch by Rebecca West, 'Arnold Bennett Himself' (1932). The first and second of the three volumes of 'The Journals of Arnold Bennett' were published in 1932, and the third volume in 1933. A separate volume published by Bennett during his lifetime covers the year 1929.

CHAPTER X

GEORGIAN NOVELISTS

THE English novel, rich as it is in great names and superb achievement, cannot be said to be altogether fortunate in its artistic tradition. George Moore, himself a competent practitioner, said of it in an interview published in the 'Fortnightly Review' for October, 1917: "The English novel remains as it was in the beginning—a drawing-room entertainment addressed chiefly to ladies. Men are not expected to put their best thoughts into novels, but into poetry and into essays, and, as man is a creature of habit, the novel remains the weakest part of English literature. The ambition of the English story-teller of the eighteenth century was to amuse the drawing-room, and I do not think the ambition of any story-teller since has been different."

After making very considerable allowance for Moore's habitual tendency to hyperbole, one must admit that there is a germ of truth in what he says. The great masters, from Fielding to Dickens, were negligent not merely of style but of structure, and the nineteenth century added to the lax artistic traditions of the eighteenth the limitations of Victorian prudishness. The attempts of George Eliot, Meredith, Hardy, Wells and Galsworthy, to enrich the social and intellectual content of the novel left it still somewhat indeterminate and amorphous as a type. George Moore in a series of novels dating from the mid 'eighties to the mid 'nineties endeavoured to establish in English fiction the freedom of treatment with regard to subject and the careful attention to regularity of form which Flaubert and Maupassant had established as accepted standards for the French novel; but 'Esther Waters' (1894) was the only work of Moore's which had enough circulation to exert any widespread influence. In the last decade of the nineteenth century Meredith, who had fallen foul of Mrs. Grundy as early as 1859 in 'The Ordeal of Richard Feverel,' made a notable contribution to the philosophical discussion of sex relations in the trio of novels beginning with 'One of our Conquerors' (1891) and closing with 'The Amazing Marriage' (1895); during the same period Hardy made headway in the same direction with 'Tess of the D'Ubervilles' (1891) and 'Jude the Obscure' (1895); but the critics' attack upon the latter novel was so violent that Hardy abandoned novel-writing in disgust at the restrictions imposed by popular taste and prevailing critical opinion. Samuel Butler's posthumous novel 'The Way of all Flesh' (1903) was a distinct landmark in the movement towards a freer treatment of sex; it by no means won the battle, but it encouraged the others. Wells in 'Tono-Bungay' and 'Ann Veronica' (1909) exercised considerable liberty, which at the time encountered a good deal of hostile criticism, though now these novels seem mild enough. A little later Galsworthy in 'The Dark Flower' treated the theme of sex with courageous frankness but with a delicate reserve which avoided offence. Arnold Bennett kept abreast of the current without making any particular advance, being, as has been noted above, more interested in improving the form of the novel than in enlarging its scope.

The accession of George V in 1910 offers a convenient

line of division, and if we agree to call the Wells-Gals-worthy-Bennett group "Edwardians," it is safe to say that the movement in English fiction for the full, frank, and free treatment of the subject of sex arrived at its height with the Georgians—the group of younger novelists who came to the front after the beginning of King George's reign, including D. H. Lawrence, Hugh Walpole, Gilbert Cannan, and Compton Mackenzie. They were the "new novelists" commended by Henry James, in his noteworthy essay of 1914, for hugging the shore of the real in matters of sex instead of flying to the open sea of sentiment at the least sign of difficulty. In 'A Novelist on Novels' (1918) W. L. George asserted that British writers had not yet attained complete freedom in dealing with sex, which still, in his opinion, played a much larger part in life than in English fiction. His opinion was fiercely contradicted at the time, but subsequent experience showed that there were much further limits than either the novelists or the critics had as yet realized.

It was a change not only in literary fashions but in manners, in morals, and in current opinion. The psycho-analytic theories of Freud and Jung, the investigations into the morbid psychology of sex by Havelock Ellis, the growing licence of French fiction from Zola to Proust all had a share in the change, but it was not entirely a matter of literature or science; it was part of the general breakdown of Puritan inhibitions, which was encouraged, though not originated, by the War. A general relaxation of sexual morality was brought about by the removal of the men on service from the restraining influences of home surroundings and local opinion and the inclination to allow them every indulgence when they returned from the front on leave. As the subject of the sex impulse is in itself of very limited interest, the attention of the younger novelists was soon attracted to its more morbid manifestations: Rosamond Lehmann's 'Dusty Answer' and Radcliffe Hall's 'Well of Loneliness' were conspicuous examples of this tendency, which soon exhausted itself, the subject being obviously one more suited to physiological or to psychological investigation than to treatment in fiction. Virginia Woolf in 'Jacob's Room' (1922) and 'Orlando' (1928) got back to the eighteenth century fashion of regarding sex with humorous detachment—as one of her admirers puts it, "with steady and amused comprehension." Florinda in 'Jacob's Room' said she was a virgin. "But whether or not she was a virgin seems a matter of no importance whatever—unless, indeed, it is the only thing of any importance at all." In London "not a square in snow or fog lacked its amorous couple. All plays turned on the same subject; yet we say it is a matter of no importance at all." In 'Orlando' the subject of sex is treated with the same sprightly detachment. On the whole it seems preferable to the elaborate but depressing lucubrations of James Joyce and D. H. Lawrence. The former's 'Ulysses' (printed in Paris, 1922) and the latter's 'Lady Chatterley's Lover' (printed in Florence, 1928) marked new depths of what had previously been regarded as indecency.

Henry James, in the essay on 'The New Novel' referred to above, not only congratulated the new Georgian novelists on the courage with which they tackled the sex question, but also on the genial force of their saturation in and possession of their material. What he criticized in them with great severity was their failure to exercise the power of selection. Even on the "slice of life" theory the novelist's duty of selection cannot be evaded. There can be no such thing as an amorphous slice; it has been *born* of naught else but measured excision. Reasons have been the fairies waiting on its cradle: "How can a slice of life be anything but illustrational of the loaf, and how can illustration not immediately bristle with every sign of the extracted and related state? The relation is at once to what the thing comes from and to what it waits upon —which last is our act of recognition. We accordingly appreciate it in proportion as it so accounts for itself; the quantity and the intensity of its reference are the measure of our knowledge of it." What then Henry James finds missing in this group of Georgian novelists is treatment, composition, structure, fusion, a centre of interest, and he ascribes this to the pernicious influence of Tolstoy, "the great illustrative master-hand on all this ground of the disconnection of method from matter."

In an incisive article in the London 'Nation' published soon after Henry James's essay, his judgment of the facts is admitted, but a different explanation is suggested. The new novels are "social documents, imaginative history, crusades, reactions, biology, or natural science," but they are not works of art; they lack style, and they lack form. Their accumulation of material circumstance is "the inevitable result of the autobiographical obsession obtruding upon the critical, the measuring, the selective faculty. The energy of an unconscious self-expression is too much for them."

This is an interesting theory, and it would not be difficult to cite particular novels or parts of novels which lend it support, but it is hardly tenable in view of the variety of the work of the Georgian novelists, or even the variety of the work of any one of them. Every novelist reproduces more or less indirectly his own experience and observation. De Maupassant, one of the most objective of writers of fiction, says: "We can only vary our characters by altering the age, the sex, the social position and all the circumstances of life of that *ego* which nature has in fact enclosed in an insurmountable barrier of organs of sense. Skill consists in not betraying this *ego* to the reader, under the various masks which we employ to cover it."

Here and there in the work of this group of the Georgian novelists, one may discern (as in the work of their predecessors) autobiography more or less assimilated to the artistic purpose they have in view; but the charge of unassimilated autobiography cannot be brought with justice against their work as a whole, or, indeed against that of any particular author. The characteristic of the novels of which both Henry James and the 'Nation' critic complained may have still another explanation. What Henry James condemns as a disregard of the essential principles of art and what the alternative view holds to be unconscious self-absorption may be really a deliberate effort to produce the effect of the variety—even the haphazard confusion—of life. The grouping of character and circumstance round a central theme may be an aim they have not merely not endeavoured to attain, but have consciously striven to avoid, and to criticize them for not reaching it is simply to disapprove of the theory of art they have taken over, either from the older English novelists or from the Russians. Fortunately we have, in Hugh Walpole's little book about Joseph Conrad, a statement (by one of themselves) of the aims and models these novelists had in view. He says: "The influence of the French novel, which was at its strongest between the years of 1885 and 1895, was towards Realism, and the influence of the Russian novel, which has certainly been very strongly marked in England during the last years, is all towards Romantic-Realism. If we wished to know exactly what is meant by Romantic-Realism, such a novel as 'The Brothers Karamazov,' such a play as 'The Cherry

Orchard' are there before us, as the best possible examples. We might say, in a word, that 'Karamazov' has, in the England of 1915, taken the place that was occupied, in 1890, by 'Madame Bovary.' "

Now 'Madame Bovary' is exactly the treatment of "a case" according to the method Henry James, in theory and practice, approved; the looser structure of the Russian authors Walpole mentions—if indeed it can be called structure at all—is that adopted by the younger English school. That Henry James should find them lacking in this respect is not surprising; but his criticism goes back to a discussion of the fundamental principles of the art of fiction to which there is no end. We may regret that the new novelists were apparently so little interested in the form of their work, or, if one agrees with Henry James, that they were influenced by the evil example of the Russians, but obviously we must take them for what they are, since it is fruitless to condemn them for what they are not. There will certainly be those who will contend that in spite of the apparent lack of a central interest, there is a subtler unity to be discerned, and that this more delicate and fluid creation represents a higher artistic standard than the more obvious and artificial construction of the older French school. The apparent formlessness which the older English novelists enjoyed in the innocence of childhood may have been adopted by the Georgians not from thoughtlessness, or lack of skill, or unconscious self-absorption, but from deliberate design.

In process of time the "new" Georgians became no longer "new" or even young, and lost their hold on the public, with the exception of D. H. Lawrence, who never had any great popularity to lose but retained the high opinion of the critics. The Edwardian group for a while recovered their place in the sun, especially Galsworthy.

Wells was too preachy for the younger generation of Georgians, and Bennett was ridiculed as old-fashioned. Mrs. Woolf, the leader of the younger Georgians, dismissed the whole Edwardian trio as "materialists." "It is because they are concerned not with the spirit but with the body that they have disappointed us, and left us with the feeling that the sooner English fiction turns its back on them, as politely as may be, and marches, if only into the desert, the better for its soul." Galsworthy, she argues, is deficient in vitality; the serious characters of Wells are merely bores; and Bennett's method is simply the accumulation of physical detail. In an essay entitled 'Mr. Bennett and Mrs. Brown,' read in 1924 to the Cambridge academic society called "The Heretics," Mrs. Woolf pictured herself as a younger novelist asking the Edwardians how to set about the creation of a character, say Mrs. Brown. "And they said, 'Begin by saying that her father kept a shop in Harrogate. Ascertain the rent. Ascertain the wages of shop assistants in the years 1878. Discover what her mother died of. Describe cancer. Describe calico. Describe . . .' But I cried 'Stop! Stop!' And I regret to say that I threw that ugly, that clumsy, that incongruous tool out of the window, for I knew that if I began describing the cancer and the calico, my Mrs. Brown, that vision to which I cling, though I know no way of imparting it to you, would have been dulled and tarnished and vanished for ever."

Whether the method Mrs. Woolf ultimately adopted really advanced the English novel on its destined way is a matter for later discussion. She is not inclined to overestimate her own achievements or those of her contemporaries. In her opinion the novelists of the first quarter of the twentieth century fall far behind those of the first quarter of the nineteenth century, because they lack faith.

"The most sincere of them will only tell us what it is that happens to himself. They cannot make a world because they are not free of other human beings. They cannot tell stories because they do not believe the stories are true. For certainty of that kind is the condition which makes it possible to write. To believe that your impressions hold good for others is to be released from the cramp and confinement of personality. It is to be free, as Scott was free, to explore, with a vigor which still holds us spellbound, the whole world of adventure and romance. It is also the first step in that mysterious process in which Jane Austen was so great an adept. The little grain of experience once selected, believed in, and set outside herself, could be put precisely in its place, and she was then free to make of it, by a process which never yields its secrets to the analyst, into that complete statement which is literature."

D. H. LAWRENCE (1885–1930)

Since the death of David Herbert Lawrence, the biographical, epistolary, and critical material about his erratic life and enigmatic personality has been intimidating in its amount and bewildering in its contradictoriness. But from the mass of inconsistencies, denials, and rebuttals, some definite conclusions make themselves clear. The popular conception of Lawrence as tormented and driven by the demon of sex has been shown to be completely erroneous. So far as being "the husband of one wife" went, he might have been a candidate for the bishopric in the primitive Christian Church; "from first to last Lawrence was for fidelity in marriage." Sex, as an end in itself, he held to be disaster, and any kind of sexual perversion he regarded with horror; it was for him a hopeless sin, "the sin against the Holy Ghost." Although he claimed a large freedom in literary expression and vocabulary, his sense of personal decency was easily offended—amounting almost to prudishness; he had a marked distaste for what he regarded as the laxity of the European Continent in such matters and clung to the end of his life to the English tradition in which he grew up.

He was born in a coalminer's cottage on the borders of Nottinghamshire and Derbyshire—the scene in which all his earlier, and perhaps his best work is cast. His mother was a woman of character and refinement and some education, and encouraged the boy to win a scholarship at Nottingham High School, which he left at sixteen to become a junior clerk and later a pupil-teacher in an elementary school, receiving instruction from the headmaster before and after the day's work. From eighteen to twenty he was a student at the Nottingham Day Training College, and for five years he taught school near London—until he got his first two novels published.

'The White Peacock,' Lawrence's first novel, is a work of promise rather than of performance. He writes well—in descriptive passages, such as this: "I was born in September, and love it best of all the months. There is no heat, no hurry, no thirst and weariness in corn harvest as there is in the hay. If the season is late, as is usual with us, then mid-September sees the corn still standing in stook. The mornings come slowly. The earth is like a woman married and fading; she does not leap up with a laugh for the first fresh kiss of dawn, but slowly, quietly, unexpectantly lies watching the waking of each new day. The blue mist, like memory in the eyes of a neglected wife, never goes from the wooded hill, and only at noon creeps from the near hedges. There is no bird to put a song in the throat of morning; only the crow's voice speaks during the day. Perhaps there is the regular breathing hush of the scythe—even the fretful jar of the mowing machine. But next day, in the morning, all is still again. The lying corn is wet, and when you have bound it, and lift the heavy sheaf to make the stook, the tresses of oats wreathe round each other and droop mournfully."

But in this first book he had no command of dialogue or perhaps not enough knowledge of how educated people talk. The teller of the story reports himself as saying to a girl about her eyes: "To have such soft, vulnerable eyes as you used makes one feel nervous and irascible. But you have clothed over the sensitiveness of yours, haven't you?—like naked life, naked defenceless protoplasm they were, is it not so?" This is a conversation between two young people in a Nottinghamshire public house parlour, and after this we are not surprised that they "drifted into a discussion of Strauss and Débussy"—whom the novelist (or his proofreader) did not yet know well enough to spell the name correctly. In the same chapter the servant makes the hero think of "the girl in Tchekoff's story," and an old woman lying in a bed suggests Guy de Maupassant's 'Toine.' Lawrence had been doing a lot of reading in London and he had not yet digested it.

His second novel, 'The Trespasser,' is written in an easier style, but is an ordinary story of an irregular love affair ending in suicide. It was only in his third novel, 'Sons and Lovers,' that he struck back to the memories of his childhood and the speech of his youth. His mother had died just before his first novel was published—the great disappointment of his life—and it was no doubt her memory that inspired the central figure of Mrs. Morel, who is, perhaps unnecessarily (for the purposes of the story), enriched with an education unusual in a collier's cottage. But once this little improbability is overcome, the fortunes of the Morel family are unrolled with uncommon skill and power. The father—drunken, sometimes violent—is not without features that make him human and natural; the mother is magnificently realized. The dialogue, now chiefly dialect, reproduces with astonishing verve and colour the forthright, picturesque colloquialism of the collier folk. Miriam, the farmer's daughter who discusses Michael Angelo and reads Baudelaire and Verlaine, is less alive; and Clara, who plays profane love to Miriam's spirituality, is a fleshly woman—nothing more —but the children of the Morel household are astonishingly real and vivid. One is a little disappointed that the eldest William should be so suddenly cut off after winning our intense interest, but his brother Paul takes his place in the reader's as well as in his mother's heart. Her consuming affection for him, her jealousy of other women, her absolute devotion masking itself under ordinary sayings and doings, is a triumph of feeling and expression, and in the last crisis of her death the novelist finds for the stricken son the words of utter simplicity and sincerity —the cry of the heart.

Lawrence said himself: "The first part of 'Sons and Lovers' is all autobiography," and there is no doubt that his hero passes through his own youthful experiences. His mother's absorbing affection for him—and his for her—prevented him from giving himself wholly to another woman. He wrote in his essay 'Fantasia of the Unconscious' (1922): "You will not easily get a man to believe that his carnal love for the woman he has made his wife is as high a love as that he felt for his mother." And that, according to J. Middleton Murry ('Son of Woman'), is the history of Lawrence's own life. Mrs. Carswell, on the other hand, in 'The Savage Pilgrimage,'

contends that Lawrence determined before his marriage
that "never again would he be mothered by any woman.
He would even put behind him that first mothering that
had meant more than anything in his youth." This view
seems to be borne out by a letter from Lawrence written
in 1913 in which he says: "I had a devil of a time getting
a bit weaned from my mother, at the age of twenty-two."
But that he was weaned seems to be indicated by a poem
addressed to his first love, Miriam, before his mother's
death:

I thought that love would do all things, but now I know I am
    wrong.
There are depths below depths, my darling, where love does
    not belong,
Where the fight that is fight for being, is fought throughout
    the long
Young years, and the old must not win, not even if they love
    and are strong.

It was Miriam who started Lawrence on his literary
career by sending this and other poems to Ford Madox
Hueffer, editor of 'The English Review.' Hueffer had
Lawrence's first novel, 'The White Peacock,' published
by Heinemann, who refused 'Sons and Lovers' on account
of its extreme sexuality—he pronounced it "one of the
dirtiest books I ever read." But as published by Duckworth it won favourable reviews and had a fair sale. It is
still held by many readers, including competent critics,
to be the best novel Lawrence ever did.

All the love affairs in these early novels had to do with
incidents in Lawrence's youth which he had left behind
him when he met the woman who was to become his wife,
Frieda, daughter of Baron von Richthofen, who had been
Governor of Alsace-Lorraine when it belonged to Ger-

many. She was older than Lawrence and had three children when he first knew her as the wife of a professor at Nottingham University College, which he had attended as a student. Lawrence and Frieda went to Germany together in the summer of 1912, and made their way on foot into Italy and afterwards back to Bavaria. After Frieda's divorce they were married in London in the early summer of 1914. Neither of them had any money and Lawrence was unable to pay the costs awarded against him in the divorce suit. He twice had severe attacks of pneumonia in his youth, and when he was twenty-six the doctor warned him that if he went on teaching he would have consumption. His first novel brought him less than fifty pounds, and the second about the same; his 'Love Poems' sold only a hundred copies; his play was a failure. "What joy to receive three pounds out of the sweet heavens!" he writes; "I call that manna." It was not that they were wasteful or extravagant, but they had not enough money to live on, not even in the simplest fashion; they were "poor as mice." He tried to write unobjectionable novels, but found he could not do it. "I can only write what I feel pretty strongly about: and that, at present, is the relation between men and women. After all, it is *the* problem of today, the establishment of a new relation, or the readjustment of the old one, between men and women." But he did not lose confidence in himself or in the future. "I *know* I can write bigger stuff than any man in England," he said, and he prophesied that success would come before he was forty-five; it did, but it was too late.

At the time of his marriage, happy in his union to the woman he loved, and relieved from immediate money anxiety by a grant of fifty pounds from the Royal Literary Fund, Lawrence, in spite of his physical frailty, gave the impression of extraordinary vitality. "There was," says

Mrs. Carswell, "a swift and flamelike quality, . . . a fine,
rare beauty in Lawrence, with his deep-set jewel-like eyes,
thick dust-coloured hair, pointed underlip of notable
sweetness, fine hands, and rapid but never restless movements." His love for his handsome German blonde found
expression in the cycle of poems 'Look! We have Come
Through!' not published till some years later; and he
felt himself arrived at man's estate, grew a beard, and
began to set his thoughts into some systematic order.
The prevalent shibboleths which divided the political and
intellectual worlds—nationalism and internationalism,
capitalism and socialism, socialism and communism,
Christianity and paganism—did not interest him. Christianity seemed to him. "based on the love of self, the
love of property, one degree removed. Why should I care
for my neighbour's property, or my neighbour's life, if I
do not care for my own? If the truth of my spirit is all that
matters to me, in the last issue, then on behalf of my
neighbour, all I care for is the truth of *his* spirit." In his
own way, Lawrence was deeply religious, a modern mystic,
and all these issues seemed to him material issues, or at
the best, mental—things of the mind, not of the whole
man. "My great religion," he wrote to a friend in 1913,
"is a belief in the blood, the flesh, as being wiser than the
intellect. We can go wrong in our minds. But what our
blood feels and believes and says is always true. The
intellect is only a bit and a bridle. What do I care about
knowledge? All I want is to answer to my blood, direct,
without fribbling intervention of mind, or moral or what-
not." These ideas Lawrence developed in a new novel
entitled 'The Rainbow,' the iris of sex, uniting the two
infinities of darkness and light, the two eternities of the
past and the future. There was a great deal in the book
about sexual intercourse, conceived in this spirit, but

capable of misinterpretation by the ordinary reader. To Lady Cynthia Asquith, who was evidently puzzled by 'The Rainbow' and asked him what was its meaning, its message, he replied: "I don't know myself what it is: except that the older world is done for, toppling on top of us: and that it's no use the men looking to the women for salvation, nor the women looking to sensuous satisfaction for their fulfilment. There must be a new world." To Mrs. Carswell he wrote a little later in the same year (1916): "What we want is the fulfilment of our desires, down to the deepest and most spiritual desire. The body is immediate, the spirit is beyond: first the leaves and then the flower: but the plant is an integral whole: therefore every desire, to the very deepest. And I shall find my deepest desire to be a wish for pure, unadulterated relationship with the universe, for truth in being. My pure relationship with one woman is marriage, physical and spiritual: with another, is another form of happiness, according to our nature. And so on for ever."

None of this was made clear to the reader of 'The Rainbow' in the book itself, and as soon as it was published in the fall of 1915 it was pounced upon by a society for the protection of public morals. Within six weeks it was condemned by a London police court as "obscene," and the whole edition was destroyed by magisterial order. The blow not only shattered Lawrence's hope of making money by publishing this novel at that time, but of publishing anything else in the immediate future. It ruined his health and broke his spirit. He and his wife retired to a cottage in Cornwall, for which they had to pay only five pounds a year, and lived there in obscurity, doing their own household work. Lawrence had no fundamental feeling for nationality. "I feel no passion for my own land, nor my own house, nor my own furniture, nor my own money. . . . I know that for me war is wrong. I know that if the Germans wanted my little house, I would rather give it them than fight for it: because my little house is not important enough to me. . . . To fight for possessions, goods, is what my soul *will not do.*" He had a German wife, and they sang German songs together to the accompaniment of an old piano he had bought for a few pounds. He applied for a passport to go to America and the Government refused it, "in the interest of the national service." His cottage was searched by the military, and though nothing was found of an incriminating nature he was ordered to leave Cornwall within three days. In October, 1917, he got back to London "at the fag end of poverty," with less than five pounds in his pocket and no resources beyond the bounty of his friends. He had been previously examined for military service and rejected on account of his physical condition. In 1918 he was called up for reëxamination and passed in Grade 3. Fortunately the Armistice came before he could be summoned for active service. In the winter he had a bad attack of influenza, but he was cheered by a legacy from Rupert Brooke, which helped him on his way to Italy when (in 1919) passports were obtainable. Money was also coming in to him from New York for the American issue of 'Look! We Have Come Through' and the first edition of his novel 'Women in Love' (1920), for which he had been vainly trying for four years to find an English publisher. Meanwhile Lawrence had prepared for the English market another story "quite amusing and quite moral," which he called 'The Lost Girl,' adding "She's not morally lost, poor darling . . . marries an Italian." The story opens in a mining town in Lawrence's native county of Nottinghamshire, and begins with what Gissing called "stark realism

218 English Literature in the Twentieth Century

in the sphere of the ignobly decent." The misfortunes of the heroine's father, who is an unsuccessful shopkeeper, are followed painstakingly for a hundred pages, and the general effect, if not, as Gissing said it would be, "intolerably tedious," is at least mildly dull. The author himself says on p. 95: "Now so far the story of Alvina is commonplace enough. It is more or less the story of thousands of girls. They all find work. It is the ordinary solution of everything. And if we were dealing with an ordinary girl we should have to continue mildly and dully down the long years of employment; or, at the best, marriage with some dull school-teacher or office-clerk." But the author goes on to say: "There have been enough stories about ordinary people. . . . We detest ordinary people. We are in peril of our lives from them: and in peril of our souls too, for they would damn us one and all to the ordinary. Every individual should, by nature, have his extraordinary points."

Now the extraordinary point about Alvina is a smothered flame of passion, which breaks out to compel her to reject her commonplace suitors and to surrender herself before marriage to an Italian variety artiste, who takes her off to his native hills in the Abruzzi. Both the passionate and the picturesque sides of this theme are congenial to Lawrence, and he treats them with characteristic distinction, leaving Alvina at the end of the story alone in the wilds (her husband being called off to the War), and expecting the birth of her first child. It is a finely told story, especially in the last hundred pages; in the centre of the book, the transition from the girl of English middle-class traditions to the woman who abandons herself to passion is difficult to manage, but when she has made up her mind to the man as her mate, the story moves more easily. There are few pages to distress the readers who dislike the intensity of Lawrence's concern with sex, and apart from these the novel has much to commend it to those likely to be attracted by the less exceptional phases of his genius.

'Women in Love' carries on the theme and some of the characters of 'The Rainbow'; it is chiefly of interest as a transition to the author's more philosophical view of sex, considered in relation to individuality. "Love," says the chief spokesman, "is one of the emotions like all the others . . . just part of human relationship, no more." Sex should be used not as a means of sensual gratification or for the procreation of children, or to give to a defective personality the sensation of fulfilment, but to gain knowledge of another personality, "never to be seen with the eye, or known with the mind, only known as a palpable revelation of living otherness." But the philosophy is not closely interwoven with the story, and this makes the book hard reading. The principal characters are all excessively neurotic, over-sexed, and over-strained, and their continual analysis, conveyed mainly by dialogue, of their desires and impulses produces an impression of artificiality. The lover who says at a picnic to the lady he shortly afterwards marries, "When the stream of synthetic creation lapses, we find ourselves part of the inverse process, the flood of destructive creation," philosophizes too much and inopportunely, and most readers will take him for a bore as well as a prig. Lawrence had seized his new idea, but he had not yet succeeded in embodying it in the appropriate form of narrative fiction.

'Aaron's Rod,' which he had begun in England and finished in Italy, shows a very distinct growth in thought and style; the author has completely assimilated his material, and manages his dialogue easily and naturally, though it ranges from the humblest themes to the highest.

The story begins in the familiar Midland mining district, where the hero is a check-weighman, and secretary to the Miners' Union for his colliery; but he is a man of very exceptional taste and talent for music and philosophy, exceptional not only in his position in life, but in any position. The opening chapters are still in the manner of Gissing, but after the hero has been emancipated from his family and his surroundings by his flight, first to London and then to Florence, the book is continued according to the prescription of Meredith, that the novel should be "fortified by philosophy"; Lawrence, however, imitates no predecessor, but is an independent artist, with a style and manner of his own. His theme is still sex, but sex as conceived in a very curious relation to individual character and society. For the author's new point of view, which has an obvious relation to his studies in psychological analysis, the hero is naturally the main exponent and example. Aaron deserted his wife, not because he was in love with another woman, or because he was not in love with his wife, but because at home his soul was not free. "Love was a battle in which each party strove for the mastery of the other's soul," and neither would give way. The author thus analyses and interprets his hero's impulse to flight in a passage introduced about midway in the book:

"Born in him was a spirit which could not worship women: no, and would not. Could not and would not. It was not in him. In early days, he tried to pretend it was in him. But through his plaintive and homage-rendering love of a young husband was always, for the woman, discernible the arrogance of self-unyielding male. He never yielded himself: never. All his mad loving was only an effort. Afterwards, he was as devilishly unyielded as ever. And it was an instinct in her, that her man must yield to her, so that she should envelop him, yielding, in her all-beneficent love. She was quite sure that her love was all-beneficent. Of this no shadow of doubt. She was quite sure that the highest her man could ever know or ever reach was to be perfectly enveloped in her all-beneficent love. This was her idea of marriage. She held it not as an idea, but as a profound impulse and instinct: an instinct developed in her by the age in which she lived. All that was deepest and most sacred in her feeling centred in this belief."

The whole novel is a plea for the freeing of men from the dominance of woman exercised in and through love. Aaron realized as he meditates further on his own position and experience that "love, even in its intensest, was only an attribute of the human soul: one of its incomprehensible gestures. And to fling down the whole soul in one gesture of finality in love was as much a criminal suicide as to jump off a church tower or a mountain peak. Let a man give himself as much as he liked in love, to seven thousand extremities, he must never give himself *away*."

Lilly, the argumentative exponent of the individualistic side of this story, says in the course of a long summing-up at the end of the book: "You *are* yourself and so be yourself. Stick to it and abide by it. Passion or no passion, ecstasy or no ecstasy, urge or no urge, there's no goal outside you, where you can consummate like an eagle flying into the sun, or a moth into a candle. There's no goal outside you—and there's no God outside you. No God, whom you can get to and rest in. None . . . There is only one thing, your own very self. So you'd better stick to it. You can't be any bigger than just yourself, so you needn't drag God in. You've got one job, and no more. There inside you lies your own very self, like a germinating egg, your precious Easter egg of your own soul.

There it is, developing bit by bit, from one single egg-cell which you were at your conception in your mother's womb, on and on to the strange and peculiar complication in unity which never stops till you die—if then."

This stark individualism was curiously combined in Lawrence with a desire to found a community: he had even chosen the site. He was encouraged by the sale of his works in the United States. 'The Rainbow' had been republished in New York; and 'Women in Love,' 'Aaron's Rod,' 'Sea and Sardinia,' 'Psycho-analysis and the Unconscious,' 'A Fantasia of the Unconscious,' and 'Studies in Classic American Literature' all appeared there before they were published in England. It was natural for Lawrence, who was thoroughly disgusted with the old world, to turn his eyes across the Atlantic, and the scene he chose for his colony, to be founded on "a union in the unconsciousness, not in the consciousness," was Fort Myers on the West Coast of Florida. There, he wrote to J. M. Murry and Katharine Mansfield, his chosen companions, we can "live blithely by a big river, where there are fish, and in the forest behind wild turkeys and quails: there we make songs and poems and stories and dramas, in a Vale of Avalon, in the Hesperides, among the Loves." Murry did not respond very enthusiastically to the invitation and the project was left in abeyance, until at Taormina, Sicily, in the autumn of 1921, Lawrence received from a wealthy American writer, Mabel Dodge Sterne Luhan, the offer of a house in Taos, New Mexico. Lawrence replied that they were "keen on coming," but wanted particulars as to cost of housekeeping: "We are *very* practical, do all our own work, even the washing, cooking, floor-cleaning and everything here in Taormina." Also he was not strong enough to face America yet; he wanted to see something of Buddhism, so he was coming round by Ceylon, for which accordingly they sailed in January, 1922. Buddhism did not make a favourable impression on Lawrence, nor did the natives, so he went on to Australia, where he had "room to be alone" and gathered material for 'Kangaroo,' a novel of working-class life and labour organizations in Australia.

In his own odd fashion, Lawrence had a keen desire to be in a right relation to society, in the way of service, or, preferably, of leadership. He writes in 'Fantasia': "Our leaders have not loved men; they have loved ideas, and have been willing to sacrifice passionate men on the altars of the blood-drinking ever-ash-thirsty ideal. Has President Wilson, or Karl Marx, or Bernard Shaw ever felt one hot blood-pulse of love for the workingman, the half-conscious, deluded workingman? . . . But oh, I would like to save him alive, in his living, spontaneous, original being. I can't help it. It is my passionate instinct. I would like him to give me back the responsibility for general affairs, a responsibility which he can't acquit, and which saps his life. I would like him to give me back the responsibility for the future. I would like him to give me back the responsibility for thought, for direction. I wish we could take hope and belief together. I would undertake my share of the responsibility, if he gave me his belief." What Lawrence wanted was a human relationship between men "deeper than the deeps of sex. Deeper than property, deeper than fatherhood, deeper than marriage, deeper than love. So deep that it is love-less. The stark, loveless, wordless unison of two men who have come to the bottom of themselves. This is the nucleus of a new society, the clue to a new world-epoch." Lawrence had looked for such a comradely relationship—a sort of primitive blood-brotherhood—among the agricultural labourers he worked with in Cornwall and found no response. The Italian peasants were equally disappointing; so were the Buddhists of Ceylon. He found no satisfaction in Australia, none among either the whites or the Indians of New Mexico, which he next visited. His "savage pilgrimage" was continued to Mexico City, which was too Americanized for his taste; he felt sympathetic to the "dark-faced gods" of Old Mexico, and strove to embody their mysterious beauty in 'The Plumed Serpent,' which he counted the best novel he had yet written. But he returned to England in 1923 with his desire to discover the right relationship of man to man still unsatisfied. On his final return to England (after a second visit to New Mexico and Mexico in 1924), Lawrence wrote to an American friend: "What ails me is the absolute frustration of my primeval societal instinct. The hero illusion starts with the individualist illusion, and all resistances ensue. I think societal instinct much deeper than sex instinct—and societal repression much more devastating. There is no repression of the sexual individual comparable to the repression of the societal man in me, by the individual ego, my own and everybody else's. I am weary even of my own individuality, and simply nauseated by other people's."

The last years of Lawrence's life were still years of conflict and disappointment. He wrote of his American publisher in 1924: "He still hovers on the brink of bankruptcy and keeps me on the edge of the same"; his London publications brought in very little. Yet at a London dinner in 1923 he was saluted by his fellow-craftsmen as "the greatest of us all." According to Mabel Dodge, Lawrence put his head on the table and wept; according to Mrs. Carswell he fainted and had to be carried to his taxi. But they both agree that next morning Lawrence felt humiliated and thought he had made a fool of himself.

Lawrence's last novel, 'Lady Chatterley's Lover,' again attacked the problem of sex, with greater freedom of phraseology than he had ever used before. His own opinion of it was that it was "very *verbally* improper— the last word in all its meanings!—but very truly moral." He had it typed by a Florence woman who knew English, and after doing five chapters she refused to go any further—it was "too indecent." Lawrence had it set up by compositors who knew only Italian and sold by a Florentine publisher; but before long five piratical editions had appeared in the United States. Lawrence felt himself very badly used: it turned his stomach that he "who loathed sexuality so deeply," should be considered a sexuality specialist. The novel, he contended, was "not really improper— I always labour at the same thing, to make the sex relation valid and precious, instead of shameful." "I want," he said to another lady, "to make an *adjustment in consciousness* to the basic physical realities. You mustn't think I advocate perpetual sex. Far from it. Nothing nauseates me more than promiscuous sex in and out of season." His last word on the subject, written within a year of his death, was this: "I write in all honesty and in the sincere belief that the human consciousness needs badly now to have the doors freely opened into the dark chamber of horrors of 'sex'—it is no chamber of horrors really, of course—and I feel the language needs to be freed of various artificial taboos on words and expressions. All these taboos and shut doors only make for social insanity. I do my work, and take the reward of insult, since it is to be expected."

He thought it an "unkind destiny" that he was so often in trouble, and complained that his friends did not stand by him. Copies of 'Lady Chatterley's Lover' were held up in the English Post Office and criminal proceedings were threatened. The manuscript of his poems 'Pansies' (*Pensées*, Thoughts), was confiscated on its way through the mail. He had taken to painting as an amusement, and an exhibition of his work was closed by the police, who would have seized some of the reproductions in the gallery as indecent, if they had not discovered, just in time, that they were by William Blake, with whose eccentric genius Lawrence had, indeed, a good deal in common. Lawrence was in fact a poet-philosopher, more poet than philosopher, and more philosopher than artist. He derided the cry of "art for art's sake" and said his motto was "art for my sake." He had ideas that he was eager to get out of himself, and he had no intention of conciliating or considering the public in the task of delivering his soul. If he had chosen to write novel after novel in the manner of 'Sons and Lovers' and 'A Lost Girl,' he could have made a great deal of money; but he did not care for money. He preferred to live in the same fashion as his working-class forbears, washing his own shirt because he loathed servants, creeping around and poisoning the atmosphere! His wife was devoted to him, in spite of their frequent and sometimes violent quarrels, and she worked at household tasks as hard as Lawrence himself, notwithstanding her upbringing as a well-to-do aristocrat. He said he had quarrelled with all his friends. But they always came back to him. An American girl who knew him well described him as "one of the most fascinating men I ever met. The first time I ever saw him, he talked for a whole afternoon, almost steadily. . . . It pours out of him like an inspired message, and no matter how much you may differ when you are away from him, or how little you are able to follow his own particular mysticism, he makes you believe it when he is with you."

.That is perhaps as near as we can get to the actual

Lawrence, poet, mystic, and prophet—by no means of smooth things. The public of his day can hardly be blamed for not understanding him: he gave them so little help. Even his most intelligent and familiar friends were often at a loss. His closest friends in the earlier part of his literary career were J. M. Murry, Katharine Mansfield, and Catherine Carswell; in the middle period, Mabel Dodge saw more of him than anyone else who has left a printed record of Lawrence as he was in those years of wandering; in the last years, his best friend was Aldous Huxley. Yet upon each of these writers Lawrence made an impression not only different from that of each of the others, but often contradictory, not merely in details but in crucial points. It is no wonder that the reading public differed even more widely in their estimates of Lawrence's personality and of his literary work. Of his skill as a writer, there can be no more question than of his sincerity and originality as a thinker; the pity is that he so often failed to use that skill to make his meaning clear. His detailed analysis of the phenomena of sex is frequently taken in exactly the contrary sense to that which Lawrence intended. It will be better understood with the lapse of time, and it seems likely that his frankness in discussing sexual facts in plain words will not in the near future be so offensive to the general eye and ear as it was when the objectionable passages were written. The more serious obstacle to his permanent fame is that, in his novels and poems alike, he is hard reading. The fate of George Meredith looks ominous when we consider the future of D. H. Lawrence. Meredith's assault upon the prudery and conservatism of his day now no longer excites the hostility of the most squeamish; but he is no longer read, first because he does not tell a straight story; and secondly, because he calls upon the reader to do too much hard thinking. On either count, one does not see how Lawrence can get through; he too thought that the novel should be "fortified by philosophy," and he too refused to accept it as the novelist's first duty to tell a tale that would hold the average reader's attention.

HUGH WALPOLE (1884–   )

Walpole's father became Bishop of Edinburgh in 1910, after holding the incumbency of St. Mary's Pro-Cathedral, Auckland, New Zealand, 1882–9, and the professorship of dogmatic theology in the General Theological Seminary, New York, 1889–96. Hugh Seymour Walpole (to give him his full name) is presumably the "Hugh Seymour" of 'The Golden Scarecrow,' who "was sent from Ceylon, where his parents lived, to be educated in England. His relations having, for the most part, settled in foreign countries, he spent his holidays as a minute and pale-faced 'paying guest' in various houses where other children were of more importance than he, or where children as a race were of no importance at all."

"Hugh Seymour" is described by his creator (or biographer) as a short-sighted, sensitive child who did not care very greatly for reading but told himself long stories of "trains of elephants, ropes and ropes of pearls, towers of ivory, peacocks, and strange meals of saffron buns, roast chicken, and gingerbread. He was bullied at school until his appointment as his dormitory's storyteller gave him a certain status."

Cornwall is dimly suggested as the scene of this story of childhood, and Cornwall was certainly the scene of the three "studies in place" (as he afterwards called them) with which Walpole began his literary career. His most successful novel, 'The Duchess of Wrexe,' was written at Polperro in that county, August 1912–January 1914, and the author's fondness for its romantic coast may be connected with family friendships formed by his father as tutor at the Chancellor's School at Truro, 1877–82. But this was before Hugh Walpole was born, and one may be very sure that it was neither this school nor King's School, Canterbury, at which he himself was educated, that stood for model for the third and most remarkable of his "studies of place"—'Mr. Perrin and Mr. Traill.' "Moffatt's" is a second-rate boarding school for middle-class boys, presented from the point of view of the staff, one of whom thus describes the type: "There are thousands of them all over the country—places where the men are underpaid, with no prospects, herded together, all of them hating each other, wanting, perhaps, towards the end of term, to cut each other's throats. You must not be friends with the Head, because then we shall think that you are spying on us. You must not be friends with us, because then the Head will hear of it, and will immediately hate you because he will think that you are conspiring against him. You must not be friends with the boys, because then we shall all hate you and they will despise you. You will be quite alone. . . . Here we are—fifteen men—all hating each other, loathing everything that the other man does—the way he eats, the way he moves, the way he teaches. We sleep next door to each other, we eat together, we meet all day until late at night—hating each other."

The situation is, one hopes, not typical—the speaker is a disappointed and embittered man—but it is a possible one where a small number of overworked, nervous and uncongenial teachers are cooped up together under an unsympathetic or selfseeking Headmaster. It is worked out in the story, perhaps with an undue indulgence in physical violence, but with undoubted power. The life of the teaching staff is presented skilfully and forcefully, their petty cares, squabbles, and resentments, and the most guilty of them (always omitting the unspeakable Headmaster who looms in the background as the evil genius of the scene) is represented as a victim of underpay, overwork, and overstrained nerves. Conditions have improved in schools of this type since the story was written, but the lot of the private schoolteacher is still far from what it should be, either for his own sake or for those under his care, and Walpole did a public service in drawing attention to it so effectively.

Walpole's story of university life, 'The Prelude to Adventure,' owes merely its external machinery to the fact that he was at Emmanuel College, Cambridge. It is classed by him as a 'prologue'—to what, is not clear. It is the story of the murder of one undergraduate by another—a murder inexplicably committed, inexplicably undiscovered, inexplicably confessed, and inexplicably condoned. Even as a study of the external conditions of university life it has very slight value.

The other prologue, 'Fortitude'—though again one does not see to what, unless Walpole had in mind the writing of a continuation—is a very much firmer and stronger piece of work. The scene is mainly in Cornwall or in London, and there is a wealth of well-conceived characters. The theme of the story is set forth in the opening sentence: " 'Tisn't life that matters! 'Tis the courage you bring to it," and the plot follows the vicissitudes of the hero, Peter Westcott, from boyhood to manhood, in his conflicts with various antagonists, without and within. We leave him

almost vanquished, baffled but triumphant, for he is still
fighting, and the work as a whole attains the effect aimed
at, in addition to many excellent strokes in detail.

'The Duchess of Wrexe' had also an ambitious theme.
The Duchess herself is an excellent character study, but beyond this Walpole aimed at the portrayal of a disappear-
ing class—the Autocrats. "You *must* have your quarter-
ings, and you must look down on those who haven't. But,
more than that, everything must be preserved, and continual ceremonies, dignities, chastities, restraints, pomps
and circumstances. Above all, no one must be admitted
within the company who is not of the noblest, the stupid-
est, the narrowest."

The Duchess is beaten, and at the end of the story we
are given a glimpse of the rising city of the new age—
"instead of this old house, the hooded furniture, the anger
at all freedom of thought, the jealousy of all enterprise,
the slander and the malice, an age of a universal Brotherhood, of unselfishness, restraint, charity, tolerance"—
but upon this prospect descended the curtain of the War,
and Walpole went off to Russia to serve with the Russian
Red Cross, 1914–16. The outcome was 'The Dark Forest'
—a romantic treatment of his experiences on the Russian
front, done in the Russian manner. It was greatly admired, perhaps most of all by those who took on hearsay
the great Russian models which it was supposed to follow
and which in fact it followed more in form than in spirit,
as is generally the case with deliberate imitations.

'The Green Mirror,' which resumed the series of 'The
Rising City,' was again a study of London life, with a
tyrannical mother, entrenched in family tradition and,
like the Duchess, ultimately defeated, as its central figure.
It is remarkable as an analysis of a small section of the
upper middle class in England, but suffered somewhat in

interest from the restriction of the field and the lack of vitality of all but the principal character.

Walpole's production after the War hardly fulfilled the promise of his beginnings. 'The Secret City' is a further outcome of his Russian experiences, but the Russian situation had changed so astonishingly during the time he was engaged on the novel as to rob it of all but temporary interest. 'Jeremy' and 'Jeremy and Hamlet' are clever and amusing tales of boyhood. 'The Captives' is a careful study of one of those obscure religious communities which are still a feature of English life in its back-eddies. ' 'The Young Enchanted' is a definite effort to deal with postwar England and the point of view of the younger generation; incidentally Walpole brings back his old hero, Peter Westcott, and leaves him with the promise of a happy ending to all his troubles. In both the novels last mentioned, Walpole shows an increasing tendency to romance in characterization and incident.

'The Cathedral' is a greater work, both in achievement and in promise. In it Walpole reveals to us the life of "the Close" with a sympathetic and critical insight that need not fear comparison with Anthony Trollope. "Polchester" reminds one at times of Durham or Truro or Canterbury, though it is none of these; it is a city devised by the novelist's imagination to make clear and real to us the inner workings of English ecclesiastical society. The novel is something more than "a study in place," to use the phrase by which the author described some of his earlier work; it has a centre of spiritual interest, and its "treatment" would have delighted the heart of Henry James. Without ever forgetting that the novelist's first duty is to tell a story and to make his characters live, Walpole implicitly suggests the gravest danger of ecclesiastical institutionalism—the danger that the Cathedral may become an end in itself instead of a means, something that comes between the worshipper and God, even to the very clergy who serve in it an obstacle instead of a help to the life of the spirit.

'The Cathedral' was—not very successfully—dramatized in 1932, and in the intervening decade Walpole put out a number of novels, most of them inferior to his earlier work. The series begun with 'Rogue Herries' in 1930 recaptured popular favour to some extent, but as a novelist Walpole did not hold his own against younger competitors. By way of consolation, he was exceedingly successful as a lecturer and journalist, and became very well known, in both capacities, to the American public.

GILBERT CANNAN (1884–   )

Gilbert Cannan was educated at the University of Manchester and King's College, Cambridge, read for the Bar, and served a brief apprenticeship to the writer's craft as dramatic critic for the London 'Star,' 1909–10. He was also engaged in the translation (1910–13) of 'Jean Christophe' by Romain Rolland, who, along with Samuel Butler, of whom Cannan published a critical study in 1915, had considerable influence upon his original novels. In the critical study of Butler he sets forth his own ideas of what the English novel should be: "Irony is one of the essential ingredients of your true novel, which is a special species distinct from the romance, and begins with the application in 'Don Quixote' of irony to romance. A novel is an epic with its wings clipped, that is, with its action and characters viewed ironically. The modern story in which action and characters are viewed sentimentally is not, properly speaking, a novel at all. . . . As for the story in which action and characters are regarded only in relation to political and sociological considerations, that is a fearful wild-fowl, wingless, featherless, strange and indecent."

As to form, he says more specifically elsewhere: "The happy, leisurely technique of Fielding is unsuited to the purposes of the modern novel. The French technique is too rigorous, the Russian too large for our insular temper. Besides, as we are insisting upon our character and striving to retrieve it, all that we learn or borrow must be assimilated to it. Easy imitation lends itself too readily to our deplorable sentimentality, and adds to our enormous pile of too-easily-written books. . . . Our own writers are either too near their emotions or too near their facts. They cannot arrange both in due proportion in their fable, yet they labour with such astonishing zest and hopefulness that it is not unreasonable to be sanguine as to the creation of a form and a technique which will make it possible for a whole generation to produce richly."

Cannan tried the Butler manner in 'Little Brother,' 'Old Mole' and 'Old Mole's Novel,' without any great success, for he had not Butler's stock of original ideas or his quizzical humour, but in 'Round the Corner,' although it has an obvious relation to 'The Way of All Flesh,' he achieved a more independent and original piece of work, conscientious, if not inspired. He was much more successful in 'Mendel,' though here again there is an unconcealed indebtedness to 'Jean Christophe,' which is more than once referred to in the course of the book. But in this instance Cannan surpassed his model, avoiding the *longueurs* of the French original and keeping the talk about art within much severer bounds than Jean Christophe's interminable divagations about music. Cannan's young Jewish painter is also a more original conception than Romain Rolland's hero, and his father, mother and brothers are all admirably realized. The arrival of this family of Polish Jews in London and their settlement in Whitechapel is wonderfully described, and their attitude to the London life they touch only at a few points (chiefly of pain and discomfort) is consistently maintained throughout. They are weird people, according to English notions, and yet Cannan has made them entirely comprehensible, and even likeable, especially the absolutely Jewish father and mother. The half Jewish children become less sympathetic; the hero's character is very carefully worked out, with its oriental passion only veneered by the manners and ideas he acquires from the English people he meets in his artistic career, but in vitality and solidity the figure of the mother, with her strong affection, limited ideas, and shrewd observations, is the masterpiece of the book.

'Pugs and Peacocks' is the first of a series (continued in 'Sembal') dealing with the distracted state of English society during and after the War "not from any political or sociological point of view, but to discover the light thrown upon human nature by abnormal events and conditions." The first novel of the series, in spite of its fantastic title, is an ambitious and serious study of a group of conscientious objectors, whose idiosyncracies are set forth with underlying sympathy, but not without a good deal of pungent humour. The hero is a Trinity College (Cambridge) don, a distinguished mathematician, of aristocratic connections, who goes to prison for a technical breach of the law against correspondence with Germany. The parallel with a well-known Cambridge philosopher is uncomfortably close, and no doubt other identifications of the "Liberty Defence" Association could be made; in any case these "queer" characters, with their strange mixture of sincerity and the desire to advertise themselves at other people's expense, are strongly realized.

There was a notable falling off in Cannan's later work in fiction and in the public interest in it; perhaps more than any other member of this group he failed to fulfil the promise of his early achievements.

COMPTON MACKENZIE (1883–   )

Compton Mackenzie, whose parents were well known and highly esteemed under their stage names of Edmund Compton and Virginia Bateman, showed early signs of literary versatility. He had become an editor (of the 'Oxford Point of View') before he left Magdalen College in 1904, and within a few years after had produced a comedy, published a volume of poems, and written an Alhambra revue. After his marriage he retired to Cornwall, and from this rustic seclusion sent his first novel, 'The Passionate Elopement,' to one publisher after another until it was accepted in 1911 and scored an immediate success. It is "an eighteenth century exercise in concentration and flexibility," and gives little hint of the very different style and manner he adopted in 'Carnival.' This is a realistic study of the life and character, especially in her childhood and youth, of a London ballet girl, conducted with admirable skill and verve until the author whisks her away from the glare of the footlights to meet an untimely death by the Cornish sea. There seems no call or excuse for this hurried ending, as the character might just as well have been taken over, as

some of the others were, into the author's subsequent
work. His plan of detailed realistic incident demands extensive space, and though it is difficult to bring a novel
written on this scale to a satisfactory conclusion, sudden
death is not a solution of the problem. The story really
breaks into two parts, and the second part is out of
proportion and out of tone with the first.

In 'Sinister Street' the novelist took a much larger
canvas and found himself more at ease. The two parts
relate with abundant detail the childhood and youth,
school days and love affairs of Michael and Stella Fane,
the offspring of an irregular union in the English upper
class. The development of the characters of the two
children under their peculiar social conditions is wonderfully done, and the conflict in Michael's nature between
the sensualist and the ascetic is movingly presented. 'Guy
and Pauline' is a detached idyll arising out of Michael's
life at Oxford, but even at the end of this third novel the
young people, after rich and varied experiences, are left
still at the beginning of their careers. The author's task
was twice interrupted, in 1913 by a physical breakdown,
which drove him to Capri for a rest, and in 1915 by
volunteering for the ill-fated expedition to the Dardanelles. In 'Sylvia Scarlett' he made a fresh start, with
an entirely new set of characters, but about halfway
through the book the old ones begin to come back again,
and by the end it is evident that the real crisis in the lives
of Michael Fane and Sylvia Scarlett is still to come. It
does come in 'Sylvia and Michael,' which rounds out the
series, with the help of a minor appendix in 'The Vanity
Girl.'

The detailed method adopted by Compton Mackenzie
has obvious dangers, and he does not altogether escape
them. He has inexhaustible inventiveness of incident,

but his versatility betrays him at times into the irrelevant and the insignificant—not the loose, easy-going scheme of the Russians, which is not at all motiveless, but the merely episodical manner of Smollett, the multiplication of incident for its own sake. Take for instance the battle royal between two of Sylvia's early lovers, in the course of which Danny Lewis knocks Jay Cohen into a slop-pail: "Danny kicked off the slop-pail, and invited Cohen to stand up to him; but when he did get on his feet, he ran to the door and reached the stairs just as Mrs. Gonner was wearily ascending to find out what was happening. He tried to stop himself by clutching the knob of the baluster, which broke; the result was that he dragged Mrs. Gonner with him in a glissade which ended behind the counter. The confusion in the shop became general: Mr. Gonner cut his thumb, and the sight of the blood caused a woman who was eating a sausage to choke; another customer took advantage of the row to snatch a side of bacon and try to escape, but another customer with a finer moral sense prevented him; a dog, who was sniffing in the entrance, saw the bacon on the floor and tried to seize it, but getting his tail trodden upon by somebody, he took fright and bit a small boy, who was waiting to change a shilling into coppers." In the midst of the hubbub, Sylvia makes her escape, but one fails to see what all this has to do with the development of her character or what influence it has on her future career. It may excite the laughter of the groundlings, but it makes the judicious grieve, for the author had shown himself capable of better things. 'Sinister Street' was a very solid and remarkable accomplishment for a novelist of Compton Mackenzie's years and experience, and it seemed a pity for so fine a talent to waste itself on such mere *tours de force* as 'Poor Relations' and 'Rich Relatives.'

'The Altar Steps' is a study of the Anglo-Catholic move-ment in the Church of England, centred in the life-history of a boy, who, at the age of fifteen, vows himself to the priesthood, and on his seventeenth birthday is vouch-safed what the author describes as "the miracle of St. Mary Magdalene's intervention" in the summary taking-off, by the fall of her image, of the blasphemous and too ardent lover of a girl the young hero admires. Up to the point of this crudely melodramatic episode, Mark Lidder-dale's boyhood is charmingly recounted, with many de-lightful touches of humour, and the novelist holds the scales fairly even between the Anglo-Catholic party and its opponents, though his sympathies are obviously on the side of his hero's faith.

The character of Mark Lidderdale is carefully and sympathetically developed, not only in his youth, but in the further unfolding of the inner life and struggles with the world in 'The Parson's Progress.'

ALDOUS HUXLEY (1894–)

Aldous Huxley was born about a decade later than the group whom Henry James called the "new novelists," and he arrived at maturity just in time to feel and express the disillusionment that accompanied and followed the War. He was the grandson of the Victorian scientist, Thomas Henry Huxley, and the grandnephew of Matthew Arnold; his father, Leonard Huxley, was editor of the 'Cornhill Magazine,' and his mother's sister, Mrs. Humphrey Ward, was a famous novelist in her day. He had, as he himself put it, "a perhaps excessively intellectual upbringing," and (again to use his own phrase) he "was very conventionally educated at Eton and at Oxford," where he studied English literature under that most stimulating of teachers, Professor Walter Raleigh.

It is no wonder that Aldous Huxley showed a precocious literary gift, and shared with Rupert Brooke the credit (or discredit) of introducing a note of youthful cynicism into Georgian poetry. Brooke was a little older, and the cynical note is obvious in his 'Poems' of 1911; Huxley published his first volume of poems five years later, but the combination of cynicism with a cold intellectual sensuality in 'Leda' (1918) was new and attracted attention. The same notes were sounded again in Huxley's early novels from 'Crome Yellow' to 'Point Counterpoint,' in which the concrete and detached presentation of sexual indulgence, robbed of all romance, gave many readers the impression that he was not condemning but condoning the moral laxity of the society he depicted with so much sardonic humour. It was not until he published 'Brave New World' (1932) that it was generally realized that he was a keen satirist of the follies and vices of his age, and that his satire involved, if not ideals, at any rate moral or intellectual standards as a background against which popular imbecilities and fashionable extravagances were displayed. The 'Brave New World' of the ironical title is modern mechanical civilization as it seems to the novelist likely to develop in the next two or three centuries. The phrase is Miranda's ejaculatory expression of admiration in 'The Tempest' when for the first time she set eyes on men other than her father and her lover. Shakespeare knew that the western world Miranda admired in her ingenuous ignorance had its Calibans as well as Prosperos, and its drunken suitors and treacherous conspirators as well as its handsome lovers and wise counsellors. So, the satirist points out to us, the Utopia of modern science and industry, when it is achieved in the materialized millennium still to be, will not be at all what modern scientists and industrialists imagine. Looking forward two or three centuries, Huxley forecasts a world highly mechanized and scientifically controlled, but intellectually, morally, and spiritually little (if at all) in advance of the England of Shakespeare.

Ford is the Messiah of the new religion, — its votaries say "in the year of Our Ford," ejaculate "Fordy," "By Ford," and so on. Mechanization is perfect—everyone has his own helicopter—but literature, art, and morals have gone to the dogs. It is an indecency to have a mother, and fathers are unknown—babies are produced in bottles—but sexual promiscuity is universal—"everyone is for everyone." Democracy has given place to absolute despotism administered by experts, the "technocracy" of modern industrialism. In accordance with modern psychology—or some of it—children are "conditioned" before birth and after it educated (in their sleep) to be of Class A (Alphas), and so on down to Epsilons, who do the dirty and menial work not yet performed by machinery. They like their work (seven and a half hours a day) and their amusements—games and unrestricted promiscuity and the "feelies"—the last an emotional debauch by means of the tactile and olfactory nerves which has supplanted the movies and the talkies; and if they should become discontented a dose of *soma*—a drug which gives the exhilaration of intoxication without the subsequent headache—puts everything right again. The hours of labour might be cut in half, but it is found that the manual workers do not know what to do with excessive leisure and take to drinking too much *soma*. Literature is strictly censored and opinions that produce unrest are barred. "Happiness and stability," not truth and beauty, are the watchwords of the new regime. "Mass production demanded the shift." You can make all the people healthy and happy, in a material way; but not wise, or good. "Industrial civilization is only possible when there's no self-denial. Self-indulgence up to the very limits imposed by hygiene and economics. . . . Chastity means passion, chastity means neurasthenia. And passion and neurasthenia mean instability. And instability means the end of civilization. You can't have a lasting civilization without plenty of pleasant vices."

Huxley's aim was to "arrive technically at a perfect fusion of the novel and the essay." It was in this fashion that Fielding in the eighteenth century attempted to give form to the embryonic formlessness of the yet undeveloped English novel; but Fielding kept his essays clearly separated from and almost independent of his story; and the reader who is pursuing only the story may skip the essays with impunity. In Huxley's novels the essays are incorporated in the story—fused with it—and the reader must swallow the gilt with the gingerbread. Huxley is a much better essayist than a novelist, and though the satiric novel gives him a wider opportunity to present concrete examples of passing follies without assuming too openly the attitude of the moralist, the more intelligent reader would prefer his essay unencumbered by the ornamental envelope of fiction, and the ordinary devourer of novels finds the philosophic element either boring, or bewildering, or both.

Perhaps the most successful compromise Huxley has achieved between narrative and satire is in his travel books. He travels widely and brings to the countries he visits a lively curiosity, a pungent wit, intellectual keenness, astonishing erudition, and moral earnestness—something more than the "passionate misanthropy" which some critics have regarded as his chief characteristic. He attempts to preserve an attitude of detachment from conventional standards, but it is obvious that he has standards, for he does not hesitate to condemn directly, or indirectly by scathing irony, the shortcomings of his own age. Thus, on a voyage in the Pacific, a wireless bulletin in the ship newspaper informed him that "Mrs. X. of Los Angeles, girl wife of Dr. X. aged 79, has been arrested for driving her automobile along the railroad track, whistling like a locomotive." The consequent domestic differences of Dr. and Mrs. X. were for a day or two made known to every traveller on all the oceans of the world. Then suddenly, by the caprice of the anonymous powers which purvey wireless news, "the name of Mrs. X. no longer rippled out toward Aldebaran and the spiral nebulæ," but all the world which cared to listen was informed that "Bebe Daniels had fallen off her horse and received contusions." "Faraday and Clerk Maxwell," comments the essayist, "had not lived in vain. . . . The modern civilization of the West, which is the creation of perhaps a hundred men of genius, assisted by a few thousand intelligent and industrious disciples, exists for the millions, whose minds are indistinguishable in quality from those of the average humans of the paleolithic age. The ideas of a handful of supermen are exploited so as to serve the profit and pleasure of the innumerable subtermen, or men *tout court*. The contemporary cave man listens in on instruments which he owes to the inspired labors of superior and, by comparison, divine intelligences. Negroid music shoots across the void into his ears, and the wisdom of such sages as Dr. Frank Crane; racing results, and bedtime stories, and the true tale of a young Mrs. X. of Los Angeles. The fire of Prometheus is put to the strangest uses. Gods propose, men dispose. The world in which we live may not be the best of all possible worlds: it is certainly the most fantastic."

Aldous Huxley is clearly one of "the spirits who deny." He has no faith in the ancient religions or in new nostrums. If it is objected to his onslaught upon mechanical industrialism that the evil consequences he foresees will be prevented by the education of the masses and the production of a superior race, he retorts that the proof of the educational pudding is in the eating. "If by some miracle the dreams of the educationists were realized and the majority of human beings began to take an exclusive interest in the things of the mind, the whole industrial system would instantly collapse. Given modern machinery, there can be no industrial prosperity without mass production. Mass production is impossible without mass consumption. Other things being equal, consumption varies inversely with the intensity of mental life. A man who is exclusively interested in the things of the mind will be quite happy (in Pascal's phrase) sitting quietly in a room. A man who has no interest in the things of the mind will be bored to death if he has to sit quietly in a room. Lacking thoughts with which to distract himself, he must acquire things to take their place; incapable of mental travel, he must move about in the body. In a word, he is the ideal consumer, the mass consumer of objects and of transport."

Hugh I'Anson Fausset, in a review published in the 'Manchester Guardian' of February 12, 1932, commenting upon Aldous Huxley's "characteristic inability to believe really in anything," says: "There is nothing which he cannot appreciate intellectually or fancifully conceive. But there is also nothing which he can imaginatively affirm. Consequently his relation to life is one of constant revulsion. He is at once allured and repelled by science or sex, the primitive or the artificial, romanticism or religion. And his treatment of each is falsified by this revulsion. He can only exploit his power destructively or as a means to exceedingly witty entertainment, as he does in this book. It fails both as satire and romance because it is controlled by no inward conviction. The dread of sentiment and the habit of disillusionment are too strong for him. It is easier to exploit the possibilities of mental death than to meet the demands of creative life."

VIRGINIA WOOLF

Virginia Woolf belongs, by right of ability and of ancestry, to the group of intellectuals known in London as the Bloomsbury school. Her father was Sir Leslie Stephen, one of the best Victorian essayists, the editor of the 'Cornhill Magazine' and of the 'Dictionary of National Biography.' Her mother, who was connected with the brilliant Prinsep family, was also a writer. Her sister, Vanessa, is an artist, and married Clive Bell, the critic. Her half-brother is Gerald Duckworth, the publisher, and H. A. L. Fisher, Master of New College, Oxford, is a cousin. With her husband, Leonard Woolf, who is a well-known publicist, she collaborated in two of her early stories.

Brought up in this cloistered academic environment, and hampered by ill-health, Virginia Woolf had little contact with the rude facts of life; but she had free access to classical literature, in any language in which she chose to read it. Off-hand phrases in her essays such as "Every second Englishman reads French" and "Ladies desire Mozart and Einstein" indicate a standard of intellectual interest confined to a very small circle. She began her professional work as a writer for the London 'Times Literary Supplement,' the most erudite and the least popular of the English weeklies, and after her marriage she was actively concerned with her husband, first at Richmond, on the outskirts of London, and afterwards in Bloomsbury, near the British Museum Library and the University of London, in the publication by the Hogarth Press of the work of the leading intellectuals of the younger school of poetry, fiction and philosophy. Writing for various periodicals and publishing a small volume of short essays, she became known soon after the War as a keen critic with a brilliant style, classical tastes, and advanced views, her sympathies lying more often with the English writers of the eighteenth century than with those of the nineteenth.

In fiction her favourite authors were Laurence Sterne and Jane Austen. Her first novels were studies of cultivated English middle-class life, with little incident and well-regulated passion, in the manner of Jane Austen; the characters were clearly and delicately, but not powerfully drawn, and seemed lacking in vitality. 'The Voyage Out'—said to have been done when the writer was twenty-four, but not published till 1915—is the story of a young girl's first leaving home for a foreign country, her engagement and early death. 'Night and Day' (1919) has even less movement, being mainly concerned with the deliberately correct relations to each other of five young people, three women and two men, who become engaged to the wrong partners in the dance of life, gradually disentangle themselves, and join up with the right ones, a single young woman being necessarily left over to concern herself with disinterested political agitation on behalf of her sex. But in the early 'twenties Mrs. Woolf gave her mind to a problem which was just then attracting a great deal of attention—the problem of "time" in the novel.

It was not a new problem, for a passage in Aristotle's analysis of Greek tragedy had raised the issue of whether the time of the action should coincide with the time of representation, and the Renaissance critics in Italian, French, and English had discussed the question of dramatic time fully and exhaustively. The employment of narrative instead of representation gave the novelists a larger liberty, and they made ample use of it, extending the time of their stories over months, years, and even generations. Sterne succeeded in making two or three books of 'The Life and Opinions of Tristram Shandy' before he got his hero born, and saw no reason why he should not publish "two volumes of Shandyism every year for forty years to come." Some of the Victorian novelists were hardly less generous with themselves and their readers; but no one attempted before the twentieth century to fill large extents of time with a detailed analysis of the inner life of the principal characters—the psychological analysis of their emotions, thoughts, and impulses. Marcel Proust published the first volume of his huge series 'A la Recherche du Temps Perdu,' 'In Search of Time Past,' in 1913, but it gained little attention till after the War, and Virginia Woolf did not read Proust till 1922. She must, however, have been acquainted with the work of Dorothy Richardson, who had begun to pursue the psychological adventures of her heroine through a series of novels begun in 1915. James Joyce's 'Ulysses', which took 732 pages to unfold the emotional and intellectual reactions of his hero during a single day, was not published till 1922, but parts of it had been printed in the 'Little Review' of April, 1919, and had attracted Virginia Woolf's attention at that time. In sketches published in the same year, she made use of the new method of the "interior monologue" or soliloquy, to exhibit what William James had long before called "the stream of consciousness."

The first novel in which Virginia Woolf used this method was 'Jacob's Room,' published in 1922, but her use of the method is her own—neither that of Proust, nor that of Joyce, nor that of Dorothy Richardson. The closest parallel with Joyce is to be found in her next novel, 'Mrs. Dalloway,' in which the action is also confined to a single day; but otherwise it has little in common with Joyce's manner. Neither 'Jacob's Room' nor 'Mrs. Dalloway' made any great impression on the public, but with her next novel, 'To the Lighthouse,' the name of Virginia Woolf began to make itself known to the general reader. The Ramsay family—in which the parents have been identified with Virginia Woolf's own father and mother—are a more interesting and lifelike group than any she had yet dealt with, and the movements of their spiritual consciousness are indicated with subtlety but without so much subtlety as to make it too difficult for the general reader to understand. The plot, such as it is, is conveyed in a few brief factual statements, enclosed by the author, for the greater convenience of the average reader, in square brackets; the following are examples:

"Mr. Ramsay, stumbling along a passage one dark morning, stretched his arms out, but Mrs. Ramsay having died rather suddenly the night before, his arms, though stretched out, remained empty."

"Prue Ramsay, leaning on her father's arm, was given in marriage. What, people said, could have been more fitting? And, they added, how beautiful she looked!"

"Prue Ramsay died that summer in some illness connected with childbirth, which was indeed a tragedy, people said, everything, they said, had promised so well."

"A shell exploded. Twenty or thirty young men were blown up in France, among them Andrew Ramsay, whose death, mercifully, was instantaneous."

This device relieved the author of the necessity of narrating external incidents, (for which Virginia Woolf has neither inclination, nor, it would appear, any great ability) and left her free to follow her bent for psychological analysis and subtle allusion.

'Orlando' was the success of the season 1928–9, and established Virginia Woolf's reputation. Instead of restricting the time of the action to one day, as in 'Mrs. Dalloway,' it extends it to more than three centuries, from early in the reign of Queen Elizabeth to the twelfth stroke of midnight, October 11, 1928. Orlando, the character running through the whole, is identified in her changing modes (including that of sex) with leading members of the Sackville family from Thomas Sackville, a favourite courtier of Queen Elizabeth and part-author of the first English tragedy, to Victoria Sackville-West, a personal friend of Virginia Woolf's and herself an author of poems and novels of modern life, notably 'The Edwardians,' 'All Passion Spent,' and 'A Family History.' In real life she is the wife of Harold Nicolson, son of Lord Carnock, and a well-known literary critic; her poem 'The Land' is quoted as written by Orlando, and her portrait appears in the novel as that of Orlando in one of her later phases. Knole Castle, the ancestral home of the Sackvilles, which dates back to the fifteenth century or earlier, with its seven large courts (one for each day in the week), 52 staircases, and 365 windows, is pictured again and again in 'Orlando' as the main scene of the story. The novel, though it is ironically called a biography, is really a fantastic celebration of the great House of Knole with allusions to the adventures and achievements of its most notable inhabitants. As the Sackvilles have figured, from one generation to another, in the diplomatic, political, literary, and scandalous chronicles of England, there was abundant opportunity for Virginia Woolf to display her wit and her learning, as well as to bring back to life the shadowy scenes and personalities of the past.

'The Waves' (1931) is a still more ambitious attempt to convey the movement of life, or of a group of lives, without having recourse to the worn expedient of an ordered narrative. The idea of the title is that of Meredith's lines at the end of 'Modern Love':

> In tragic hints here see what evermore
> Moves dark as yonder midnight ocean's force,
> Thundering like ramping hosts of warrior horse,
> To throw that faint thin line upon the shore!

The time element in 'The Waves' is indicated by the rising of the sun in the childhood of the six characters, its attainment of its full height as they reach maturity, its setting as they too decline; the waves are the symbol of the passions that move them, calm and blue in their childhood, swift in their youth, and angry in their maturity; at the end "the waves broke upon the shore." The characters are a group of six children—three boys and three girls—and one character outside the group, the Percival they all admire, whose death in India is in a sense the catastrophe of the story. There is no connected narrative, no dialogue, not even a clear record by an individual character such as might be written in a letter or entered in a diary—merely a series of "interior monologues" setting forth the mood, motives, or point of view of each character at a certain moment as interpreted by their creator, just as Shakespeare in the soliloquies of Hamlet and Macbeth puts in his own imaginative language the thoughts and emotions he ascribes to those characters in a particular situation. The difference is that Virginia Woolf's whole story, such as it is, is revealed by these soliloquies, which include a necessary minimum of the element of narrative, conveyed by inference rather than told directly.

It is no wonder that the critics were puzzled, even as to the classification of 'The Waves.' Is it a novel or a prose poem? One says it is "a novel of first importance, one of the few which have come in our own day with so much as a small chance to survive the rigorous test of time." Another says it is not a novel at all, but "a kind of symphonic poem with themes and thematic development in prose. . . . The texture of the prose is a warp of sensory impressions woven into woof of poetical abstraction." The last sentence is a plausible explanation of the fact that the children in their soliloquies use words no child would employ; one speaks of a bush under which they were telling stories as "lit by pendent currants like candelabra."

But whether 'The Waves' is a new and significant development of the novel, or merely "a jumping-off place" from it does not greatly matter. The method is new, but its difficulty does not arise altogether from its novelty; it must always be, from its inherent conditions, a difficult method, even for the intelligent reader. Gerald Gould, who has been reviewing Georgian novels ever since they began, expresses the opinion that "a reader gifted with exceptional memory and concentration . . . might, with firm labour, disentangle the individualities presented, and

keep them sufficiently sharp and clear to obtain a retro-
spective excitement." The question is whether the re-
sultant thrill would be exciting enough to repay the labour
of concentration and recollection. Certainly there are
few to whom it would be an easy task. And without accepting the Tolstoy dictum that all great literature appeals
directly to the common people, one feels that a literary
work that only a very select few can understand has not
a great chance of survival. Robert Herrick, one of the
foremost American novelists and a critic of unusual
knowledge and acumen, in a review of Virginia Woolf's
novels generally sympathetic in tone, nevertheless regards
her work as presenting a "multiple reflection of a dying
race, a twilight of small souls," and fears that "her
progress from concern with the dreary particulars to her
forlorn universals is but the rationalization of the intellectual in face of futility."

It is hardly possible to discuss the achievement of
Virginia Woolf in simple terms, for her work is new
and strange and elusive in its significance. It may be
that she is trying to force into the novel, which has
hitherto depended for its interest mainly upon its narrative framework, an intellectual content it is not capable
of conveying. She is certainly much more at her ease in
such critical essays as are included in the first and second
'Common Reader' or such flashes of original wit as 'Mr.
Bennett and Mrs. Brown' and 'A Room of One's Own.'
It must be left to the future to decide whether her contribution to the development of the novel is a renewal
of an outworn form of fiction or merely an eccentricity—
a yielding to the temptation to gratify the craze for
novelty. But it can hardly be doubted that her contributions to literary criticism are of permanent value and
interest, both for the brilliance of their style and for

their sympathetic insight into the lasting qualities of the authors she admires. Her power of appreciation, though not always extending to her immediate predecessors, is, for the mass of English literature, both liberal and enthusiastic.

BIBLIOGRAPHY

D. H. LAWRENCE

NOVELS

1911   'The White Peacock.'
1912   'The Trespasser.'
1913   'Sons and Lovers.'
1915   'The Rainbow.'
1920   'Women in Love.'
       'The Lost Girl.'
1922   'Aaron's Rod.'
1923   'Kangaroo.'
1926   'The Plumed Serpent.'
1928   'Lady Chatterley's Lover.'

SHORT STORIES

1914   'The Prussian Officer.'
1922   'England, My England.'
1923   'The Captain's Doll,' 'The Fox,' and 'The Ladybird.'
1925   'St. Mawr.'
1928   'The Woman Who Rode Away.'
1930   'The Virgin and the Gipsy.'
1933   'The Lovely Lady.'

ESSAYS AND TRAVEL BOOKS

1915   'The Crown.'
1916   'Twilight in Italy.'
1921   'Sea and Sardinia.'
       'Psycho-analysis and the Unconscious.'
1922   'Fantasia of the Unconscious.'
1923   'Studies in Classic American Literature.'
1925   'Reflections on the Death of a Porcupine.'

1927   'Mornings in Mexico.'
1931   'The Man who Died.' (Published in a briefer form in the 'Forum,' 1928, as 'The Escaped Cock.')
       'Apocalypse.'
1932   'Etruscan Places.' (Published in 'World To-day,' 1928.)

PLAYS

1914   'The Widowing of Mrs. Holroyd.'
1920   'Touch and Go.'
1926   'David.'

POEMS

1913   'Love Poems.'
1916   'Amores.'
1917   'Look! We have Come Through.'
1918   'New Poems.'
1919   'Bay.'
1921   'Tortoises.'
1923   'Birds, Beasts and Flowers.'
1929   'Pansies.'
1932   'Last Poems.'

BIOGRAPHICAL AND CRITICAL

John Middleton Murry, 'Son of Woman, The Story of D. H. Lawrence,' 1931.
Aldous Huxley (Ed.), 'The Letters of D. H. Lawrence, 1932.
Mabel Dodge Luhan, 'Lorenzo in Taos,' 1932.
Catherine Carswell, 'The Savage Pilgrimage, a Narrative of D. H. Lawrence,' 1932.
Ada Lawrence and Stuart Gelder, 'Young Lorenzo, The Early Life of D. H. Lawrence,' 1932.
   There is a bibliography by E. D. McDonald (Philadelphia, 1925 and 1931).

JAMES JOYCE

1907   'Chamber Music.' (Poems.)
1914   'Dubliners.' (Short stories.)
1916   'A Portrait of the Artist as a Young Man.' (Novel.)
1918   'Exiles.' (Play.)
1922   'Ulysses.' (Novel.)

Hugh Walpole

1909	'The Wooden Horse.'
1910	'Marmaduke at Forty.'
1911	'Mr. Perrin and Mr. Traill.'
1912	'The Prelude to Adventure.'
1913	'Fortitude.'
1914	'The Duchess of Wrexe.'
1915	'The Golden Scarecrow.'
1916	'The Dark Forest.'
1918	'The Green Mirror.'
1919	'The Secret City.'
	'Jeremy.'
1920	'The Captives.'
1921	'The Young Enchanted.'
1922	'Jeremy and Hamlet.'
	'The Cathedral.'
1924	'The Old Ladies.'
1925	'Portrait of a Man with Red Hair.'
1926	'Harmer John.'
1929	'Hans Frost.'
1930	'Rogue Herries.'
1931	'Judith Paris.'
1932	'The Fortress.'

Gilbert Cannan

1909	'Peter Homunculus.'
1910	'Devious Ways.'
1910–13	'John Christopher.' (Translation.)
1912	'Little Brother.'
1913	'Round the Corner.'
1914	'Old Mole.'
	'Old Mole's Novel.'
1915	'Young Earnest.'
1916	'Mendel.'
1917	'The Stucco House.'
1918	'Mummery.'
1919	'Pink Roses.'
1920	'Time and Eternity.'
	'Pugs and Peacocks.'

1922 'Sembal.'
1923 'Annette and Bennett.'
1924 'The House of Prophecy.'

COMPTON MACKENZIE

1907 'Poems.'
1911 'The Passionate Elopement.'
1912 'Carnival.'
1913 'Sinister Street,' Vol. 1.
1914 'Sinister Street,' Vol. 2.
1915 'Guy and Pauline.'
1918 'Sylvia Scarlett.'
     'Sylvia and Michael.'
1919 'Poor Relations.'
1920 'The Vanity Girl.
     'Rich Relatives.'
1922 'The Altar Steps.'
     'The Seven Ages of Woman.'
1924 'The Heavenly Ladder.'
1925 'Coral.'
1926 'Fairy Gold.'
1927 'Vestal Fire.'
1932 'Our Street.'

ALDOUS HUXLEY

NOVELS

1921 'Crome Yellow.'
1923 'Antic Hay.'
1925 'Those Barren Leaves.'
1928 'Point Counterpoint.'
1932 'Brave New World.'

ESSAYS AND TRAVEL BOOKS

1920 'Three Critical Essays on Modern English Poetry.'
1926 'Jesting Pilate.'
1927 'Essays New and Old.'
1928 'Proper Studies.'

Virginia Woolf

NOVELS

1915   'The Voyage Out.'
1919   'Night and Day.'
1922   'Jacob's Room.'
1925   'Mrs. Dalloway.'
1927   'To the Lighthouse.'
1928   'Orlando.'
1931   'The Waves.'

ESSAYS AND SKETCHES

1921   'Monday or Tuesday.'
1924   'Mr. Bennett and Mrs. Brown.'
1925   'The Common Reader.'
1929   'A Room of One's Own.'
1932   'The Second Common Reader.'

CHAPTER XI

ESSAYS, JOURNALISM AND TRAVEL

IT may be doubted whether the twentieth century produced any great fiction, but there can be no question
that it produced a large quantity of good writing by
essayists and writers for periodicals—journalism, as it
was practised by Carlyle, Macaulay, Lamb, Hazlitt, and
De Quincey about a century earlier. Evidently the way
in which an essay is first published—whether it is with
other articles in a periodical or by itself in a book—does
not go far towards enabling us to decide whether it is
literature, *i.e.*, writing of permanent interest and value,
or merely journalism, destined for immediate consumption
and the funereal oblivion of newspaper or magazine files.
It is difficult for contemporary opinion to distinguish
between the two classes of writers. Some, who claim only
to be journalists, may leave behind them a body of significant literature, and others, accepted by their contemporaries as leading men of letters, may attract little attention after their immediate vogue has passed.

WILLIAM HENRY HUDSON (1841–1922)

Hudson is one of these writers upon whose place in
the annals of literature it is difficult to make a final de-
cision. Edward Garnett says it was the publication of
'The Naturalist in La Plata' (1892) and 'Idle Days in

Patagonia' (1893), which made Hudson famous; but according to the 'Manchester Guardian' not a single work of his had a circulation of a thousand copies up to 1910, when 'A Shepherd's Life' just topped the thousand mark. A Civil Service pension of £150 was awarded to Hudson in 1901 "in recognition of the originality of his writings on natural history," and it was not till twenty years later—in the year before his death—that he was able to resign it on the ground that he needed it no longer, as his books brought him in enough to live on. In the twenty years intervening he had made two remarkable successes in 'Green Mansions: A Romance of the Tropical Forest' (1904) and 'Far Away and Long Ago: A History of My Early Life' (1918). But to the end he was a writer prized by the discerning few rather than by a large circle of readers.

This lack of widespread popularity was not due to any difficulty of style or of subject: he wrote clearly, easily, and with distinction; and there was nothing esoteric about his subjects or his manner of treating them. There was, however, a certain aloofness in his attitude towards the public, and even in his bearing towards his intimates. This is admitted by his friend Morley Roberts, who thus records his impression of Hudson as he first knew him in 1880: "His height was about six feet three inches when he stood upright, which he rarely did. He wore a short-cropped beard and an untrimmed moustache: his hair in his youth was dark brown and in later years grizzled. His eyes were more or less hazel and deeply set, with heavy brow ridges and well-marked eyebrows: his nose, large and prominent and by no means symmetrical. His complexion was sallow, and his ears, though well-formed, as large in proportion as his hands and feet. As much might be said of thousands. But it was Hudson's whole aspect that showed the man. It marked him with a rare stamp. It was at once kindly and formidable. He looked like a half-tamed hawk which at any moment might take to the skies and return no more to those earth-bound creatures with whom he had made his temporary home. His sight was keen: his curiosity insatiable. As he walked the street he observed everything and everybody. Had he been a draughtsman he could have drawn them from memory. He was as much the field-naturalist in London as in the country. In town, for beasts and birds he substituted the whole race of man. This gave him his air of interested armed detachment."

This reserved bearing and habitual reticence made the simplest facts about Hudson unknown till after his death. He was born near Buenos Ayres, where his father, who came from Massachusetts, had taken up a sheep farm; his grandfather was a Devon man; his mother was of an old Puritan family from Maine. After his father's death in 1868 Hudson sailed for England, and never again left the British Isles; he always counted himself an Englishman and was formally naturalized in 1900. He married an Englishwoman much older than himself in 1876 and for many years they endured a life of privation in London, sometimes almost starving; "for one week they lived on a tin of cocoa and milk." Always of Bohemian tastes and habits, Hudson earned a pittance by writing for magazines and published his first book 'The Purple Land that England Lost' in 1885. It was a failure, and he had little more success with an anonymous romance 'A Crystal Age' (1887), in which he imagined an ideal community given to simple agricultural pursuits and the study of music, living without industrial competition or sexual desire, the business of reproduction being assigned to a Queen Mother and King Father selected by the tribe.

Hudson was next engaged in a descriptive catalogue of the birds of the Argentine Republic, and then wrote a pamphlet for the Society for the Protection of Birds protesting against the use of osprey plumes for aigrettes. But it was 'The Naturalist in La Plata,' and 'Idle Days in Patagonia' that first attracted attention to Hudson's unusual skill and charm as a writer on nature and the life of the open air; and it was not until the turn of the century that the grant of a government pension put him beyond the reach of want.

'Green Mansions,' on which Hudson had been engaged for some years, came out in 1904 and established his reputation as a writer of romance. The figure of Rima, the birdwoman, impressed the popular imagination, and after Hudson's death was made the centre of a sculptured memorial to him at the Bird Sanctuary in Hyde Park. The sculptor was Epstein, and his bold and original work excited a great deal of interest, as well as not a little hostile comment.

Theodore Roosevelt wrote a commendatory introduction for 'The Purple Land' and John Galsworthy one for 'Green Mansions.' Both books became well known in England and in the United States. Hudson's rambles about Hampshire, Wiltshire, and Cornwall revealed him as a lover of the land of his adoption, and a passionate admirer of the simplicity of nature in haunts of birds and men removed from industrialism and urbanization. He devoted his energies and what money he could save to the protection of bird life in England and his efforts in that direction had permanent results; the bird sanctuaries established in various parts of the British Isles are mainly owing to his influence. Success came to him too late for it not to have a bitter tang, but it encouraged him to do some of his best work.

'Far Away and Long Ago,' the account of his youth in the Argentine which he completed when seventy-seven years of age, has an astonishing verve and freshness. It could be said of him as of Moses: "his eye was not dim, nor his natural force abated." John Galsworthy more than once recorded his conviction that Hudson was a "rare and potent force," "a very great writer," and, in his opinion, "the most valuable our age has possessed. He is, of living writers that I read, the rarest spirit, and has the clearest gift of conveying to me the nature of that spirit." "Hudson was the rarest, the most unique, personality of his time, the one whose understanding stepped farthest out of the merely human ring, the one who succeeded best to see the face of nature as it is." What Galsworthy prized in Hudson was his passion for the simpler life of the open spaces, his sympathy for the birds and beasts and simple folk who dwelt there, and his power to reproduce the spirit of such places and their inhabitants. The life of men in cities was alien to Hudson, and whenever he could he fled from it to the wilds where he felt himself at home. He wrote in 'Hampshire Days': "The blue sky, the brown soil beneath, the grass, the trees, the animals, the wind, the rain and stars are never strange to me; for I am in, and of, and am one with them; and my flesh and the soil are one, and the heat in my blood and in the sunshine are one, and the winds and the tempests and my passions are one."

EDMUND GOSSE (1849–1928)

Edmund Gosse was a man of letters before he was a journalist. In the days of the Pre-Raphaelite Brotherhood he was the friend of Rossetti and Swinburne. As a poet, as he said himself, he belonged "to the age of the Franco-German War, of the Introduction of Japanese Art into Europe, of the discoveries of Huxley and Haeckel, and of the Oxford lectures of Matthew Arnold." An article of his in the 'Fortnightly Review' introduced Ibsen to the British public, and he did the 'Life and Letters' of Donne long before that seventeenth century poet became the craze of the twentieth.

But it was not till the twentieth century that Gosse attained that commanding eminence in journalism and literary criticism which he enjoyed in the two decades before his death. His half century of life in the nineteenth was occupied first by a hard struggle for a livelihood and for freedom from the shackles of the narrow environment into which he was born; and secondly, by bitter quarrels in which his reputation as a literary historian did not come off unscathed, though to the next generation they seemed small matters of accuracy in detail and neglect to verify his references, of little account in comparison with his general competence as a critic. Long years of work in the Civil Service and his appointment as Librarian to the House of Lords at length set him free to enjoy the harvest of a life of study of literature and personal acquaintance with the leading figures of the Victorian literary world. His weekly column of literary criticism and reminiscence in the London 'Sunday Times,' continued by him up to the very day of his death, was distinguished (as J. C. Squire testified on behalf of the younger generation) by "qualities of memory, judgment, energy, and grace which were the envy of his juniors."

It was in 1908 that he published 'Father and Son,' the volume of autobiography which established his position in the literary world and secured for him a permanent place in literary history. His father, Philip Henry Gosse, was known to the public as a fellow of the Royal Society and a distinguished zoölogist; in private life he was the leader of an obscure evangelical sect. His attempts to reconcile the results of modern science with a literal interpretation of the first chapter of Genesis seemed merely ludicrous to the next generation, which accepted evolution and had no patience with narrow sectarianism. It was Edmund Gosse's difficult task to exhibit his father as a sincere believer in evangelical religion and himself as an unfortunate child exposed to all the extravagances of religious fanaticism and responding to them with childish fervour. He accomplished this with a revealing frankness which enlisted the reader's full sympathy and with a discerning tact which left the curious combination of his father's mental and spiritual make-up still worthy of respect. As a document of the Victorian transition in religious faith it is unsurpassed, and in combination with its intrinsic interest as a historical record it has literary qualities which should win for it the attention of posterity as a study of a spiritual crisis in a young man's life.

C. E. MONTAGUE (1867–1928)

Of Irish descent, Charles Edward Montague was born near London and educated at the City of London School and Balliol College, Oxford. An article written by him as an undergraduate for the 'Oxford Magazine' attracted the attention of C. P. Scott, editor of the 'Manchester Guardian,' and at twenty-three Montague became one of the group of brilliant journalists whom Scott gathered about

him during his long and distinguished editorship, which
made the name of the 'Guardian' known all over the
world. Montague applied himself strenuously to learn the
craft of journalism and after a dozen years or so became
chief editorial writer; when Scott as a member of Par-
liament was in London, Montague, though still second
in command, was virtually in control of the policy of the
paper. He married Scott's only daughter, made Manchester his home, and was adopted by the community as
one of its leading citizens. In the office of the 'Guardian'
he saw and practised journalism at its best; of what it
might be at its worst he wrote an amusing story, ' A Hind
Let Loose' (1910), described by himself as "only a sort
of overgrown skit, or narrative farce, about various
kinds of rotten journalism." A more serious effort about
one side of his journalistic activity—dramatic criticism—
found its way into book form as 'Dramatic Values'
(1911). He had almost completed a quarter of a century
of useful and distinguished newspaper work when the
outbreak of the War changed the whole current of his
life. He was forty-seven years of age, he had a wife and
seven children, the 'Guardian' had opposed the entrance
of Great Britain into the War, but after the inevitable
step was taken Montague had written editorials advising
young men to serve, and he felt that it would be incon-
sistent for him not to serve himself. He accordingly enlisted as a private, fought in the trenches, was invalided
home, returned to France as an Intelligence officer, and
was assigned to duty as censor and guide to "distinguished
visitors" to the Western front. The end of the War found
him at Mons, and two months later he was back at his
desk in Manchester. His attitude to the War was one of
unusual detachment; he wrote in the midst of the struggle
in his private diary:

Yes, of course it was sin
  And no Christ would say 'Fight
  For the right'—
But we *had* to win.

When the chaplain would bluster and blow
  About laying the rod
  Of God
On the back of 'His foe,'

I knew it was all just a form,
  And there was no fiery sword,
  And the Lord
Was not in the storm.

Yet—to have stood aside
  Hoarding my fortunate life
  With my wife
While the other men died!

Some sort of god, good or bad,
  Would have kept me longing in vain
  To be slain
As I am, if I had.

He was appalled by the waste of human life, the evil passions aroused, the professional jealousy, incompetence, and stupidity of those in high office. He wrote in his diary in the winter of 1916–17: "If we were a band of brothers for one month, I believe we should have won the war. If we could all forget decorations and promotions for six months, it would be over too. If we, outside the trenches, bore what men in the trenches do, it would be over too. If all these miracles happened together, it would be over at once." But of all this he did not breathe a word so long as he wore the uniform. Only when he was a free citizen again, he gave vent to what he had felt—and thousands of others unable to express their thoughts and emotions—in 'Disenchantment' (1922). It was powerfully written and made a great impression both in England and America. The following year he relieved his soul further in a collection of stories of the War entitled 'Fiery Particles'—in allusion to Byron's lines referring to the death of Keats: " 'Tis strange the mind, that very fiery particle, Should let itself be snuffed out by an article." The War gave life and vigour also to the most potent scenes of his novel 'Rough Justice,' published in 1926, the year following his retirement from the 'Guardian' after thirty-five years' service, if one counts in the War years. He retired to a cottage at Burford in the Cotswolds and returned to Manchester only to fulfil his duties as a Governor of the University of Manchester, which had in 1926 given him an honorary degree. It was on one of these official visits that he caught a chill which developed into acute pneumonia and ended in his death in the city of his adoption. He had served it well as a brilliant and conscientious journalist; but he was more than this—more even than a writer of distinction known by his work in England and America—he was one of the great personalities of his time.

H. W. NEVINSON (1856–   )

Like C. E. Montague, Henry W. Nevinson had a streak of Don Quixote in his composition. Born and brought up in conventional surroundings, a home atmosphere of conservative politics and evangelical religion, educated at Shrewsbury School and Christ Church, Oxford, he was unhappy in his youth because of his excessive shyness and inability to make friends. An enthusiasm for Carlyle

led him to the Weimar of Goethe and back to the East
End of London, where he took an active part in the settlement work then fashionable; in Germany he came to the
remarkable conclusion that the elevation of the poverty-
stricken masses in England was to be accomplished by
way of military service, and on his return he drilled the
young men of the East End Settlement with conscientious
ardour; these activities are reflected in two early books on
German literature and one on life in the East End, entitled 'Neighbours of Ours'; but Nevinson had not yet
found his way. It was opened to him in 1897 when he
was sent by the 'Daily Chronicle' to Greece to write letters from the front during the war with the Turks then
impending. The War lasted only thirty days, but it gave
Nevinson an opportunity to show the stuff he had in him,
and on his return to England he was offered a permanent
position on the 'Chronicle,' which he held for the next
half-dozen years. Of this period the chief event was the
Boer War, in which Nevinson served as the 'Chronicle'
correspondent, going through the siege of Ladysmith and
being present at the declaration of peace at Pretoria.

Nevinson had a knack of getting on the unpopular side;
he always took the part of the underdog. During the great
coal strike of 1893 he proclaimed as his principles (amid
general disapproval) the maxims "The Workers are always right" and "The Workers, right or wrong," and he
maintained them during all subsequent controversies,
strikes, and social disturbances. He was, of course, a
Pro-Boer, and had his clothes ripped off his back by a
London mob. He was for the Greeks, Macedonians, and
Albanians against the Turks, for the Russian proletariat
against the Czar, for the natives of Africa and India
against their oppressors, for the revolutionists in Spain
and the rebels in Morocco, for the Home Rulers in Ireland and the suffragettes in England. Where there was an

uprising against injustice, he rushed to its support; where there were helpless victims of oppression, he ran all kinds of risk in their defence. This was notably the case in his account of his journey in the Angola Province of Central Africa and the Cocoa Islands of New Guinea, and his exposure of the Portugese Slave Trade in those parts, published in 1906 under the title 'A Modern Slavery.' His attack upon the abuses in the cocoa trade provoked violent indignation among powerful interests in England, but Nevinson stuck to his guns and had the satisfaction of seeing some of the worst evils corrected.

Adventures fall to the adventurous, and this was not the only occasion on which Nevinson went looking for trouble—and found it. On all these issues he wrote numberless articles and many books, of which the best are his autobiographical series: 'Changes and Chances' (1923), 'More Changes, More Chances' (1926), and 'Last Changes, Last Chances' (1928). During the Great War he was in Belgium, France, the Dardanelles, Salonika, Egypt, Germany after the Armistice, Ireland before the treaty of 1921; at Washington during the International Conference of that year, in Germany during the Ruhr occupation, in Palestine in 1926, and in 1928 in the Near East for the twelfth time. Wherever he found himself he was a knight errant of the Press, ever ready to use his keen intelligence and full knowledge in defence of liberty and justice.

G. K. CHESTERTON (1874–   )

Gilbert Keith Chesterton was born in London and educated at St. Paul's School and the Slade School of Art. He very soon gave up art to write for the newspapers and in 1900 obtained a permanent post on the London 'Daily News.' He is, says one of his biographers, "always the journalist, writing for the day only." But in journalism he stoutly maintained an independent position, writing against Liberalism for a dozen years in the 'Daily News,' which was the leading Liberal organ, and leaving it in 1913 to write in the 'Daily Herald,' a Socialist Labour paper, with the principles of which he had even less sympathy. His attitude was one of reaction against the Radicalism then becoming fashionable. He said of Bernard Shaw: "Most people either say that they agree with Bernard Shaw or that they do not understand him. I am the only person who understands him, and I do not agree with him." He borrowed from Shaw's armoury two of his most potent weapons—half-humorous dogmatic assertion and ingenious paradox. But while Shaw, as a Puritan revolutionist, compared things as they are with things as they might be in the future—to their great improvement —Chesterton, as a Catholic and a Medievalist, compared things with what they had been in the past—to their great disadvantage in the present. This attitude of devotion to unpopular views he maintained with determined courage and brilliant rhetorical effects. When the intellectuals were pressing for more liberal divorce, he was declaring himself against any divorce at all: "Keeping to one woman is a small price for so much as seeing one woman. To complain that I could only be married once was like complaining that I had only been born once. It was incommensurate with the terrible excitement of which one was talking. It showed, not an exaggerated sensibility to sex, but a curious insensibility to it. A man is a fool who complains that he cannot enter Eden by five gates at once. Polygamy is a lack of the realization of sex; it is like a man plucking five pears in mere absence of mind." It is doubtful whether this kind of advocacy was of much service to the cause it defended, but it was amusing to read.

There is hardly any kind of literary composition that Chesterton has not tried—poetry, drama, the novel, the short story, history, biography, criticism, and the essay in all its forms. He wrote a book on 'The Victorian Age in Literature,' and discussed in other volumes Charles Dickens, Robert Browning, Robert Louis Stevenson, Rudyard Kipling, George Moore, Bernard Shaw, and H. G. Wells—all from his personal point of view and in his characteristic style of epigram and paradox. The most considerable body of his work would be classed under the heading of miscellaneous essays—as Stuart Sherman put it, "the bag of a journalistic sportsman who has been shooting contemporary follies as they fly." Among a dozen or so volumes under various titles, 'All Things Considered' may be accounted typical, and of it the author himself says: "I cannot understand the people who take literature seriously; but I can love them, and I do. Out of my love for them I warn them to keep clear of this book. It is a collection of crude and shapeless papers upon current or rather flying subjects; and they must be published pretty much as they stand. They were written, as a rule, at the last moment; they were handed in the moment before it was too late, and I do not think the commonwealth would have been shaken to its foundations if they had been handed in the moment after."

The disadvantage of Chesterton's attitude as compared with that of Shaw is that while the latter attempted to put the clock forward, the former attempted to put it back. Shaw's prophecies of the socialistic millenium may prove platitudinous or absurd, but in either case they are likely to be more interesting to posterity than the praises of a time gone by, which recedes further and further into the past. Still, in his own day, Chesterton was a valiant champion of causes that seemed to most people to be lost, and defended forlorn hopes with courage, tenacity, and a brilliance which was not merely verbal but intellectual. He was a hard hitter—not always without malice, as when he described Thomas Hardy as "a sort of village atheist brooding and blaspheming over the village idiot," but for the most part his extravagances were merely controversial, and for many years his ponderous bulk was one of the most familiar and popular figures in the London world of letters and journalism.

BERTRAND RUSSELL (1872–   )

Bertrand Arthur William Russell, younger son of Lord Amberley, grandson of the Lord John Russell who in 1932 passed the first Reform Act, succeeded to the Earldom in 1931, but this is the least of his titles to distinction. He is the most gifted of that little band of English scientists and philosophers who in recent years have endeavoured to make the most abstruse problems clear to the general public. Inheriting a family tradition of devotion to humanity he was an eager student. "From the age of eleven," he writes, "when I began the study of Euclid, I had a passionate interest in mathematics, combined with a belief that science must be the source of all human progress. Youthful ambition made me wish to be the benefactor of mankind, the more so as I lived in an atmosphere in which public spirit was taken for granted. I hoped to pass from mathematics to science, and lived a solitary life amid day dreams such as may

274 *English Literature in the Twentieth Century*

have inspired Galileo or Descartes in adolescence. But it turned out that while not without aptitude in pure mathematics, I was completely destitute of the concrete kinds of skill which are necessary in science. . . . At the same time I found myself increasingly attracted to philosophy, not, as is often the case, by the hope of ethical or theological comfort, but by the wish to discover whether we possess anything that can be called knowledge. At the age of fifteen, I recorded in my diary that no fact seemed indubitable except consciousness. (Now I no longer make this exception.)"

When he arrived at maturity he devoted himself to the most abstruse and difficult of mathematical problems, the testing of fundamental principles which most students of mathematics take for granted. After twenty years' study, he published in 'Principia Mathematica' (in collaboration with Professor A. N. Whitehead) "all that I could hope to contribute to the solution of the problem. . . . The main question remained of course unanswered; but incidentally we had been led to the invention of a new method in philosophy and a new branch of mathematics."

With the advent of the War he found abstract pursuits impossible, and plunged into international politics. Invited to Harvard University, he was refused permission to sail by the British Government "in the national interest," being already notorious as an ardent pacifist. A pamphlet he wrote for the No-Conscription Fellowship, which was held to be likely to discourage recruiting, led to his imprisonment under the Defence of the Realm Act in 1916 for two months. In 1918 he served a further sentence of six months for an article on the entry of the United States into the War.

After the War, he travelled in Russia and China, was divorced, married again, and, becoming the father of two children, interested himself, with his usual originality and absorption, in the problem of education. 'Education and the Good Life' is probably the best known and most influential of his publications, but he has also written on Bolshevism, the problem of China, industrial civilization, mathematical philosophy, 'The Analysis of Mind,' 'The Analysis of Matter,' 'The ABC of Atoms,' 'The ABC of Relativity, 'Marriage and Morals,' 'The Conquest of Happiness,' and 'The Scientific Outlook.' His remarkable gift of clear exposition has enabled him to bring to the knowledge of a wide public the implications of recent theories of mathematical physics, about which he speaks with distinterested authority; his radical views of public and international questions naturally meet with less general acceptance, but even those who disagree with him on political issues respect him for his independence of mind and his undoubted devotion to what he believes to be the truth.

T. E. LAWRENCE (1888–   )

Among the many remarkable figures thrown up by the War, no Englishman more impressed the popular imagination than "Lawrence of Arabia," or "El Aurans," as he was known to the desert tribes among whom he worked and fought. Born in North Wales, and educated at Jesus College, Oxford, from which he graduated with first class honours, he was able to satisfy by means of a travelling scholarship his youthful dream of exploring Northern Syria. After this he was a member of the British Museum expedition which excavated the Hittite city of Carchemish, on the Euphrates. In 1913 he was engaged in surveying the Sinai peninsula for the Palestine Exploration Fund. When Turkey came into the War he was sent to Egypt to draw maps for the Intelligence Service, but office work was distasteful to him, and none the less so when it was combined with military discipline. In the years before the War he had wandered about Arabia and acquired a knowledge of the language, so that when the Arab revolt developed in 1915 and its leader, Feisal, son of the Sherif of Mecca, applied to the British for help, it was natural that Lawrence should be sent to investigate.

Lawrence gives a characteristic account of his first meeting with Feisal in a desert camp: "Tafas said something to a slave who stood there with silver-hilted sword in hand. He led me to an inner court, on whose further side, framed between the uprights of a black doorway, stood a white figure waiting tensely for me. I felt at first glance that this was the man I had come to Arabia to seek —the leader who would bring the Arab revolt to full glory. Feisal looked very tall and pillar-like, very slender, in his long white silk robes and his brown headcloth bound with a brilliant scarlet and gold cord. His eyelids were dropped; and his black beard and colorless face were like a mask against the strange, still watchfulness of his body. His hands were crossed in front of him on his dagger."

After formal greetings, Feisal asked "And do you like our place here in Wadi Safra?" "Well," answered Lawrence, "but it is far from Damascus." Lawrence knew that the dream of Feisal and of the silent, intent figures who surrounded him, was the establishment of Arab independence with Damascus as its centre. The word "Damascus" fell into their midst like a sword. "There was a quiver. Then everybody present stiffened where he sat, and held his breath for a silent minute. Feisal relieved the strain with a smile and the remark, "Praise be to

God, there are Turks nearer us than that." The two men understood each other and were able to work together. Lawrence was shrewd enough to submit outwardly to Feisal's authority, and in no way to attempt to over-shadow him. But Lawrence knew how to capture the Arab confidence. Riding on a camel and dressed as an Arab wanderer, he made a four-hundred-mile round of the Turkish positions without misadventure and used the knowledge thus acquired to lead a dash across the desert and capture the important seaport of Akaba. Relying on this achievement he visited General Allenby, the new British commander in Egypt, and obtained from him authority to support the Arab revolt with money, with material, and with military advisers, of whom Lawrence himself was the chief.

Lawrence's part, for which he was admirably qualified, was to harass the Turks by leading Arab bands to cut the railway, blow up bridges, destroy armoured trains, and otherwise distract the Turks' attention—and their troops —from Allenby's main attack on Palestine. The policy was successful, and before the end of 1917 Lawrence was able to fly over from Akaba to accompany Allenby on his triumphal entry into Jerusalem.

About this time Lawrence became aware of a complication which he had not foreseen or expected. He liked the Arabs and sympathized with their ambition for an Arab empire centering on the ancient capital of Damascus. But in the chess game of European diplomacy, by a secret pact which later became known as the Sykes-Picot agreement, Damascus had been assigned to the French sphere of influence to balance the award of Mesopotamia to England. Lawrence wished to resign, but his influence on the Arab raiders under Feisal was necessary to the completion of Allenby's plans. Much against his will, Lawrence stayed with his Arab friends until the British and Arab forces entered Damascus and set up a temporary Arab government. He was among the very few—perhaps the solitary individual—in the triumphant throng who knew that the Arab expectations could not be fulfilled. In the book 'Seven Pillars of Wisdom' he wrote years later, he put on record the sense of desolation which possessed him, the overwhelming feeling of bitterness that in being faithful to his own country he had in a sense betrayed his Arab friends.

"Later I was sitting alone in my room working and thinking out as firm a way as the turbulent memories of the day allowed, when the muezzins began to send their call of last prayer through the moist night over the illuminations of the feasting city. One, with a ringing voice of special sweetness, cried into my window from a near mosque. I found myself involuntarily distinguishing his words: 'God alone is great: I testify that there are no gods but God: and Mohammed is his Prophet. Come to prayer: come to security. God alone is great: there is no god—but God.'

"At the close he dropped his voice two tones, almost to speaking level, and softly added: 'And he is very good to us this day, O people of Damascus.' The clamour hushed, as everyone seemed to obey the call to prayer on this their first night of perfect freedom. While my fancy, in the overwhelming pause, showed me my loneliness and lack of reason in their movement: since only for me, of all the hearers, was the event sorrowful and the phrase meaningless."

On Armistice Day, November 11, 1918, Lawrence returned home, and under orders reluctantly took a humble part at Versailles in the framing of the peace treaty which assigned Damascus to the French, who very soon ousted Feisal. Lawrence pleaded the cause of the Arabs as well as he could with the British Government and the British public, and when Winston Churchill took control of the Colonial Office in 1921, he was able to open the way for Arab independence in Mesopotamia with his friend Feisal as King of Irak. It was not an ideal solution, but Lawrence was satisfied that it was the best he could do. He could retire from politics with his mind at rest.

In 1922 he enlisted in the Royal Air Force as a private and became Aircraftsman T. E. Shaw. After some misadventures his book 'Seven Pillars of Wisdom' was published in a very expensive limited edition in 1926; even at what seemed an extravagant price, it made a heavy loss, and to meet this Lawrence edited in 1927 a popular abridgement under the title 'Revolt in the Desert,' which had a very large sale.

The literary merits of Lawrence—and even some features of his personal character and achievements—have been much discussed. Professor A. S. Noad, to whose study of Lawrence the present writer is largely indebted, says of him: "The purely 'travel-book' part of Lawrence's book, the disclosure to western eyes of the strange, narrow, fanatical Arab world, has been done better elsewhere— notably in Doughty's vast 'Arabia Deserta.' As a depicter of famous or interesting personages there are many living today who can outdo him. But what adventurer of similar calibre has left such a record of his thoughts and feelings, not in distant retrospect, but noted in the midst of tingling hours of action? The number of that select company is very small in the whole range of literature."

To Lawrence himself the discussions of what he had written and what he had done must have been largely indifferent. He secluded himself on the northwest frontier of India, and gave his attention to the routine duties of the Air Force and the translation of Homer. His version of the Odyssey appeared in 1932. It seems likely to be classed with that of Samuel Butler as one of the freaks of an eccentric genius whose caprices must remain an enigma to the ordinary run of humanity.

CHAPTER XII

LYTTON STRACHEY

IN the early years of the twentieth century H. A. L. Fisher, an Oxford don, read in the 'Independent Review' a notice of a translation of 'Vauvenargues' over the signature of G. Lytton Strachey. He was impressed by the reviewer's knowledge of French literature, his insight into the French genius, and the skill and precision with which his criticisms were expressed. On inquiry he found that the unknown critic was the son of Sir Richard Strachey, the cousin of the editor of 'The Spectator,' St. Loe Strachey, and a scholar of Trinity College, Cambridge. Later, Mr. Fisher became Minister of Education, President of the British Academy, and Warden of New College, Oxford, but at this time these honours had not yet fallen upon him. He was, however, editor in chief of a modest but meritorious series of handbooks called the 'Home University of Modern Knowledge,' and it happened that about this time the publishers wished to add to the series a small volume on French literature. Their idea was to engage for the task some well-known English authority on French literature, such as Edmund Gosse, but Mr. Fisher persuaded them to give the opportunity to the young Cambridge scholar with whose excellence as a critic of French literature he had been so much impressed.

"I well remember," Mr. Fisher writes, "my first interview with Strachey, a sensitive, ungainly youth, awkward in his bearing, and presenting an appearance of great physical debility, as if he had recently risen from the bed of an invalid. His voice was faint and squeaky. His pale face was at that time closely shaven. The long red beard of Lamb's portrait, which has made him so familiar, was a thing of the future. He was very silent, but uncannily quick and comprehending. I told him that I wanted him to write a sketch of French literature in fifty thousand words, and showed him J. W. Mackail's 'Latin Literature,' with which he was not then acquainted, as a model which he might be content to follow. He assented to my proposal with rare economy of speech, and with none of the usual expressions of diffidence, which an editor is accustomed to hear from an untried author to whom he has offered a task of exceptional difficulty. In a very few months the manuscript of the outlines of French literature was in my hands. It was a masterpiece of imaginative and scholarly appreciation, and an extraordinary achievement for so young a writer."

Naturally, this small handbook, on its publication in 1912, attracted little attention from the general reading public, few of whom would be led to read any book about French literature, even if it did not bear the modest title of 'Landmarks in French Literature,' and present the usual appearance of an educational textbook. Nor did the essays on French and English authors which young Strachey published from time to time in the early years of the century in various literary reviews and periodicals make any particular impression, although when these were gathered together and published as a volume in 1922 under the title 'Books and Characters, French and English,' it was easy to see that the characteristics which Mr. Fisher saw in Strachey's work were there. But the public did not recognize them until Strachey published in

1918 what was really his first book of biography, 'Eminent Victorians.' In addition to scholarly insight and an incisive style, Strachey showed a power to conceive and execute a vivid biographical sketch in a manner which was not unfamiliar to French literature but was almost unknown in English. At the same time he fell in with a tendency which was strongly prevalent at this time, not only in literary but in social and political circles—an inclination to reject the authorities of Victorian life and letters and to subject them to a revaluation which exhibited their virtues and failings in an altogether different perspective. It was the process known in the United States as "debunking," which has become the most popular literary sport of the younger generation during the last dozen years. It would be too much to claim for Strachey that he originated this movement, but he certainly contributed greatly to its popular influence, and in biography he may be fairly regarded, not only as its originator, but as its most successful practitioner.

In 'Eminent Victorians' he took four characters which had been greatly admired and idealized by their contemporaries. The first was Cardinal Manning, who in the latter years of his life had become almost a mystical figure in London society. He was given precedence even of princes and played a leading part in public affairs, especially on questions of labour, politics, and education. He was idolized by the poor and venerated by the rich; his worn, ascetic face and commanding figure impressed those who differed most widely from his opinions on politics and religion. Strachey takes the character and career of Manning and analyzes it with merciless keenness and detachment, telling the story of his long contest with the other English Cardinal, Newman, and suggesting that unscrupulous ambition had perhaps as much to do with

Manning's success as fervent piety and disinterested devotion to the public welfare. In the same spirit he subjects to cold, scientific scrutiny the popular conception of Florence Nightingale, "the Lady with the Lamp," founder of modern nursing, who rescued the British soldier from the unspeakable horrors of the military hospitals in the Crimea. Strachey does not take away from Florence Nightingale's well-established reputation as a ministering angel, but he shows that there was an entirely different side to her character, that she was, in fact, possessed by a demon of energy and organization. Born in a superior situation, she had rejected the comfortable life of love and marriage in the English upper class. When a suitor presented himself, she analyzed the situation with a detached clearness showing an extraordinary knowledge of her own nature. "I have an intellectual nature which requires satisfaction, and that would find it in him. I have a passional nature which requires satisfaction, and that would find it in him. I have a moral, an active nature, which requires satisfaction, and that would not find it in his life." What she wished to do was to found "something like a Protestant sisterhood, without vows, for women of educated feelings." She succeeded, in spite of parental opposition, in obtaining a few months' training as a nurse, and when the London 'Times' war correspondent revealed the disorganization of the military hospitals during the Crimean campaign, she organized a corps of thirty-eight nurses to remedy their deficiencies. From the military authorities, with the exception of the War Minister, Sidney Herbert, she received no encouragement, but violent and obstinate opposition. On one occasion 27,000 shirts sent out at her instance were kept unpacked for three weeks, although the sick and wounded lay half-naked and shivering from want of clothing. Later, in defiance of doctors and generals, she paid for her own supplies and ordered them to be taken out of the Customs House and unpacked on her own responsibility. Her principal opponent was a Dr. Hall who had been made a K.C.B. and resented all criticism of, or interference with, his maladministration; Florence Nightingale said he ought to be called "Knight of the Crimean Burial-ground," and as she did actually succeed in reducing the mortality from forty-two to twenty-two per thousand, there seems to be some justification for the slur upon his title.

Strachey fell with equally merciless rigour upon the popular reputation of another Victorian reformer, Dr. Thomas Arnold, father of Matthew Arnold and head-master of Rugby School, who had re-organized the public school system and given it the form and spirit which still prevail in English secondary education. Strachey pointed out that, excellent as the system might be on the side of manners and even of morals, it left much to be desired on the intellectual side, and had a serious fault in the over-emphasis on athletics. C. E. Montague, who was educated at the City of London School, and W. H. Nevinson, who was a product of the English public school system at Shrewsbury, one of its most renowned centres, offered criticisms of equal pungency which were not resented, perhaps because neither barbed his shaft with the irony which made Strachey's attack upon Arnold hard to forgive and impossible to forget. "The earnest enthusiast who strove to make his pupils Christian gentlemen and who governed his school according to the principles of the Old Testament has proved to be the founder of the wor-ship of athletics and the worship of good form. Upon those two poles our public schools have turned for so long that we have almost come to believe that such is

their essential nature, and that an English public school-
boy who wears the wrong clothes and takes no interest in
football is a contradiction in terms."

Even less pardonable was Strachey's treatment of the
fourth "eminent Victorian," General Gordon, whose heroic sacrifice of his life at the siege of Khartoum had en-
shrined his memory in popular affection. Strachey's profoundly sceptical turn of mind made him quite unable to
appreciate the mystical side of Gordon's nature. He introduces Gordon to his reader as a solitary English gentleman engaged in looking for Biblical sites (including that
of the Garden of Eden) in the neighbourhood of Jerusalem; and then passes to Gordon's suppression of the
Taiping rebellion, led by Hong-siu-tsuen, a Chinese
schoolmaster and a convert to Christianity, in whose fe-
vered brain Evangelical Protestantism had gone through
an extraordinary transformation. "His theogony," says
Strachey, "included the wife of God, or the celestial
Mother, the wife of Jesus, or the celestial daughter-
in-law, and a sister of Jesus, whom he married to
one of his lieutenants, who thus became the celestial
son-in-law; the Holy Ghost, however, was eliminated.
His mission was to root out Demons and Manchus from
the face of the earth, and to establish *Taiping*, the reign
of eternal peace. In the meantime, retiring into the depths
of his palace, he left the further conduct of earthly opera-
tions to his lieutenants, upon whom he bestowed the title
of 'Wangs' (kings), while he himself, surrounded by
thirty wives and one hundred concubines devoted his
energies to the spiritual side of his mission." Strachey's
obvious and half-expressed intention is to parallel the
religious vagaries of Hong-siu-tsuen with those of Gordon
himself, who was employed by the Chinese Government to
suppress them. An exposition, by no means sympathetic, of

Gordon's own highly unconventional beliefs immediately follows, and then an account of his experiences as Governor of Equatorial Africa, the region about the Upper Nile recently annexed by the Khedive of Egypt. All this is by way of introduction to the real story of the rebellion in the Soudan under a fanatical religious leader, the Mahdi, who succeeded in defeating the Khedive's armies and isolating the Egyptian garrison of Khartoum. How Mr. Gladstone's Government was induced to send out Gordon to evacuate the Khartoum garrison, and how Gordon persisted in staying to die with them is one of the strangest chapters in modern political history. Strachey treats it throughout in the spirit of irony, and ends with the satirical comment: "At any rate it had all ended very happily—in a glorious slaughter of twenty thousand Arabs, a vast addition to the British Empire, and a step in the Peerage for Sir Evelyn Baring."

When it became known that the next victim of the acid test was to be Queen Victoria herself, it was generally expected that the conventional figure of the Beloved Queen would suffer severely in the course of the experiment, but when the book was published in 1921, its tone turned out to be not particularly iconoclastic. It was obviously the most ambitious undertaking of Strachey's career, and by his success in it his reputation must stand or fall. It was a supremely difficult task to extricate Victoria's real character and achievement from the mass of conventional appreciation and official documentation in which it was enveloped. But Strachey was unusually well qualified for it by his natural genius and scholarly habit of life, his personal contact with the later years of the Victorian era, and his absolute detachment from Victorian prepossessions and prejudices. In the limitations of the Queen's character and environment he found abundant opportunity for mordant irony, but his general attitude towards his subject is one of sympathy. This is indicated in his comment on Victoria's childish exclamation when she first realized the prospect of her succession to the throne: "I will be good." "The words were something more than a conventional protestation, something more than the expression of a superimposed desire; they were, in their limitation and their intensity, their egotism and their humility, an instinctive summary of the dominating qualities of a life." And as we follow the young queen through the vicissitudes of marriage, maternity, and widowhood until in her secluded authority she becomes an almost mythical embodiment of Victorian ideals and aspirations, we are conscious of her essential greatness in spite of all her shortcomings. So, in her middle life, when the English Court receives a visit from Napoleon III and the beautiful Empress Eugénie, Strachey writes: "Victoria became much attached to the Empress, whose looks and graces she admired without a touch of jealousy. Eugénie, indeed, in the plenitude of her beauty, exquisitely dressed in wonderful Parisian crinolines which set off to perfection her tall and willowy figure, might well have caused some heartburning in the breast of her hostess, who, very short, rather stout, quite plain, in garish middle-class garments, could hardly be expected to feel at her best in such company. But Victoria had no misgivings. To her it mattered nothing that her face turned red in the heat and that her purple pork-pie hat was of last year's fashion, while Eugénie, cool and modish, floated in an infinitude of flounces by her side. She was Queen of England, and was not that enough? It certainly seemed to be; true majesty was hers, and she knew it. More than once, when the two were together in public, it was the woman to whom, as it seemed, nature and art had given so little, who, by the sheer force of an inherent grandeur, completely threw her adorned and beautiful companion into the shade."

By the end of her reign, Strachey notes that while the power of the sovereign had appreciably diminished, the prestige of the sovereign had enormously grown. Victoria took no interest and had no part in the social, political, scientific, and industrial changes which made the Victorian era memorable; but the great majority of the nation prized goodness above every other quality and they recognized that the Queen had kept the promise she made at the age of twelve—to be good. Her sincerity speaks equally in her last message to the nation at the time of the second Jubilee in 1897. "From my heart I thank my beloved people. May God bless them!" "The long journey was nearly done. But the traveller, who had come so far, and through such strange experiences, moved on with the old unfaltering step. The girl, the wife, the aged woman, were the same: vitality, conscientiousness, pride, and simplicity were hers to the latest hour."

Strachey's 'Queen Victoria' was at once recognized as not merely a brilliant performance but a great achievement, and it had a very large sale on both sides of the Atlantic. The author established himself with his mother and sister in Gordon Square, near the house of Virginia Woolf, to whom his greatest work is dedicated. In the remainder of his life he accomplished nothing equal to his 'Queen Victoria.' He waited seven years before putting out 'Elizabeth and Essex' (1928), which (mainly perhaps on the strength of Strachey's previous achievements) attained an enormous sale. It was highly praised, too, by the critics; in the opinion of Dr. J. W. Krutch, it is the work which places Strachey's reputation beyond merely contemporary fame. "It is writing of a kind whose goodness has nothing of mere fashion about it." To others, however, it seemed inferior to 'Queen Victoria'—less sane in judgment, too much affected by the modern craze for psycho-analysis. Elizabeth's character is conceived almost exclusively in the light of a supposed peculiarity in her physical organization. So, she is imagined as "an old creature, fantastically dressed, still tall, though bent, with hair dyed red above her pale visage, long blackening teeth, a high domineering nose, and eyes that were at once deep-set and starting forward—fierce, terrifying eyes, in whose dark blue depths something frantic lurked—something almost maniacal." And in the end Elizabeth's motives for sending Essex to the scaffold are represented to be not reasons of state, anxiety for the safety of her throne or concern for the welfare of her subjects, but a kind of mad sexual jealousy, a fear that as an old and worn woman of sixty-seven she cannot hope to keep a lover of less than half her age. Such a theory seems to belong rather to the realm of sentimental romance than that of sober history.

In his last book, published the year before his death, 'Portraits in Miniature' (1931), Strachey is again seen at his best, but he is dealing with smaller subjects, necessarily on a smaller scale. We have a group of grotesques —half-forgotten people who, but for some oddity, would have been forgotten altogether—and a group of historians of the eighteenth and nineteenth centuries. In the latter group the best portrait is that of Gibbon, whose 'Decline and Fall' is praised as "one of the chief monuments of classic art in European literature. His whole genius was preëminently classical: order, lucidity, balance, precision —the great 'classical qualities'—dominate his work."

Strachey had himself in generous measure these great classical qualities, which distinguish his work from that of his Victorian predecessors. He had also a personal tang of scepticism and cynicism, peculiarly characteristic of his own time. He expressed perhaps more clearly and fully than any of his contemporaries the new standards of value which constitute the revolt from Victorianism. In biography as a literary genre he effected a change of tone and manner which amounted to a revolution; and he remains the ablest exponent of the new form. Among his numerous followers in many tongues not even the best—Philip Guedalla in English, Emil Ludwig in German, and André Maurois in French—have equalled their master in weight of learning, critical acumen, and brilliance of style. If one in a hundred among his imitators had learnt from him the necessity for scholarship, insight, and artistry, we should have less cause to lament the truth of Strachey's epigram: "There are fewer good lives written than spent."

CHAPTER XIII

MASEFIELD AND THE NEW GEORGIAN POETS

THERE is general agreement among the critics that so far the twentieth century is not a great poetic period. The principal poetic achievement of the first decade was 'The Dynasts' (1904–8) by Thomas Hardy, who continued his poetic activity up to his death in 1928; Meredith and Swinburne both survived till 1909, but all these great names obviously belong to the Victorian era. When Masefield succeeded to the Laureateship in 1930, many readers, even students of English literature, would have been unable to say who had occupied the position since the death of Tennyson in 1892. William Archer in the introduction to his survey of the 'Poets of the Younger Generation' (1902), remarked a "general tendency among cultivated people to assume that English poetry has of late entered on a temporary or permanent period of decadence," and he was so far from denying this assumption that all he claimed for the thirty-odd writers included in his review was that they were all "true poets, however small may be the bulk of their work, however unequal its merit." Whether they were major or minor poets he left to the judgment of posterity; and posterity so far has not ventured to promote any one of the 33 to first poetic rank, though (among those who have died since) the work of John Davidson (1857–1909) and Francis Thompson (1859–1907) has stood the test of time. The fact that the lives of both were made miserable by poverty as well as ill-health indicates a lack of appreciation by the contemporary public, which did not find either Davidson's scientific materialism or Thompson's imaginative mysticism to its taste; but the former's 'Fleet Street Eclogues' (1893 and 1896) and 'Ballads' (1894, 1897, and 1899) were in their own way as genuine additions to English poetry as Thompson's 'The Hound of Heaven' (1893), 'Sister Songs' (1895) and 'New Poems' (1897), which had their own little band of convinced and enthusiastic admirers.

But it was not until the new century was well advanced that a more hopeful and appreciative spirit was to be remarked. When the little collection entitled 'Georgian Poetry 1911–12' was issued in the latter year, it was "in the belief that English poetry is now once again putting on a new strength and beauty, and that we are at the beginning of another 'Georgian period' which may take rank in due time with the several great poetic ages of the past." The modest ʼnterprise met with a cordial reception from the public, ʌnd was followed by two other volumes, 'Georgian Poetry 1913–15' and 'Georgian Poetry 1916–17,' not perhaps quite equal to the first endeavour, either in merit or in the impression made on the public, but going far to sustain the spirit of hopefulness the first volume had engendered. Professor Gilbert Murray, in the preface to a similar collection, 'Oxford Poetry 1910–13' (which also had annual successors) spoke (in September, 1913) of the "feeling of vivid expectancy which the Georgian volume raised in many lovers of English verse." This feeling was wide-spread, and it received further encouragement from 'New Numbers' (1914) by Wilfrid Wilson Gibson, Rupert Brooke, Lascelles Abercrombie, and John Drinkwater, the first of a series of collections of verse intended to be published quarterly; but across this brilliant dawn there fell the black shadow of the Great War.

JOHN MASEFIELD (1874–   )

The new poets of the first decade did not form a group coherent or influential enough to be called the Edwardians, but among them there is no question that John Masefield made the most impression on the public. He continued the English poetic tradition from Chaucer to Kipling, and, taking it up at a time when the last-mentioned was enormously popular, he naturally came under the Kipling influence. Some of his earlier ballads, such as 'Cargoes,' have the Kipling tang, but he soon broke away from this to a subtler and less mechanical style which was all his own, having more in common with the melody of Chaucer than with any modern poet. His point of view, however, was entirely modern and democratic, in accordance with the spirit of the time and his own experience of life.

Masefield was born in Ledbury, Herefordshire, and began his connection with the sea on the training ship Conway in the Mersey. Then he worked "before the mast" on the sailing ship Gil Croix, and visited South America and other parts of the world, enduring hardship and enjoying adventures by land and sea. Stranded in the United States in his early twenties, he worked on a Connecticut farm, in a Yonkers carpet factory, and in a bakery in Forty-sixth Street, New York City. Legend has it that he tried to pick up a few coppers by singing in the streets of New York, and served at the bar of a saloon, kept by Luke O'Connor, at the corner of Christopher Street and Greenwich Avenue. But in a newspaper interview given during his visit to New York in 1933 Masefield said that he had never risen to the high rank of bartender. All he did was to wash the glasses: he never served any drinks to customers. He also "fetched up bottles from the cellar, polished the brasswork, and swept the floor." In any case, Masefield had abundant opportunity to make acquaintance with working people in their hours of toil and of relaxation and acquired a store of knowledge which he was to turn to poetical account in later years. Meanwhile, he cherished dreams of writing literature and fed his soul on Malory's 'Morte d'Arthur' and a seventy-five cent copy of Chaucer.

Returning to England, he had the good fortune to fall in with W. B. Yeats, to whose influence and encouragement he was greatly indebted. But while Yeats found his greatest interest in Irish myth and mysticism, Masefield was profoundly English in his modern realism and his love of the sea. His love of the sea is not only a racial instinct, but springs directly from his personal experience, not from any literary influence or tradition. He might have said with his hero Dauber:

> It's not been done, the sea, not yet been done,
> From the inside by one who really knows.

He did it from the inside in 'Salt Water Ballads,' his first volume of verse, and for a long time his sea poems remained his most characteristic achievement. He reproduced the tang, look, and movement of the sea; in the unspeakable beauty of ships he found his first inspiration:

> When I saw
> Her masts across the river rising queenly,
> Built out of so much chaos brought to law,
> I learned the power of knowing how to draw,
> Of beating thought into the perfect line,
> I vowed to make that power of beauty mine.

Beyond and above all this, Masefield realized and rendered the life of seafaring men—not merely their wild romantic adventures on sea and shore—yarns "of ships and mermaids, of topsail sheets and slings," but the hard everyday experiences of the common sailor—it was only here that he found "life and life's romance":

The sailor, the stoker of steamers, the man with the clout,
The chantyman bent at the halyards putting a tune to the
      shout,
The drowsy man at the wheel and the tired look-out.

Others may sing of the wine and the wealth and the mirth,
The portly presence of potentates goodly in girth;
Mine be the dirt and the dross, the dust and scum of the earth!

Theirs be the music, the colour, the glory, the gold;
Mine be a handful of ashes, a mouthful of mould.
Of the maimed, of the halt and the blind in the rain and the
      cold—
Of these shall my songs be fashioned, my tales be told.

He could write of these because he had himself known their experiences—not merely "wild days in a pampero off the Plate" with surf-swimming between rollers, but

Days of labour also, loading, hauling;
Long days at winch or capstan, heaving, pawling;
The days with oxen, dragging stone from blasting,
And dusty days in mills, and hot days masting.

These are the things, he tells us in his 'Biography,' that made him:

Not alone the ships
But men hard-palmed from tallying-on to whips,
The two close friends of nearly twenty years,
Sea-followers both, sea-wrestlers and sea-peers,

> Whose feet with mine wore many a bolthead bright
> Treading the decks beneath the riding light.

To a keen human sympathy with the humble and oppressed, Masefield added, even in his earlier poems, a
delicate sense of beauty and a questioning mind. His
"Seekers" are looking for "the City of God and the haunt
where beauty dwells," and in spite of the "Waste" of
human life, he is confident that "Death brings another
April to the soul." His love poems, 'Her Heart,' 'Being
Her Friend' and 'Born for Nought Else,' have the right
simple charm and music, and so has 'Beauty':

> I have heard the song of the blossoms and the old chant of
>   the sea,
> And seen strange lands from under the arched white sails
>   of ships;
> But the loveliest things of beauty God ever has showed to me,
> Are her voice, and her hair, and eyes, and the dear red curve of
>   her lips.

Masefield might well have been content with the reputation won by his sea poems and ballads; but in 'The
Everlasting Mercy' he attempted an entirely new style.
It is the story of a drunken poacher's conversion as told
by himself. A single stanza will give some idea of the
effects attempted:

> "You closhy put"—
> "You bloody liar"—
> "This is my field."
> "This is my wire."
> "I'm ruler here."
> "You ain't."
> "I am."
> "I'll fight you for it."
> "Right, by damn."

> "Not now, though, I've a-sprained my thumb,
> We'll fight after the harvest hum.
> And Silas Jones, that bookie wide,
> Will make a purse five pounds a side."
> Those were the words, that was the place
> By which God brought me into grace.

This, with the description of the prize fight that follows, shows a great deal of metrical versatility and literary skill, but at times one hardly knows whether the poet is aiming at a burlesque effect, thus:

> Jack chucked her chin, and Jim accost her
> With bits out of the "Maid of Gloster."
> And fifteen arms went round her waist.
> (And then men ask, Are Barmaids chaste?)

The last line may be attributed to the hero of the story (though it is not altogether in character), but the poet must take the responsibility for such rhymes as "is and was—Caiaphas," "honest schism—pauperism," "knows his—disposes," "offence—Testaments," which would only be excusable if the poacher were the author of the poem.

'The Widow in the Bye Street,' like the two long poems that followed it, is in Chaucerian stanza, which Masefield manages with great skill, though he occasionally slips into grotesqueness, rhyming "bastard—lasted," and "Susan's —nuisance" and ending one stanza thus:

> And then swept out repeating one sweet name
> "Anna, O Anna," to the evening star.
> Anna was sipping whiskey in the bar.

And again:

> She sighed, to hint that pleasure's grave was dug,
> And smiled within to see him such a mug.

The tale of Jimmy's love for the faithless Anna and his slaying of her paramour is told with no sparing of plain words, but the attempt to regard this story of murder and sensuality *sub specie æternitatis* is unsuccessful. Like Chaucer, Masefield, moralizes upon destiny:

> So the four souls, ranged, the chessboard set,
> The dark, invisible hand of secret Fate
> Brought it to come to being that they met
> After so many years of lying in wait.
> While we least think it he prepares his Mate.
> Mate, and the King's pawn played, it never ceases
> Though all the earth is dust of taken pieces.

The story fails because its psychology is not deep enough to be interesting; in 'The Everlasting Mercy' the hero tells his own story; here it is the author who narrates, and the loss is hardly made up by the addition of descriptive passages, though some of these are of great beauty:

> All through the night the stream ran to the sea,
> The different waters always saying the same,
> Cat-like, and then a tinkle, never glee,
> A lonely little child alone in shame.
> An otter snapped a thorn twig when he came,
> It drifted down, it passed the Hazel Mill,
> It passed the Springs; but Jimmy stayed there still.

'Dauber' gains the interest of a really attractive central character with a touch of romance and above all it gains the interest of the sea, where Masefield is at home and has room for both his narrative and descriptive powers so that his imagination warms to its task and gives us some of his best work.

In 'The Daffodil Fields' Masefield reverted to a somewhat melodramatic story of rustic love and jealousy ending in mutual slaughter, but the workmanship is fine, and the characters clearly drawn. The Chaucerian stanza is retained, but with the last line an Alexandrine, which takes it part way over to the Spenserian, but falls between the two. There are brilliant passages, but as a whole the poem does not attain the cumulative effect of 'Dauber.'

All four poems attracted a great deal of attention and there was much discussion, praise and dispraise, alike of detail and general conception. It was agreed that they were remarkable, original in their method of treatment and metrical handling, but most, even of the appreciative critics, had reservations, and the general impression was that Masefield could do better work—had indeed done better work in the poems of the sea. The outbreak of the War gave him a great occasion and he rose to it easily and perfectly. 'August, 1914' is not only the best of the numberless poems the War produced, but it is bound to take its place as a classic in the long and glorious history of English poetry. With a few quiet strokes he realized the beauty of the English landscape, enriched by the affection of unknown generations, who, "century after century held these farms" and knew what it meant to answer the summons of War:

> Yet heard the news, and went discouraged home,
> And brooded by the fire with heavy mind,
> With such dumb loving of the Berkshire loam
> As breaks the dumb hearts of the English kind.
>
> Then sadly rose and left the well-loved Downs
> And so, by ship to sea, and knew no more
> The fields of home, the byres, the market towns,
> Nor the dear outline of the English shore.
>
> But knew the misery of the soaking trench,
> The freezing in the rigging, the despair

In the revolting second of the wrench
When the blind soul is flung upon the air.

And died (uncouthly, most) in foreign lands
For some idea but dimly understood
Of an English city never built by hands,
Which love of England prompted and made good.

The grave elegiac mood of 'August, 1914' prepares the reader for the high philosophy of 'Lollingdon Downs.'

What is this life which uses living cells
It knows not how nor why, for no known end,
This soul of man upon whose fragile shells
Of blood and brain his very powers depend.
Pour out its little blood or touch its brain,
The thing is helpless, gone, no longer known;
The carrion cells are never man again,
No hand relights the little candle blown.

He finds no answer to his restless questioning of here and hereafter:

It may be, that we cease; we cannot tell.
Even if we cease, life is a miracle.

Most of all is he puzzled by man:

This atom which contains the whole,
This miracle which needs adjuncts so strange,
This, which imagined God and is the soul.

If its business is not mainly earth, why should it demand such heavy chains to sense?

A heavenly thing demands a swifter birth,
A quicker hand to act intelligence;
An earthlier thing were better like the rose,
At peace with clay from which its beauty grows.

"We are neither heaven nor earth, but men," he concludes, and God is of our own making:

> Let that which is to come be as it may,
> Darkness, extinction, justice, life intense,
> The flies are happy in the summer day,
> Flies will be happy many summers hence.
>
> And when the hour has struck, comes death or change,
> Which, whether good or ill, we cannot tell,
> But the blind planet will wander through her range
> Bearing men like us who will serve as well.
> The sun will rise, the winds that ever move
> Will blow our dust that once were men in love.

After the War, Masefield's gift of narrative poetry woke to new life in 'Reynard the Fox.' First comes the description of the meet, with its lively and tender reminiscences of Chaucer, not unworthily introduced, for nothing better of its kind has been written in English since the Prologue to the Canterbury Tales. The verse has vigour of movement and variety of colour, and the strongly individualized characters of the English countryside are presented in a few dashing but powerful strokes. The run, narrated from the point of view of the fox, is magnificently done, and the reader's sympathies, thoroughly awakened by Reynard's craft and pluck. are left glowing by his final escape, another fox being sacrificed to the hounds at the last moment, so that everybody rests content with a happy ending. So stirring a tale in verse had not been seen in English for many a day, and it is very likely to remain Masefield's supreme achievement in narrative.

'Right Royal,' the story of a steeplechase, though good, was not so good, in spite of many excellences in detail. The same is true of 'King Cole,' a narrative poem dealing with the vicissitudes of a travelling circus. In both, especially in the latter, the effect is weakened by the introduction of supernatural elements; and neither poem has the rush and force of 'Reynard.'

Masefield's appointment as Poet Laureate in 1930 proved, as in so many other cases, a recognition of good work done rather than an incentive to better work still to be accomplished. There was a general feeling that the honour was well deserved in view of Masefield's character and achievement as a diligent student and a careful editor, a critic of insight and independent judgment, a dramatist of unusual power, an excellent storyteller in prose as well as in verse, and one of the best descriptive writers of the day. His poetry unites very varied qualities—a keen instinct for beauty, metrical versatility, skill in swift narrative and vivid description of nature, reasoning powers of a high order, and sympathetic contact with subject ranging from the wrongs and sorrows of the humblest and most degraded to the philosophic questionings which beset the keenest intellects of our time.

Through repeated lecture tours and readings of his own poetry on both sides of the Atlantic, as well as on the European Continent, Masefield became well known and regarded with much affection. His genuine simplicity, unassuming modesty, and quietness of demeanour have the charm of an older day, and his attitude of mind forms a pleasing contrast to the restlessness and cynicism of more recent English poetry. He kept his faith in humanity, though he had seen it at its worst as well as at its best; and the idealism which sustained him in his earlier struggles with adversity withstood the temptations of popularity and worldly success. In an address to the students of Aberdeen University he gave a word of encouragement to the eager literary aspirant which is at the same time a summary of his own spiritual biography: "You begin as a writer. You are filled with the energy of youth, and you believe that you can reform the whole profession of literature. You go on in that good faith as long as youth lasts. After a few years you look at what you have done. You see simply that you have been young and that youth is gone. You see that you have not discovered what life is, nor what is behind life, and that your work is past and that you are so many years to the bad. But then you think; 'Well, I have at least rid myself of some of the nonsense that was in me.' You think that perhaps you have some greater power over your material, some greater sense of the value and colour of words. Then you turn again to your work, and after the lapse of some years you look again at what you have done. You see that you know nothing about life. Life is infinitely more mysterious than anything you can say. You can't probe its mysteries; you know nothing about it. Then you will be filled with despair. You turn again to your work. You realize that somewhere outside life there come gleams and suggestions—a kind of butterflies floating into this world from somewhere. You have, yourself, the determination that you will follow these butterflies of the soul and find that you will come at last to some country that is quite close to this life of ours. You will be able to enter into it and make it visible to the rest of mankind, and then you go on in that faith. You may never get to that country. But the belief that that country exists tends to make it possible to all the rest of mankind, because all mankind, since the beginning of man, has been a building-up by courage and by truth and by beauty and by acts of self-sacrifice of some great invisible world to which men in moments of peril, moments of anxiety and exaltation, have access according to their power; and all efforts, no matter how feeble at first, tend to make that world greater."

RUPERT BROOKE (1887–1915)

It would be difficult to imagine a more complete contrast to Masefield's early life of struggling vagabondage than the fortune-favoured career of Rupert Brooke. The gods lavished upon him every gift of circumstance and endowment—physical beauty, a brilliant and attractive personality, every educational opportunity (he was a prize-winner at Rugby, and a fellow of King's College, Cambridge), the ease and dignity of academic life, a charming retreat at Grantchester Vicarage, congenial and sympathetic friends, devotion to a great cause, death in service on St. George's Day, and a fitting burial place in the Island of Skyros, marked since 1931 by a bronze statue, twice life-size, in view of a wide stretch of the Ægean. His loss was lamented by the leading masters of prose and verse, and the romantic ending of his career at once won public attention. The War, which stunned older writers into silence or stammering inadequacy, gave him a lofty and dignified utterance he had hitherto failed to attain. The coldest literary historian cannot but be impressed by so bright a spirit, suddenly rising to the height of a great opportunity and as suddenly extinguished by death in the service of the cause he celebrated. Whether he could have kept the pitch is a question no one can answer; but the perfect rounding of his achievement offers at least some consolation for his early death.

"I suppose," says his friend and fellow poet John

Drinkwater, "no one of his years can ever have had in greater measure the gifts that can be used to make easily swayed admiration gape, or greater temptations so to employ his qualities; and I am sure no man has ever been more wholly indifferent to any such conquests. Humour he had in abundance, but of witty insincerity no trace. Never was a personality more finely balanced. . . . It has been said that he had a strain of self-consciousness about his personal charm and brilliance, that he was a little afraid lest that side of him should claim too much attention. To answer the suggestion would be an impertinence. He was properly glad of his qualities; also, he was properly careless of them. The notion that any such matter ever occupied his mind for a moment can be nothing but ludicrous to those who knew him."

It is interesting to compare with this the personal impression made by Rupert Brooke upon Henry James as a "beautifully producible" specimen of the amenity and energy of the English tradition, of the exquisite civility, the social instincts of the race. He imagines the English as being able to say:

"Yes, this, with the imperfection of so many of our arrangements, with the persistence of so many of our mistakes, with the waste of so much of our effort and the weight of the many-coloured mantle of time that drags so redundantly about us, this natural accommodation of the English spirit, this frequent extraordinary beauty of the English aspect, this finest saturation of the English intelligence by its most immediate associations, tasting as they mainly do of the long past, this ideal image of English youth, in a word, at once radiant and reflective, are things that appeal to us as delightfully exhibitional beyond a doubt, yet as drawn, to the last fibre, from the very wealth of our conscience and the very force of our own history. We haven't, for such an instance of our genius, to reach out to strange places or across other, and otherwise productive tracts; the exemplary instance himself has well-nigh as a matter of course reached and revelled, for that is exactly our way in proportion as we feel ourselves clear. But the kind of experience so entailed, of contribution so gathered, is just what we wear easiest when we have been least stinted of it, and what our English use of makes perhaps our vividest reference to our thick-growing native determinants."

The generously perfect endowment of Brooke suggested to Henry James the question, "Why *need* he be a poet, why need he so specialize?" Well, the gods had added this gift too. Even in the poems written before he was 21, Brooke shows an almost uncanny power of deft expression. He can versify two Germans in the night train between Bologna and Milan (second class) or a sensual music lover at a Wagner concert:

> The music swells. His gross lips quiver
> His little eyes are bright with slime.
> The music swells. The women shiver
> And all the while, in perfect time,
> His pendulous stomach hangs a-shaking.

In technique, in intelligence he was already mature. He imagines the poet as going on a magnificent quest to curse God on His throne of fire, and finding—nothing:

> All the great courts were quiet as the sun,
> And full of vacant echoes; moss had grown
> Over the glassy pavement, and begun
> To creep within the dusty council-halls.
> An idle wind blew round an empty throne
> And stirred the heavy curtains on the walls.

Only in emotional experience is he immature, with the assumed maturity of extreme youth. His "heart is sick with memories," and even in the hour of "one last mad embrace" he reminds his love that

> Each crawling day
> Will pale a little your scarlet lips, each mile
> Dull the dear pain of your remembered face.

Obviously no lover is conscious of such truths in the moment of passion. In Meredith's 'Modern Love' the husband says "Ah, Yes, love dies!" but he adds in recollection "I never thought it less." With Brooke it was a thought he could never get away from. In the fine sonnet included in the poems of 1908–11 'The Hill,' the lovers defy old age and death—

> And then you suddenly cried, and turned away.

In the poems of this period Brooke has a surer touch, not merely of phrase, but of presentation. His cynicism begins to gain in humour. In 'Menelaus and Helen' he contrasts, effectively enough, the Helen of romance with the repentant wife who

> Bears
> Child on legitimate child, becomes a scold,
> Haggard with virtue.

'The One before the Last' is also in a lighter vein:

> Oh! bitter thoughts I had in plenty
> But here's the worst of it—
> I shall forget, in Nineteen-twenty,
> *You* ever hurt a bit!

'A Channel Passage' is Brooke's most outrageous example in the presentation of offensive ugliness, and it is necessary to remember that he was still young, with gifts that demanded some price to be paid, if only in the way of temptation to misuse them.

In the summer of 1913 Brooke crossed the American continent and went by way of the Pacific in the autumn to Samoa. Some of the poems suggested by the visit were published in 'New Numbers' for February and August, 1914, but a growing ripeness of thought is more fully shown in 'The Great Lover,' published along with them in the latter month and dated "Mataiea, 1914." The intervening April number contained 'Heaven,' one of his deftest ironical analyses of romance—in this case the romantic anthropomorphism of popular theology:

> Fish say, they have their stream and pond,
> But is there anything beyond?
> This life cannot be all, they swear,
> For how unpleasant if it were!
> One may not doubt that, somehow Good
> Shall come of Water and of Mud!

and so on to the faith in "wetter water, slimier slime":

> And under that Almighty Fin,
> The littlest fish may enter in.
> Oh! never fly conceals a hook,
> Fish say, in the Eternal Brook,
> But more than mundane weeds are there,
> And mud, celestially fair;
> Fat caterpillars drift around,
> And paradisal grubs are found;
> Unfading moths, immortal flies,
> And the worm that never dies.
> And in that Heaven of all their wish,
> There shall be no more land, say fish.

Upon this poem it is perhaps well to quote the comment of John Drinkwater: "When the poet elects to make brief intellectual holiday, so long as he does so in the terms of his own personality, we should do nothing but make holiday gladly with him." 'The Old Vicarage, Grantchester,' which appears to belong to an earlier date, is an altogether charming example of intellectual playfulness; the lightheartedness of 'The Chilterns' suggests that Brooke had at last got the better of the eternal antinomy between love and old age which haunted his early youth:

> And I shall find some girl perhaps,
> And a better one than you,
> With eyes as wise, but kindlier,
> And lips as soft, but true.
> And I daresay she will do.

So Rupert Brooke stood at the beginning of the war— the ideal modern Englishman with senses and intelligence all alert, a keen gift of humour, a supreme gift of expression which had hitherto not found its way. He has given us, under a thin veil, his impressions when he first heard of the war:

"As he thought 'England and Germany,' the word 'England' seemed to flash like a line of foam. . . . He was immensely surprised to perceive that the actual earth of England held for him a quality which he found in A——, and in a friend's honour, and scarcely anywhere else, a quality which, if he'd ever been sentimental enough to use the word, he'd have called 'holiness.' His astonishment grew as the full flood of 'England' swept him on from thought to thought. He felt the triumphant helplessness of a lover."

It was this that gave the sonnet series '1914' its distinguishing note. A fellow poet, Lascelles Abercrombie, has well said: "Rupert Brooke had a decided advantage

over other patriotic poets; when he celebrated the fault-
less beauty of sacrificing oneself for England, they were
his own immediate emotions that he expressed. He
knew that beauty of self-sacrifice not by any effort of
imagination, but simply because it was the thing that
entirely governed his life from the beginning of the war.
And in five sonnets he set forth the whole of it, with a
beauty of music and imagery perfectly answering to the
spiritual beauty.''

There is no question that the sonnet series is the crown-
ing glory of Brooke's poetic achievement. He was moved
to the depths of his rich nature as he had never been
before, and all his gifts of artistic endowment thrilled for
use in the supreme offering of himself and his powers to
one great object. The sacrifice was consecrated by his
death; but even without this added glory, the emotion
expressed in these five sonnets would have remained an
abiding witness of the power of England to stir the hearts
of men to devotion and to beauty.

WILFRID WILSON GIBSON

Wilfrid Gibson's poetic development is interesting in
itself, and helps us to understand the kind of work he has
come to do. He began to publish in 1902 lyrics which
had grace and charm, but were not otherwise distinguished
amid much other meritorious work of the type and time.
But in 'The Stonefolds' (1907) he turned aside from conventional romance to present the life of the rather grim
shepherd folk of his own rugged Northumbrian hills.
The form is very simply dramatic—there are only three
or four characters in each little scene and the incident is
slight, though the characterization is clear; the metre is

blank verse, which combines oddly with the North Country "thou" to give an impression of artificiality. Such a line as the following, coming from a shepherd's wife, strikes cold on the ear:

"Is this thy wisdom? Little hast thou learned."

Evidently some different medium was needed, and in 'Daily Bread' (1910) Gibson tried again. He was by this time perfectly clear about what he was trying to do, as the motto of the book shows:

All life moving to one measure—
Daily bread, daily bread—
Bread of life, and bread of labour,
Bread of bitterness and sorrow,
Hand to mouth, and no to-morrow,
Dearth for housemate, death for neighbour. . . .
Yet, when all the babes are fed,
Love, are there not crumbs to treasure?

The poet's aim was to catch the gleam of romance in everyday life without ever losing hold of reality. "Free verse" was at this time being much discussed, not only in England but in France and the United States, and it was not surprising that Gibson should try what he could do with it. It seemed to suit the subject he had chosen— the struggle of the labouring poor for daily bread—and to be capable of reproducing the effect of everyday conversation. Take such a passage as this:

And there's small blame to them
Who drink too much, at whiles.
There's little else the poor can get too much of,
And life, at best, is dull enough, God knows.
Sometimes, it's better to forget. . . .
And . . . it's a lovely dizziness.

raised by the average man against modernist painting. The average man assumes that it is the painter's first business to represent reality truly, either with the explanatory distinctness of the Pre-Raphaelites, or with the atmospheric suggestiveness of the Impressionists. The modernist painter replies that realism is not his primary aim at all; that photography can always be more realistic than he can; that his object is not to represent but to create arrangements of mass, of colour, and of line that of themselves give pleasure to the eye, in the same way that music – an art in which imitation is never of first importance – gives pleasure to the ear. The modern painter adds that many of the greatest painters of the past were not primarily realists at all; and cites the dangers of the nineteenth century habit of unselective copying. But if he is wise he admits that in creative work, nature is a helpful and even an indispensable guide; and that, if he tries to be independent of her help altogether, his work will become as barren in its way as that of the mechanical copyist. Creative work (painted perhaps entirely from imagination) is the richer in proportion as there have previously been stored up in the mind's eye the images of things actual; and when forms, colours and relations are simplified and re-combined in entirely new ways, these combinations have beauty only when the eye has been previously trained to observe.

The demand for realistic painting is a demand for something less simple than is supposed. Much can be seen, which paint cannot possibly imitate; but, granting realism as an aim, there are at least two main ways of being realistic. *Either* the painter can record what he sees without any attempt to explain its structure; *or* he can render its formation clearer to the uninstructed spectator than it would ever have been, had that spectator been confronted by the object itself. In the second case the painter will represent the object by a sharper outline and by surfaces more clearly divided into light and shade than those which actually appear upon his retina. As Mr. Roger Fry has pointed out, each reform the poet dreaming by his hearth and seeing fantastic shapes in the embers:

> Till, dazzled by the drowsy glare,
> I shut my eyes to heat and light;
> And saw, in sudden night,
> Crouched in the dripping dark,
> With steaming shoulders stark,
> The man who hews the coal to feed my fire.

These sketches give a fuller, richer impression of the life of the poor, with more colour and humour, and the poet, whether speaking in his own name or dramatically, infuses more of his own imagination into the story. Take for example 'The Hare,' which is told by a lad of seventeen who, after dreaming of taking in his hands a terror-stricken hare, follows one along the roadside and catches the same look of terror in the eyes of a girl he meets by a gipsy camp-fire. He helps her to escape from the man she is afraid of, and together they tramp the moorland trackways. One night his dream of the hare comes back to him and he wakes in a fright:

> Her place was empty in the straw. . . .
> And then, with quaking heart, I saw
> That she was standing in the night,
> A leveret cuddled to her breast. . . .
>
> I spoke no word; but, as the light
> Through banks of Eastern cloud was breaking,
> She turned, and saw that I was waking.
> And told me how she could not rest;
> And, rising in the night, she'd found
> This baby hare crouched on the ground;
> And she had nursed it quite a while.
> But, now, she'd better let it go.
> Its mother would be fretting so.
> A mother's heart. . . .

I saw her smile,
And look at me with tender eyes;
And as I looked into their light,
My foolish, fearful heart grew wise
And now, I knew that never there
I'd see again the startled hare,
Or need to dread the dreams of night.

Some critics objected to the hare episodes as too fanciful and strained, but there is no question that the execu-
tion of the poem is as beautiful as the original conception;
it is all suffused with delicate imaginative feeling, and
the verse is a delight.

Gibson returned to this form in subsequent volumes
and practised it with infinite variety of subject and tone.
'The Swing' reproduces a little servant girl's enjoyment of
a hard-won holiday:

Yesterday
She'd hardly thought she'd get away;
The mistress was that cross, and she
Had only told her after tea
That ere she left she must set to
And turn the parlour out. She knew,
Ay, well enough, that it meant more
Than two hours' work. And so at four
She'd risen this morn, and done it all
Before her mistress went to call
And batter at her bedroom door
At six to rouse her. Such a floor,
So hard to sweep; and all that brass
To polish! Any other lass
But her would have thrown up the place,
And told the mistress to her face. . . .

'Between the Lines' is a war-study, but one in Gibson's
characteristic manner. His soldier had been a draper's

assistant (dry goods clerk) and as he lies wounded in a
shell-hole he muses:

> This was different certainly,
> From selling knots of tape and reels of thread
> And knots of tape and reels of thread and knots
> Of tape and reels of thread and knots of tape,
> Day in, day out, and answering "Have you got's?"
> And "Do you keep's?" till there seemed no escape
> From everlasting serving in a shop,
> Inquiring what each customer required,
> Politely talking weather, fit to drop,
> With swollen ankles, tired. . . .

Only great imaginative sympathy and technical skill
could achieve the bringing out of the romance in the shop-
man's life at the very point at which it seems most prosaic
—its monotony. In the same volume, entitled 'Battle,'
Gibson perfected a new form of short rhymed poem
of which one example will serve better than description
or definition, 'The Father':

> That was his sort.
> It didn't matter
> What we were at
> But he must chatter
> Of this and that
> His little son
> Had said or done;
> Till, as he told
> The fiftieth time
> Without a change
> How three-year-old
> Prattled a rhyme,
> They got the range
> And cut him short.

The ironical humour of this and of many others of
these miniatures is grim enough, but it is never lacking

in sympathy, and it is extraordinarily effective. Gibson shows us the weariness, the madness, the cruelty and pain of the trenches as they appear to the common soldier, and clothes them in his own imaginative beauty of phrase and setting.

WILLIAM H. DAVIES (1872–   )

The poems of W. H. Davies need no extrinsic circumstance to commend them, but their interest is certainly enhanced by the extraordinary conditions under which he began his literary career. As he has told the whole story fully and frankly in his 'Autobiography of a Super-Tramp,' there can be no indiscretion in summarizing it here. Born in a Newport (Monmouthshire) public-house, he passed a wayward youth, which brought him at an early age into conflict with the police (he was whipped in gaol for heading a youthful gang of thieves), and as soon as he was out of his apprenticeship as a picture frame maker, he crossed the Atlantic. Falling in with a professional tramp at a small town in Connecticut, he beat his way to Chicago, begging victuals from the farmers' wives, and stealing an occasional ride on the railway. He objected to this mode of life because it gave him no chance to enrich his mind, but he kept at it through many wanderings until an attempt in Canada to board a train in motion so as to escape paying his fare deprived him of a foot. He then returned to England, and, as he had fallen in for a legacy which brought him in a few shillings a week, he decided to devote himself to literature. He read widely in free libraries and wrote a tragedy in blank verse, which, to his astonishment, was returned by one publisher after another. English tramping expeditions, combined with collecting the pennies for a one-legged "gridler" (street-singer), enabled him to save enough money to get his first poems printed, but the periodicals to which they were sent for review paid no attention to them. After vainly seeking the help of sundry charitable organizations, he took the matter into his own hands. Personal appeals (accompanied by copies of the poems) not merely brought in money but secured reviews in the leading papers, and his literary position was established forthwith. Within ten years he had published two or three considerable volumes of prose and eight little books of verse, immediately re-issued as 'Collected Poems.'

It was a most astonishing, almost an incredible achievement, and the most remarkable thing about it was that the poems made their own way when their author's romantic story was forgotten. Once well-started on his literary career, Davies made no attempt to exploit his sensational past or to find in it materials for such realistic studies of low life as were winning fame and fortune for contemporary poets. A pure lyrist, he continued to sing the graceful songs of love and nature with which he had first won the ear of the public, although such early poems as 'In a Lodging House,' 'Saints and Lodgers,' and 'The Lodging House Fire' proved that he was not unaware of the opportunity or incapable of taking advantage of it. A small Government pension (£50 a year) "in recognition of his poetical work" suffices for his simple wants:

> No maid is near,
> I have no wife;
> But here's my pipe
> And, on my life,

> With it to smoke,
>   And woo the Muse,
> To be a king
>   I would not choose.

Davies's contempt for the ordinary luxuries and comforts of life is genuine. What he sought in the life of a
tramp was freedom, and he did not find it. He quotes
himself as saying to a fellow-tramp from whom he wished
to part:—"Your life is not mine. We often go for days
without reading matter, and we know not what the world
is saying; nor what the world is doing. The beauty of
nature is for ever before my eyes, but I am certainly not
enriching my mind, for who can contemplate Nature
with any profit in the presence of others? I have no
leisure to make notes in hopes of future use and I am so
overpacking my memory with all these scenes, that when
their time comes for use, they will not then take definite
shape. I must go to work for some months, so that I
may live sparingly on my savings in some large city, where
I can cultivate my mind."

What Davies wanted was leisure, and having gained it
after a hard and painful struggle, he has used it to some
purpose. He has the genuine poet soul, born in a strange
time and in stranger surroundings, but speaking the un-
mistakably authentic accent of sincerity:

> Let me be free to wear my dreams
> Like weeds in some mad maiden's hair,
> When she believes the earth has not
> Another maid so rich and fair;
> And proudly smiles on rich and poor,
> The queen of all fair women then;
> So I, dressed in my idle dreams,
> Will think myself the king of men.

WALTER JOHN DE LA MARE (1873–   )

Davies has some charming poems about children, but the children's poet of the period is Walter de la Mare. His 'Songs of Childhood' continued in delicate verse the well-established tradition of ogres and witches, gnomes and elves, and 'Peacock Pie' has a wealth of fanciful rhymes arranged under headings such as 'Up and Down,' 'Boys and Girls,' 'Places and People,' 'Witches and Fairies,' 'Earth and Air.' But besides dainty rhymes for children, he writes more profound fancies for older readers and some that would do for both. Perhaps we should put in the latter class the poem in 'The Listeners' which tells how on a summer afternoon a little girl found her mother asleep in a chair:

> Even her hands upon her lap
> Seemed saturate with sleep.
> And as Ann peeped, a cloudlike dread
> Stole over her, and then,
> On stealthy, mouselike feet she trod,
> And tiptoed out again.

No less charmingly effective—though perhaps only for grown-ups—is the poem in the same volume entitled 'Miss Loo,'—an absent-minded maiden lady whom the poet reëmbodies from the recollections of his childhood:

> And I am sitting, dull and shy,
> And she with gaze of vacancy,
> And large hands folded on the tray,
> Musing the afternoon away;
> Her satin bosom heaving slow
> With sighs that softly ebb and flow,
> And her plain face in such dismay,
> It seems unkind to look her way.

Until all cheerful back will come
Her cheerful gleaming spirit home.
And one would think that poor Miss Loo
Asked nothing else, if she had you.

Less successful is a similar sketch in 'Motley' (1918)
of 'Mrs. Grundy,' who has

Called me, "dear Nephew," on each of those chairs,
Has gloated in righteousness, heard my prayers.
High-coifed, broad-browed, aged, suave yet grim,
A large flat face, eyes keenly dim,
Staring at nothing—that's me!—and yet,
With a hate one could never, no, never forget.

This lacks the innocence which is the chief charm of
childhood, and is so far less effective on that account, but
the little picture is clearly drawn. Perhaps under the
weight and stress of the War, de la Mare drifted away
from the simplicity of his earlier Muse into something
like mysticism. Thus, 'The Scribe' imagines himself
drawing on for ever with the ink of some tarn in the hills
the wonders of God he sees about him:

Still would remain
My wit to try—
My worn reeds broken,
The dark tarn dry,
All words forgotten—
Thou, Lord, and I.

LASCELLES ABERCROMBIE (1881–   )

Lascelles Abercrombie has no.. of the various qualities
which have given the poets already discussed, for one

reason or another, some popular appeal. His massive and acute intellect finds freer play in criticism and metaphysics than in poetry, and his verse is almost devoid of sensuous attraction of any kind. Severe alike in subject and in treatment, it appeals only to the intelligence. His first volume treats dramatically in blank verse without a touch of romance two mediæval legends, along with other subjects, all regarded on the intellectual side, and contains also a dialogue between the Body and the Soul, and an Ode to Indignation. Two more mediæval legends, 'Mary and the Bramble' and 'The Sale of St. Thomas,' followed, and were published by the author privately. A brief extract from the latter poem may give a hint of the poet's method and style. St. Thomas, bidden to take ship for the conversion of India, hesitates on the quay, not from cowardice but from prudence, until his Lord appears and sells him as a slave to the sea-captain:

> "Now, Thomas, know thy sin. It was not fear;
>   Easily may a man crouch down for fear,
>   And yet rise up on firmer knees, and face
>   The hailing storm of the world with graver courage.
>   But prudence, prudence is the deadly sin,
>   And one that groweth deep into a life,
>   With hardening roots that clutch about the breast,
>   For this refuses faith in the unknown powers
>   Within man's nature."

In 'Emblems of Love' the subject treated is still more abstruse and difficult. A 'prelude of discovery and prophecy' reveals first two warriors at the dawn of civilization; one cherishes women as the breeder of more warriors against the wolves, the other as the source of beauty and pleasure. In 'Vashti' we move a step onward in the distinction she puts to Ahasuerus:

> "Lovest thou me, or dost thou rather love
> The pleasure thou hast in me?"

She refuses herself to Ahasuerus and is driven out of the palace, but as she goes the Goddess Ishtar appears to her and reveals the future:

> "There shall be
> Of man desiring, and of woman desired,
> A single ectasy divinely formed,
> Two souls knowing themselves in one amazement.
> All that thou hatest to arouse in man
> Prepareth him for this; and thou thyself
> Art by thy very hate prepared."

Part II shows us in three dramatic episodes love in imperfection; Part III, 'Virginity and Perfection,' dramatizes the story of Judith, who is taken as an emblem of the power of the spiritual against the material. We have next a dialogue 'The Eternal Wedding,' a 'Marriage Song,' and finally an 'Epilogue,' all rendered in the same high intellectual strain. There is no question of the keenness of the intelligence at work or of the excellence of the verse; but it is a cold arid region of the mind where few can long breathe the rarefied air. Abercrombie is highly esteemed, especially by his fellow poets; but that he will ever win any large number of readers seems very improbable.

T. S. ELIOT (1888–   )

Thomas Stearns Eliot came of a well-known New England family, was born at St. Louis, and educated at Harvard, where he took his A.B. in 1909 and his A.M.

in 1910. Shortly afterwards he went to Europe, studied at the Sorbonne and Merton College, Oxford, married an Englishwoman, and became a British subject. When he came back to the United States, it was as Charles Eliot Norton Professor of Poetry at Harvard for 1932–3. In the meantime he had been recognized as the leader of a new and revolutionary school in English poetry.

The new school, though it aimed at upsetting the leading principles recognized by English poets and critics in the nineteenth century, had an earlier representative in Gerard Manly Hopkins, a Jesuit father who had great difficulty in getting his poetry understood or even printed, but is now distinguished by the new school as the greatest poet of the Victorian age, and the only one influential "for our time and the future." So says F. R. Leavis, who welcomes Hopkins as a rebel against the romantic tradition running through Tennyson and Swinburne to A. E. Housman and Rupert Brooke. Victorian poetry in general is condemned because it was not in touch with life either in substance or in form, the new thought requiring a new technique. It was in fact chiefly on the technical side that Hopkins was an innovator. He wrote:

> How to kéep—is there ány any, is there none such,
>> nowhere known some, bow or brooch or braid
>> or brace, láce, latch or catch or key to keep
> Back beauty, keep it, beauty, beauty, beauty, . . .
>> from vanishing away?

It is perfectly possible, as Sturge Moore showed in a recent number of 'The Criterion' (July, 1930), to put the thought of this into traditional form:

> How to keep beauty? is there any way?
> Is there nowhere any means to have it stay?
> Will no bow or brooch or braid,

Brace or lace
Latch or catch
Or key to lock the door lend aid
Before beauty vanishes away?

Many readers would no doubt think the Sturge Moore
rendering preferable; but F. R. Leavis points out that
he has "discarded 'back' and everything it represents;
words as he uses them have no body. He has discarded,
not merely a certain amount of music, but with the emotional crescendo and diminuendo, the plangent rise and
fall, all the action and substance of the verse."

T. S. Eliot came to initiate his own crusade, not through
the influence of Hopkins, whose poems were not published
in their entirety till 1918, but through acquaintance with
the work of the French poets, Jules Laforgue and Tristan
Corbière, whose style he imitated in French verses published in 1920, and in English poems written as early as
1909; he was also influenced by the verse forms of the
later Elizabethan dramatists, Chapman, Middleton, Web-
ster, Tourneur, and of Donne, in whose lines he particularly admired "that perpetual slight alteration of
language, words perpetually juxtaposed in new and sudden
combinations, which evidences a very high development
of the senses. . . . Sensation became word, and the word
was sensation." Of this period, "when the intellect was
immediately at the tips of the senses," Eliot regards
Shakespeare as the leading representative; the next
period, initiated in drama by Massinger, is that of
Milton.

The first considerable poem in which Eliot adopted
the new style was 'The Love Song of J. Alfred Prufrock,'
which was rejected by all the London editors to whom it
was offered (one of them remarked that it was "queer to

the point of madness"); it found its way into print in the American magazine 'Poetry' through the interposition of another young American poet, Ezra Pound, and was published in England in 1917 with other early poems in a slim volume entitled 'Prufrock and other Observations.'

Similar small volumes appeared in 1919, but Eliot won no public attention till 1922, when 'The Waste Land' was published in London and in the New York 'Dial,' which at once awarded to Eliot its prize of $2000 for literary achievement. The reviewers began to take notice, though they were still puzzled; one described the poem as "half painful wisdom, and half posing nonsense"; another regarded it as probably an attempt to hoax the American literati with "a jargon of incomprehensible phrases." Later criticism and explanation, however, compelled the most sceptical critics to take the poem seriously and it remains Eliot's most considerable achievement in verse up to the time of his return to America in 1933, when he delivered lectures at Harvard and other universities and was very warmly received.

It must be acknowledged that one's first contact with 'The Waste Land' is not encouraging. The title consists of seven lines of which three are in Latin (including five words of Greek) and one in Italian. The author's note on the title refers the reader for elucidation of the difficulties of the poem to three books on anthropology, Miss Jessie L. Weston's 'From Ritual to Romance' and the two volumes on 'Attis Adonis Osiris,' in Frazer's 'The Golden Bough.' The ordinary reader will probably prefer to accept the assurance of F. R. Leavis that it is Eliot's picture of the modern world—"a world in which the traditions are bankrupt, the cultures uprooted and withering, and the advance of civilization seems to mean death to

distinction of spirit and fineness of living." In form it is
a group of disconnected "subjective renderings of cere-
bral phenomena"—"a stream of memories and images the
like of which, a little dulled and narrowed, runs through
the brain of any educated and imaginative man whose
thoughts are sharpened by suffering." This last was
Elinor Wylie's view; but Eliot himself said that 'The
Waste Land' "was not a reflection of an attitude fundamentally melancholy, but rather a calculated piece of
poetic mosaic, deliberately (but in a sense accidentally)
designed to produce a certain series of poetic effects."
In any case, the impression produced upon understanding
readers, including Eliot's personal friends, is that it is
a poem of negation, of chaos, of despair. But it is also,
Conrad Aiken wrote, "the poetry of a highly sensitive and
shrinking individual with exceptionally acute insight and
imagination and a very fine sense of the values of word
and rhythm."

Those who, even with the help of books of reference
and ten pages of author's notes, still find the poem
puzzling may content themselves with Eliot's assurance
that "genuine poetry can communicate before it is understood"; and if they cannot find in it a narrative, dramatic, or even a metaphysical unity—the search for
any of these is, we are assured, "a wrong approach, an
approach with inappropriate expectations"—they can at
least appreciate its general musical movement and the
significance of some of the etchings of modern life which
illustrate its theme, such as that of Madame Sosostris,
famous clairvoyante, in Part I; the talk at closing time
in a London bar in Part II; or the tawdry and sordid
encounter of the typist with the carbuncular young man
in Part III. The description of their parting may be
quoted as an example of Eliot's method and manner:

> She turns and looks a moment in the glass,
> Hardly aware of her departed lover;
> Her brain allows one half-formed thought to pass:
> "Well now that's done: and I'm glad it's over."
> When lovely woman stoops to folly and
> Paces about her room again, alone,
> She smooths her hair with automatic hand,
> And puts a record on the gramophone.

It is, of course, seldom that Eliot is quite so lucid and direct. The most sanguine of his interpreters has to admit "that 'The Waste Land' can be appreciated only by a very small minority." The justification offered is that the fault is not his, but that of modern civilization. "The important works of to-day, unlike those of the past, tend to appeal only at the highest level of response, which only a tiny minority can reach, instead of at a number of levels. On the other hand, the finer values are ceasing to be a matter of even conventional concern for any except the minority capable of the highest level. Everywhere below, a process of standardization, mass-production, and levelling-down goes forward, and civilization is coming to mean a solidarity achieved by the exploitation of the most readily released responses. So that poetry in the future, if there is poetry, seems likely to matter even less to the world." In support of this view F. R. Leavis quotes the testimony of Sidgwick and Jackson, one of the most enterprising and enlightened London publishing firms, that in the decade ending 1929 they received 1000 manuscripts of new poets (exclusive of those from writers of known standing). Of these they published fifteen, by twelve authors, who shared about $350 in royalties; only two of the fifteen volumes paid their way; the net loss on the fifteen was about $700. It must be agreed that the publication of poetry is seldom profitable, either to author or publisher. Still, poetry does somehow manage to get itself published, and one is inclined to believe that a poet big enough to grapple with the complexities of modern civilization might even make a living by it. Eliot puts a great many obstacles in the way of the reading public, and this has not prevented his poems from having a considerable sale.

In the volume of criticisms entitled 'For Lancelot Andrewes' (1929), Eliot declared his general point of view to be "classicist in literature, royalist in politics, and Anglo-Catholic in religion." He announced also three volumes in preparation: 'The School of Donne,' 'The Outline of Royalism,' 'The Principles of Modern Heresy.' As a critic and a philosopher he has a keen mind and a ready pen. As a poet he belongs to an age of transition and unrest, and the refuge he has found in Anglo-Catholicism has not made his subsequent poems any easier to understand. Judgments as to his poetic importance are at present necessarily tentative and partisan. The verdict of his friend Richard Aldington is reasonably phrased and not too extravagant in its appreciation: "His thought is pessimistic and disillusioned; his modes of expression are sarcastic, and his chief weapon is an acrid wit. He is psychologically subtle and intellectually acute; his culture is extensive. He is not a democrat, though he observes popular habits. He is a cosmopolitan, but he enjoys the flavour of nationality. He writes for an audience equipped to understand him and is indifferent to popular success. His mind is exceedingly complex and moves with a rapidity incomprehensible to sluggish wits. He is perilously balanced among the rude forces of a turbulent, mechanical age; he walks the tight rope over an abyss and he knows it. His work has the gusto of peril."

BIBLIOGRAPHY

JOHN MASEFIELD

POEMS

1902 'Salt-Water Ballads.'
1903 'Ballads.'
1910 'Ballads and Poems.'
1912 'The Everlasting Mercy' ('English Review,' Oct., 1911).
'The Widow in the Bye Street' ('English Review,' Feb.)
1913 'Dauber ('English Review,' Oct., 1912).
'The Daffodil Fields' ('English Review,' Feb.).
1916 'Sonnets and Poems.'
1917 'Lollingdon Downs and other Poems.'
1919 'Reynard the Fox, or the Ghost Heath Run.'
1920 'Enslaved and other Poems.'
'Right Royal.'
1921 'King Cole.'
1923 'The Dream.'
1926 'Sonnets of Good Cheer.'
1929 'South and East.'
1931 'Minnie Maylow's Story.'
1932 'A Tale of Troy.'
'Collected Poems.'

PLAYS

1907 'The Campden Wonder.'
1909 'The Tragedy of Nan.'
1910 'The Tragedy of Pompey the Great.'
1914 'Philip the King.'
1915 'The Faithful.'
1916 'Good Friday' ('Fortnightly Review,' Dec., 1915).
'The Locked Chest.'
'The Sweeps of '98.'

1922   'Esther' (trans. from Racine).
       'Berenice' (adapted and partially translated from Racine).
       'Melloney Holtspur.'
1923   'A King's Daughter.'
1925   'The Trial of Jesus.'
1927   'Tristan and Isolt.'
1928   'The Coming of Christ.'
1929   'Easter.'

TALES AND NOVELS

1905   'A Mainsail Haul.'
1907   'A Tarpaulin Muster.'
1908   'Captain Margaret.'
1909   'Multitude and Solitude.'
1910   'Lost Endeavour.'
1911   'The Street of To-day.'
1923   'The Taking of Helen.'
1924   'Sard Harker.'
1926   'Odtaa.'
1927   'The Midnight Folk.'
1929   'The Hawbucks.'

PROSE

1911   'William Shakespeare.'
1916   'Gallipoli.'

BIOGRAPHICAL AND CRITICAL

W. H. Hamilton, 'John Masefield, a Critical Study,' 1922.
C. Biggane, 'John Masefield, A Study,' 1924.
Gilbert Thomas, 'John Masefield,' 1933.
Bibliographies by Iolo A. Williams (1921) and Charles H. Simmons (1930).

RUPERT BROOKE

1911   'Poems.'
1915   '1914 and other Poems.'
       'The Collected Poems of Rupert Brooke' (New York).
1916   'Letters from America,' with a preface by Henry James.

1918 'The Collected Poems of Rupert Brooke' (London).

There are short essays on Rupert Brooke in 'Studies of Contemporary Poets' by Mary C. Sturgeon (1916) and in 'Prose Papers' by John Drinkwater (1917). Walter de la Mare's lecture on 'Rupert Brooke and the Intellectual Imagination' was published in New York in 1921.

WILFRID WILSON GIBSON

1907 'Stonefolds.'
1910 'Akra the Slave.'
       'Daily Bread.'
1912 'Fires.'
1914 'Thoroughfares.'
       'Borderlands.'
1915 'Battle.'
1916 'Friends.'
1917 'Livelihood.'
1918 'Whin.'
1920 'Neighbours.'
1922 'Collected Verse.'
       'Krindlesyke.'
1924 'Kestrel Edge and other Plays.'
1925 'I Heard a Sailor.'
1928 'The Golden Rod.'
1932 'Islands.'

WILLIAM H. DAVIES

POEMS

1906 'The Soul's Destroyer.'
1907 'New Poems.'
1908 'Nature Poems.'
1910 'Farewell to Poesy.'
1911 'Songs of Joy.'
1913 'Foliage.'
1914 'The Birds of Paradise.'
1916 'Child Lovers.'
1920 'The Song of Life.'
       'The Hour of Magic and other Poems.'

1923 'Nature Poems.'
1924 'Secrets.'
1927 'A Poet's Calendar.'
1929 'Forty-nine Poems.'
1932 'Poems, 1930–31.'

PROSE

1907 'The Autobiography of a Super-Tramp.'
1916 'A Pilgrim in Wales.'
1918 'A Poet's Pilgrimage.'
1925 'Later Days.'
1933 'My Birds.'

WALTER DE LA MARE

1902 'Songs of Childhood.'
1904 'Henry Brocken,' a romance.
1906 'Poems.'
1910 'The Return,' a novel.
1912 'The Listeners' and other Poems.'
1913 'Peacock Pie.'
1918 'Motley and other Poems.'
1921 'Memoirs of a Midget.'
1922 'The Veil and other Poems.'
1923 'The Riddle and other Stories.'
1926 'The Connoisseurs and other Stories.'

BIOGRAPHICAL AND CRITICAL

R. L. Mégroz, 'Walter de la Mare,' 1924.
Forrest Reid, 'Walter de la Mare; a Critical Study,' 1929.

LASCELLES ABERCROMBIE

1908 'Interludes and Poems.'
1910 'St. Mary and the Bramble.'
1911 'The Sale of St. Thomas.'
1912 'Emblems of Love.'
     'Thomas Hardy; a critical study.'
1913 'Deborah, A Play in three acts.'
     'Speculative Dialogues.'
1922 'Four Short Plays.'

Thomas Stearns Eliot

POETRY

1917 'Prufrock and other Observations.'
1919 'Poems' (including 'Portrait of a Lady' and 'Sweeney among the Nightingales.')
1919 'Poems.' ('Ara Vos Prec.')
1922 'The Waste Land.'
1930 'Ash Wednesday.'

PROSE

1920 'The Sacred Wood.'
1924 'Homage to John Dryden.'
1928 'An Essay of Poetic Drama.'
1929 'For Lancelot Andrewes.'
'Dante.'
1932 'Selected Essays 1917–1932.'
'John Dryden, Poet, Dramatist, Critic.'

INDEX

(Titles mentioned only in Bibliographies are not included in the Index)